THE
POLARIZATION
MYTH

America's Surprising Consensus
on Race, Schools, and Sex

JONATHAN BUTCHER

Encounter
BOOKS

New York • London

First American edition published in 2025 by Encounter Books,
an activity of Encounter for Culture and Education, Inc.,
a nonprofit, tax-exempt corporation.
Encounter Books website address: www.encounterbooks.com

Manufactured in the United States and printed on
acid-free paper. The paper used in this publication meets
the minimum requirements of ANSI/NISO Z39.48-1992
(R 1997) (*Permanence of Paper*).

FIRST AMERICAN EDITION

LIBRARY OF CONGRESS CATALOGING-IN-PUBLICATION DATA IS AVAILABLE

Library of Congress CIP data is available online under the following
ISBN 978-1-64177-483-3.

CONTENTS

INTRODUCTION

Unless a common purpose binds them together, tribal antagonisms will drive them apart. In the century darkly ahead, civilization faces a critical question: What is it that holds a nation together?
—Arthur Schlesinger Jr., *The Disuniting of America: Reflections on a Multicultural Society*[1]

The woman on the other end of the phone has been through a lot.[2] Latasha Fields was raised by her grandmother in a "poor, black, drug-infested neighborhood," as she describes it, in Baton Rouge, Louisiana. Her mom struggled with drug addiction and spent time in prison.

I called to talk about her work with families in Chicago to help parents find quality education options for their children. But the significance of her work today is best understood by learning about her past. Years before our phone call, in her testimony before Congress in 2019, Fields said, "I basically grew up with all the typical black stigmas: the lack of motivation for education, promiscuous behavior, drugs, crime, and some family members on welfare."

Fields became a mom herself at age seventeen, which "was a major turning point in my life." Her grandmother may have only had a second-grade education, but she was a "strong hard-working woman, who showed tough love and amazing independent work ethic." Despite the "stigmas" of poverty and failure that are associated with low-income areas, Fields "didn't want to be like the rest."

"I always strived for better and wanted to beat the social norms of the black community. I did not want to be another statistic," she said in her testimony.[3]

She loved education, she said, and in our conversation we talked about how she guides families in and around Chicago who want to homeschool

I

their students. "It builds that strong family bond between parents and children," she said in our interview.

Today, Fields is an American success story. "I worked hard, graduated from high school five months pregnant," she told Congress in her testimony. "During my teenage years, I worked at Burger King as part of my high school's entrepreneurship program," She finished college with honors and is now an ordained minister, and works with her husband to help local communities.[4]

She is involved with several organizations that advocate for parental rights in education, including the Christian Home Educators Support System (CHESS) and ParentalRights.org. Fields has been recognized as an Achiever by 1776 Unites, a nonpartisan group of writers and activists working to promote education and "upward mobility," for "triumphing and living the ideals of America's founding."[5]

You don't have to agree with homeschooling, Fields's faith and the virtues that go along with it, or what constitutes "black stigma" to find her story inspiring. She began at the bottom, took responsibility for her actions, and chased the American Dream. The good life.

In fact, Fields believes there is widespread agreement that a quality education is still the path to success. "In the black community, there is more emphasis on the academics," she said in our interview, and "academic proficiency is the leading issue."[6]

Americans today may look around and see divisions in politics and culture ("Biden v. Trump," "School choice" vs. "Support public schools," or "Protect women's private spaces!" or "Respect my pronouns!"), but regardless of political party, religion, or race, people from all walks of life still value education. It is hardly controversial to say that Fields's example is inspiring. We can all agree with her that hard work pays off, and that it is noble to prioritize education so much that you would dedicate your career to helping other parents find great opportunities for their children.

★ ★ ★

In fact, Americans agree on these things and more.

But you wouldn't know this from following the news or scrolling through social media. Pollsters, news anchors, and newspaper columnists say America is polarized. The day before the 2024 presidential election, *The New Yorker* released an article titled "The Americans Prepping for a Second Civil War," which seemed to anticipate that a nation-shattering conflict would erupt no matter who won.[7] During President Joe Biden's term, a survey conducted in 2022 by FiveThirtyEight/Ipsos found that Americans ranked "political extremism or polarization" as one of their biggest concerns, which was an unusual finding compared with previous poll results. Earlier polls that had asked the same questions about Americans' top priorities usually found that the economy and foreign conflicts occupied the top spots.[8]

Yes, another election is always around the corner for Americans, and voting tallies remind us of electoral divides. In 2012, Barack Obama beat Mitt Romney by less than four percentage points in the popular vote.[9] In 2016, Hillary Clinton finished just over two percentage points ahead of Donald Trump, who nevertheless won the Electoral College.[10] In 2020, the difference was near four points again.[11] In 2024 it was fewer than two percentage points.[12] You get the idea. Some choose to describe the period spanning these elections, especially the most recent elections, only from the perspective that we are a polarized populace. Writing for the Carnegie Endowment in 2023, researcher Rachel Kleinfeld said, "The United States feels roiled by polarization. . . . Some scholars claim that Americans are so polarized they are on the brink of civil war."[13] Headlines from NBC ("Here's What's Driving American's Increasing Political Polarization"),[14] *The Atlantic* ("The Doom Spiral of Pernicious Polarization"),[15] and *The New Yorker* ("How Politics Got So Polarized"),[16] among others, have claimed that our nation is starkly divided.

Social media platforms such as Facebook and X (formerly known as Twitter) and cable news programs seem designed for people to argue. Conflict sells advertising and makes for good ratings, but if you watch the evening news or practice "doom scrolling" through social media feeds before going to bed, you would think Americans have little to nothing in common.

Hollywood is not helping. In 2024, the film studio A24 released *Civil War*, a feature starring Kirsten Dunst that portrays an America violently divided. In the film, a bloc of states has seceded from the union and characters live in a dystopian future in which the White House is calling air strikes on civilians. Not a comforting scenario. One reviewer in *The Atlantic* said the film had an "uncomfortable resonance in these political polarized times."[17]

Yet does it resonate? Or are Americans being told by "experts" that the nation is polarized, when, in fact, there is widespread agreement on issues crucial to our everyday lives?

"Experts" Say We Are Polarized

In these examples, Hollywood, the media, and political commentators—even doctors and lawyers who pontificate about political issues (sometimes referred to as the "expert" class)—contend that America is sharply divided.[18] Referring again to Hollywood, movie reviews offer a fitting illustration: Released in 1999, the film *The Boondock Saints* has an "expert" score of just 26 percent on Rotten Tomatoes (a website that provides movie reviews from audience members and film critics), while audiences awarded the movie a 91 percent favorability rating.[19] There was a 54 percentage point divide between the experts and the audience on 2001's *Super Troopers*, with audiences giving it a 90 percent score on Rotten Tomatoes compared to a meager 36 percent favorability score from film critics.[20] The disconnect went in the opposite direction for *Star Wars: The Last Jedi* (2017), with the experts giving it a 91 percent favorability rating, compared to a mere 41 percent favorability rating among the true experts—the audience of die-hard Star Wars fans.[21]

Likewise, the opinions of the "expert class" are often at odds with public opinion. "Appeals to authority" that once resonated have lost their salience in the wake of COVID-19 as skepticism of fields such as education and medicine has grown.

For example, in March 2025 *The New York Times* issued a *mea culpa*, of sorts, on the origins of the COVID-19 pandemic, publishing commentary by Zeynep Tufekci entitled "We Were Badly Misled About the Event That Changed Our Lives."[22] Indeed, we were misled—by *The New York Times*. The "experts" dismissed the "lab leak" theory as the origin of the pandemic, several times, in fact.[23] Five years on, Tufecki writes in the *Times* that

> We have since learned, however, that to promote the appearance of consensus, some officials and scientists hid or understated crucial facts, misled at least one reporter, orchestrated campaigns of supposedly independent voices and even compared notes about how to hide their communications in order to keep the public from hearing the whole story.[24]

The "experts" also held that little kids would be just fine not having access to school, their friends, reading instruction, and mask-free faces. *Slate* compared parents' concerns over prolonged school closures to a "moral panic" pushed by "overblown newspaper headlines and yelling pundits."[25] One columnist claimed kids were "more resilient than I ever dreamed possible" and had turned "lemons into lemonade."[26] But the most tone-deaf award goes to Larry Delaney, president of the Washington Education Association (Washington state's branch of the National Education Association, the nation's largest teacher union), who, in response to a question about the long-term negative effect of school closures on children responded that "…our kids are resilient. Across the country everyone has missed certain learning. So if everyone is 'behind,' I guess no one is behind."[27] He was horribly, horribly wrong.

Keeping the nation's 50 million public school children out of classrooms for a year or more had devastating consequences.[28] They missed social events like prom and homecoming, missed out on playing on sports teams and associated scholarships, some opting out of college altogether when universities went remote. Research estimates that students will have lost 5 to 6 percent of lifetime earnings, a loss of some $31 trillion to the U.S.

at large through 2100 due to the closures.[29] A significant body of research found declines in measures of student mental health.[30] For example, a report in *Perspectives on Psychological Science* documented how "the unprecedented scale and length of school closures resulted in a substantial deficit in children's learning and a deterioration in children's mental health."[31]

Yet even in 2025, Becky Pringle, president of the National Education Association, doubled down, claiming that school closures were the right approach, and that "what we needed to do was listen to the infectious disease experts."[32]

These are the "experts" who insist that Americans are polarized. As this book will argue, the truth is that the experts cannot reckon with an American public that disagrees with them.

Political Polarization vs. Polarization on the Issues

The distinction between seeing America as polarized and as a nation of competing interests is an important one. At the time of our nation's birth, our Founding Fathers knew that Americans did not agree on every issue and likely would not in the future. They knew voters would continue to break into groups representing their interests—what the Founders called "factions." (*Federalist* no. 10, a seminal essay by James Madison advocating for the adoption of our U.S. Constitution, speaks specifically to the subject of factions.) Volumes have been written about how the Founding Fathers structured our government to balance competing interests because they knew people would have different priorities for themselves and those closest to them.

There are signs, however, that the differences are not as stark as the media and others would have us believe. There is a lot Americans agree on. To begin with, when the FiveThirtyEight/Ipsos pollsters referenced above compared their results revealing general dissatisfaction with American political life with other surveys, their comparison found that "over the past decade [surveys have] seen a larger share of people cite dissatisfaction with the government or poor leadership as the nation's top issue, reaching record highs in recent years."[33] Note that the dissatisfaction here was with leadership, not the actual issues Americans deal with or read about in the news. Likewise, according to Gallup, as of December 2024 only 15 percent of voters approved of the way Congress was handling their job, and this figure had not even approached 40 percent since 2009.[34] Polling from *The New York Times* in 2024 found that 60 percent of those surveyed agree that "government is almost always wasteful and inefficient."[35]

Deflating as it may sound, Americans share a general dissatisfaction with government.

Surely there is more to this finding, though. After the second election of Trump to the presidency, a blizzard of executive orders followed, many addressing cultural issues that parents, the media, and public officials had been wrestling with for years.

Were the disagreements on these *issues*—the issues the new administration tackled in its opening weeks and months—so entrenched that America could only be headed to a civil war? What topics actually separate Americans? Given the headlines, messages from Hollywood, and close popular votes in presidential elections, Americans should be surprised to learn that they are not as divided on hot-button topics today as the experts would have us believe.

To investigate this claim, I collaborated with a polling company and surveyed more than two thousand Americans in July, August, and September of 2023, including parents, working-age adults, and adults near or in retirement, and then compared the results with research on public policy. Like the surveys commonly released by Gallup and the mainstream media, the sample is a reliable cross-section of Americans (a "nationally representative" sample) and also contains a representative sample of parents. We surveyed a smaller, not nationally representative sample of K–12 school board members because some of the most controversial issues confronting Americans today regard K–12 schools. (A summary of our respondents is available in the appendix).

The results demonstrate that Americans are not polarized on some of the most pressing issues in politics and culture today. The results also offer a bridge that connects the politics and the culture wars from the first Trump administration through President Joe Biden's administration into the second Trump White House. Policymakers do not and should not design laws and regulations based on public opinion alone, but the survey results provide a remarkable contrast to the claims that America is deeply, even dangerously, divided.

Here's what the survey uncovered:

- Americans care about character and virtue and want children in school to learn about these things (74 percent in favor).
- Americans want educators to teach civics more in school (57 percent in favor) so that students can be prepared to be contributing members of society when they grow up.
- Our respondents believe that your biological sex is fixed and want school officials to call a student by the name and pronouns that are consistent with the child's birth certificate—the name their parents lovingly gave them (60 percent).
- Respondents did not want young children taught that they can change their "gender" (61 percent) or any students to have access to books in school that depict sexual activity (69 percent).
- And Americans do not want college admissions officers to judge student applicants using racial preferences. Such preferences are the centerpiece of the "diversity, equity, and inclusion" (DEI) movement (52 percent oppose the use of racial preferences, while 23 percent agreed and 25 percent were neutral).

Figure 0.1 Americans Agree on Hot-Button Issues (General Population Results)

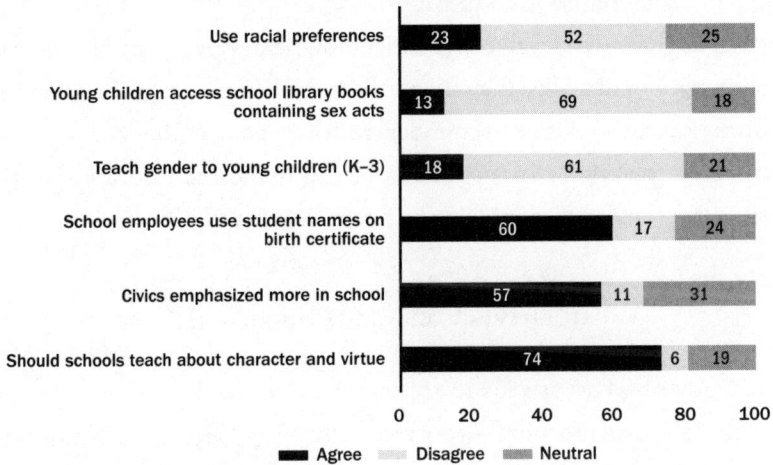

Issue	Agree	Disagree	Neutral
Use racial preferences	23	52	25
Young children access school library books containing sex acts	13	69	18
Teach gender to young children (K–3)	18	61	21
School employees use student names on birth certificate	60	17	24
Civics emphasized more in school	57	11	31
Should schools teach about character and virtue	74	6	19

0   20   40   60   80   100

■ Agree   Disagree   ■ Neutral

For information on our survey, see the appendix.

These are just a few of the topics on which this survey found high levels of agreement among respondents *on the issues.*

One survey does not settle these questions, of course. But other polling, across multiple years and across subjects, supports these results. When several surveys yield the same results over time, the findings are no longer a one-off but depict a trend, a general disposition among Americans.

If surveys reveal that, over time, a majority of respondents do not want college admissions officers to use race as the most important factor in college admissions, these results become part of our shared norms. To put a finer point on it, prevailing opinions help decide how voters and policymakers and members of communities respond to the questions they face—such as when the U.S. Supreme Court decided in 2023 that race should not be the determining factor in college admissions (see Chapter 1). Following the decision, parents, students, and university officials all had to respond to the high court's opinion in their different roles in higher education, from families choosing where their student would apply to college, to administrators determining how to evaluate

applications, to alumni deciding whether they should continue supporting their alma maters, and more.

Highlighting the levels of agreement can help strengthen communities.
Americans should realize they are not alone in their opinions. And with this
information, lawmakers can confidently design policies that are consistent
with voters' positions, robust research, and our Constitution—creating
positive outcomes for citizens, voters, families, and children.

What Surveys Can—and Cannot—Tell Us

"The study of what citizens think about politics and policy is a genuine
contribution to democracy," wrote researchers E. J. Dionne and Thomas E.
Mann on the topic of polling and surveys.[36] I agree, and that is why I wrote
this book. I explain why I chose the questions in this survey and how
lawmakers and citizens can use the widespread agreement to defend the
policies that govern communities they represent. We can better understand
each other and our friends and neighbors when we understand more about
public opinion.

Dionne and Mann are affiliated with the Brookings Institution, a
Washington, D.C.–based think tank that is structurally similar through
ideologically different from my employer, and they have researched and
commented on politics for decades. While I may not always agree with
them on the issues, I share their careful, optimistic view of the benefits of
understanding and using polling results to take the country's temperature
on subjects important to our daily lives.

No single survey is enough to explain the big questions about what
is happening around us. Neither should lawmakers adopt public policies
based on surveys alone. For this reason, I do not rely exclusively on the
results from my poll in the chapters to come. Dionne and Mann warn
analysts and consumers alike not to overstate the conclusions from polling, warning against depending on polling "as a definitive guide to public
opinion."[37] Survey questions should be carefully designed and poll a

representative sample of respondents to accurately depict the opinions of those whom they survey.

Sometimes policymakers should lean "against current public preferences," as Dionne and Mann write.[38] When evidence from research and the outcomes of public policies contradict survey results, each of us should be prepared to lean against polling results, too. Such actions are appropriate when preferences violate crucial laws protecting freedom—civil rights, for example. I argue that supposed elite institutions such as the mainstream media and universities have over-corrected on the issue of race in American life, reverting back to racial prejudice in the form of critical race theory (CRT) and its application, diversity, equity, and inclusion (DEI).

So, when my survey produced some inconclusive responses on race—the results were divided on questions pertaining to CRT and DEI, and I cannot draw conclusions about general opinions—I lean against responses that favor racial discrimination. Here, I rely on academic and policy-related research in addition to polling. This book will point out the ways in which public opinion has strayed from effective policy or how these opinions would endanger individual liberty and inhibit healthy families and communities.

With these things in mind, I compared our survey's results with the results of other reliable polling on the same or similar questions. The results create a picture of where Americans stand on important subjects concerning the nation in which we live. I am encouraged that survey results from companies and organizations such as Gallup, *The Wall Street Journal, The New York Times,* and Pew Research often agreed with the findings on many of the topics included in the poll for this book.

As in the case of the FiveThirtyEight/Ipsos survey and analysis I mentioned earlier, when I found the same results across several surveys, especially across several years, those findings became not just snapshots of public opinion but reliable indicators of common knowledge and prevailing opinions. When survey results conflicted with the research on effective policies or with laws protecting freedom, this book will explore the details to help readers sort through competing information.

Again, there were instances when the responses to this survey were not conclusive. As the chart above demonstrates, Americans agree more often than all of us may realize, but there were times when responses were mixed. When this happens, "that does not mean there is anything wrong with the public," as Dionne and Mann explain.[39] "In a democracy, citizens are typically more concerned with some matters than others, and most citizens are not continuously engaged in public affairs."[40] I agree with Dionne and Mann here and will explain in these pages what lies behind the issues in the survey, especially when the responses themselves seem to offer little in the way of explanation.

My hope is that Americans, after taking a closer look at the issues, can have better-informed debates on subjects that matter to them. I am politically conservative and won't hide my positions, but I hope to create "more light than heat"—giving people more information on key topics by laying out the prevailing opinions on the issues and findings from research literature on these topics.

★ ★ ★

The "light" in this book is urgently needed today because of how quickly policies are changing on cultural and moral subjects. On his first day in office, Trump issued more than forty executive orders, presidential memos, and other proclamations, many overturning orders from his predecessor.[41] (Biden had issued nine on his first day).[42] In his first 100 days, Trump issued some 336 orders, memos, and proclamations, including orders on the following topics:

- A clear message to the 'gender' movement saying the U.S. government will use the word "sex" to refer to "an individual's immutable biological classification";[43]
- An order rejecting surgical interventions favored by the same movement by ending federal spending for surgeries and medical interventions for minor children who want to "transition" to a different "gender";[44]

+ A statement opposing DEI and racial preferences (otherwise known as "affirmative action") in favor of meritocracy;[45]
+ An order opposing the teaching of critical race theory in K–12 classrooms;[46]
+ An order that prohibits educators from keeping quotas on how many students they suspend or expel from school according to a student's skin color or ethnicity;[47] and
+ An order showing support for school choice in K–12 schools, directly challenging the nation's largest left-wing interest groups, teacher unions.[48]

These were just a few of the orders that declared the administration's positions on issues that had dominated debates in Washington, statehouses, and the media for many years. While some argue that Americans are polarized, my research for this book found that, regardless of your opinion of Biden, Trump, Republicans, or Democrats, Americans share many of the same opinions on these issues.

★ ★ ★

The survey in this book covered more than education. Because there is so much discussion today about sex and "gender," race, library books, and the topics educators are teaching in schools, and because these issues touch Americans' lives as they go about their days, heading off to work and sending kids to school in the morning, the list of questions addressed these topics to try to capture a broad picture of what is happening around us.

Like many of my colleagues and neighbors, I have a spouse and children, which means that some of the survey questions in the poll covered subjects that affect my family, as well as others with whom I interact with on a regular basis.

For example, one of the questions asked respondents questions about K–12 student discipline policies, a topic that has a direct relationship to school safety. Statistically, school shootings are mercifully rare. When these events occur, however, they are catastrophic to the communities involved. I have experienced minor safety incidents at my child's school, and I served on a school board that asked our principal to hire a security officer to patrol school grounds. These experiences were more than enough to demonstrate for me that school safety is a crucial topic for parents and families.

★ ★ ★

To begin: Americans agree on key questions about race, schools, and sex that regularly make headlines. Considering the rather low marks that lawmakers received from survey respondents in the polls mentioned earlier (15 percent of voters approved of the way members of Congress were doing their jobs in December 2024),[49] policymakers should use these areas of agreement to rebuild trust with taxpayers and voters. Here's how.

First, Americans oppose racial discrimination. The U.S. Supreme Court has ruled against discrimination on several occasions, and in 2023 the high court held that college admissions processes that give preference to applicants based on skin color violate the Constitution. The majority opinion in this crucial case has sweeping implications for civil-rights laws even beyond universities. As Chief Justice John Roberts wrote, "Eliminating racial discrimination means eliminating *all* of it" [emphasis added].[50]

In February 2025, the U.S. Department of Education issued a letter stating that the Trump administration would enforce the high court's order. "Discrimination on the basis of race, color, or national origin is illegal and morally reprehensible," then-Acting Assistant Education Secretary Craig Trainor said.[51] He continued:

[C]olleges, universities, and K-12 schools have routinely used race as a factor in admissions, financial aid, hiring, training, and other institutional programming. In a shameful echo of a darker period in this country's history, many American schools and universities even encourage segregation by race at graduation ceremonies and in dormitories and other facilities.

He added, "If an educational institution treats a person of one race differently than it treats another person because of that person's race, the educational institution violates the law." Trainor emphasized the significance of the Civil Rights Act of 1964 and the *Students for Fair Admissions v. Harvard* and *Students for Fair Admissions v. University of North Carolina* (decided together in 2023) decision upholding civil rights.

The court's decision in the *Students for Fair Admissions* case was a seminal statement against U.S. college administrators' use of racial preferences in admissions decisions. (For decades, advocates of these preferences euphemistically called the process "affirmative action.") In these cases, the advocacy group Students for Fair Admissions filed lawsuits against Harvard and the University of North Carolina, arguing that the schools had denied admission to Asian students based on their race.[52] The high court agreed and issued a remarkable majority opinion in favor of the Civil Rights Act of 1964 and equality under the law—and against the use of racial preferences.

For years, surveys have found that the use of racial preferences is unpopular. The survey asked our sample about the use of racial preferences in admissions and what respondents think should be the most important factor in college admissions.

Leading up to the Supreme Court decision, researchers and investigators uncovered evidence that so-called DEI offices on campuses have been advocating for racist ideas, including but not limited to racial preferences in admissions, for over a decade. As Trainor's letter on the *Students for Fair Admissions* decision said, DEI offices are "smuggling racial stereotypes and explicit race-consciousness into everyday training, programming, and discipline" in education.[53] Even before the advent of DEI, college officials had incorporated racial preferences in their school policies (scholarship awards, faculty hiring, and more).

Americans' confidence in higher education has declined in recent years,[54] and if policymakers and academics want to restore public faith in post-secondary education, the public opinion on all of these subjects—racism, civil rights, college applications, and DEI—is valuable. Higher education is expensive, and enrollment is decreasing.[55] Colleges and universities nation-wide report nearly $1 trillion in revenue every year, and the total amount of college loan debt held by current and former students is $1.6 trillion[56]—a figure that is roughly equivalent to the entire economy of Brazil.[57] It is in college officials' best interest to determine what Americans want out of a four-year college experience.

College admissions decisions and taxpayer spending on DEI programs have significant consequences for families concerned about household budgets and their students' future, as well as our nation's economy. There are policies that, in recent years, state lawmakers around the country and now Donald Trump have adopted to prohibit taxpayer spending on DEI (Chapter 1).

I also talked to a college president—the first Black president of Hough-ton College, a Christian university in New York—who explains why DEI is inconsistent with civil rights and why he wants nothing to do with the discrimination it causes.

As with most of the other findings from the survey, this poll was not the only analysis to find that Americans oppose the use of race in college admissions. Furthermore, Americans agree that school officials should consider student performance on college admissions tests as the most important factor in admissions decisions. Such consistency across several surveys makes this finding especially robust and worthy of a closer look.

The questions on the use of race in college admissions and of how much university administrators consider a student's merit have implications for life outside of the academy—such as in the example of the chemist I interviewed who worked for an oil company in Oklahoma. He explained to me how his life was upended by DEI.

This book explores the roots of racial preferences, how groups on both sides are debating the question today, and what all these ideas mean for more complicated topics such as critical race theory and DEI, which frequently make headlines in the news and on social media.

Second, and on the topic of K–12 schools, Americans want educators to teach children about character and virtue. Surveys, including the survey in this book, find that parents and voters do not want schools to avoid moral issues or attempt to be neutral on values. Two subjects stood out in this survey and others that I reviewed: civics and a set of life choices known as the "success sequence."

For many years, surveys have found that Americans on both the right and the left sides of the political divide believe K–12 educators are not teaching civics enough or effectively. Civics instruction includes lessons on how our government works, on how we can be responsible citizens and participate in government at the local, state, and national levels, and on the history of our representative system. K–12 students have posted dismal scores on reliable measures of civics learning for decades. Civics resides at the intersection of history, social studies, and government, so the discussion of whether America's history is ultimately a story of victory and redemption or one of power and oppression resonates with everyone who calls this nation home.

Civics simply does not receive enough attention in schools. Should children be taught about character and virtue, qualities promoted by our Founding Fathers, or should they be taught that American life is defined by power struggles? Is life a power struggle between oppressors and the oppressed? Conservatives and liberals have different solutions for the civics crisis, but all agree that civics education is in poor shape and that improving it should be a priority.

As for the success sequence, a majority of the respondents surveyed agreed that young people should be taught the positive benefits that come from finishing high school, getting a job or enrolling in college, and getting married before having children. Researchers on the right and left side of the ideological divide have explored the research on these choices dating back nearly thirty years and found that children of married parents are more likely to experience positive outcomes—they get better grades, are less likely to go to jail or prison, and are less likely to live in poverty as adults—than their peers. Finishing high school helps graduates when they enter the workforce. The enormous positive effects of getting married before having children cannot be overstated. Putting marriage before carriage has benefits for the spouses and their children.[58]

Lessons on the success sequence are not meant to shame those who have children outside of wedlock or who do not finish high school. And no one should stay in an abusive marriage just for the sake of staying married, nor should students be forced to remain in persistently failing schools just for the sake of graduating. Each of those issues—nonmarital pregnancy, dropping out of school, spousal abuse—deserves a separate discussion that is outside the scope of this book, but there are essential benefits that flow from a set of very basic life choices around education, work, and marriage that do not receive enough attention in schools, politics, or the media.

Young students deserve to know that some 97 percent of individuals from the millennial generation (born from the early 1980s to mid-1990s) who follow the success sequence do not live in poverty when they reach prime working age.[59] Married adults are happier, and the children of intact, married parents are more likely to succeed, by any measure. We should teach children these things at age-appropriate times. (Spoiler alert: Americans *want* teachers to share this information with students.) Educators are doing students a disservice if we do not tell them and help inform the decisions they make about their lives.

Before civics and the success sequence in schools, though, Americans have still another problem: student scores in reading, perhaps the most basic and necessary of all academic subjects, have fallen to historic lows. How can we ask schools to better prepare students to be contributing members of society and understand America's founding documents when nearly 40 percent of fourth-grade students read below grade level and scores among eighth-graders are the lowest they have been since 1992?[60]

Curiously, reading has been back in the news recently, and not just because of low test scores. Inspiring success stories still capture national attention. To wit, in October 2022, Oliver James, age thirty-four, posted videos on social media of teaching himself how to read, and the posts went viral and landed him an interview on *The Today Show*.[61] James had been incarcerated, making him an underdog, the kind of come-from-behind figure

Americans love to cheer for. His videos inspired many because he learned a skill late in life that anyone holding this book often takes for granted.

The bestselling *Why Johnny Can't Read* concerned many Americans when it was released in 1955, and it raised awareness about the importance of phonics instruction. More contemporary research finds that the "cueing" or "whole word" methods of reading instruction, which until recently had replaced phonics in many classrooms, has crippled generations of students. My survey asked respondents about how best to teach reading and whether schools should use phonics-based instruction (now part of a movement called the "science of reading") or the "cueing/whole word" method, and the results strongly suggest that parents and educators need to return to phonics-based instruction and end the reading wars.

Respondents are split on the methods teachers should use in K–12 reading instruction, something that has important implications for people like James and currently incarcerated individuals (see Chapter 2). While respondents may be divided over the use of phonics or the cueing/whole word methods, all would agree that they would rather see more people working productively and contributing to society than in jail or prison. While more research is needed to make causal connections between literacy and incarceration (that is, research does not prove that illiteracy causes you to go to prison), the data strongly suggest that more effective reading instruction leads to improved academic outcomes overall, which correlate with lower incarceration rates.[62]

So, Chapter 2 surveys the debate over how to teach reading and describes the data on how cueing may have set back millions of students over several decades. This topic has a significant, perhaps even unexpected connection with criminal justice, underlining the importance of focusing on effective reading instruction, which paves the way for students to learn about virtue, civics, and the success sequence.

In writing this chapter, I interviewed parents who are part of a movement to put classic books back in schools and revitalize civics instruction. And I talked to an immigrant mother from India who defended the U.S.

Constitution at a Virginia state school board meeting and was shocked to find stiff resistance to using our founding documents in classrooms. Reading, civics, and the topic of what it means to be an American all came together in these conversations with local leaders.

Third, Americans agree that young children should not be exposed to graphic sexual content nor be taught that a person can choose one's "gender." The survey respondents, especially parents, do not want this information represented in books on school library shelves, nor do they want children taught about such things in elementary and middle school. Agreement was strongest when our survey question asked about students in kindergarten through third grade.

Furthermore, respondents agreed that school personnel should not keep secrets from parents when a child wants to change their name at school or answer to pronouns that do not correspond to the child's birth certificate. My survey and others find that Americans believe parents should know about decisions such as these that their children are making while at school. While groups such as the American Civil Liberties Union (ACLU) argue that minor-age children have a right to choose their "gender,"[63] some state lawmakers have gotten parents' message and are passing laws to reinforce parental rights.[64] This subject is one on which state lawmakers and the general public are moving in the same direction.

Affirming a minor child's decision to assume a different gender can start a process that results in irreversible changes. Many formerly "trans" youth (called "detransitioners") have come to regret the choices they made earlier in their lives. Americans also agree that boys should not participate in girls' sports, nor should girls participate in boys' athletic competitions—another topic of much discussion in Washington and in state capitol buildings. Here again, state lawmakers and the Trump administration have acted decisively in favor of children's health (Chapter 4).

I interviewed parents of children who were caught in the gender craze. They tell their stories and explain what they are doing to help other families experiencing the same things.

The survey respondents also strongly agreed that parents should have a say in the books that are available in school libraries. My earlier book, *Splintered: Critical Race Theory and the Progressive War on Truth*, explained that a radical movement was afoot to remove Shakespeare and *To Kill a Mockingbird* from schools as a way of "decolonizing" the curriculum (read: removing anything written by a White person, even if the work is a core part of the Western canon). At the same time, efforts were and are underway to add sexually explicit material to classrooms and libraries. Maia Kobabe's *Gender Queer*, for example, has been the topic of numerous reports and even school board meetings after parents discovered the graphic novel on school library shelves. Nudity, oral sex, and bodily fluids are all depicted in living color in this novel, and families have been shocked to learn that such material could find its way in front of young children in schools.[65]

The topics of "gender" and "library books in schools" involve not just card catalogues but also issues of biological truth and moral values. Chapter 4 discusses these issues in detail.

Fourth, teacher unions are arguably the strongest interest groups influencing politics today. The nation's largest teacher union, the National Education Association (NEA), has some three million members and annual revenues of more than $529 million. It can hardly even be called a union—if unions are organizations that advocate on behalf of their members. Only 7.5 percent of the NEA's expenditures are on "labor representation." The rest of the budget goes to the interest groups' own employee salaries and to lobbying on a host of issues, from opposing nuclear power to resisting the private operation of prisons.[66]

The survey asked respondents to rate unions on a scale of 1 to 10, with ratings of 1–3 being harmful and 8–10 helpful. Most of those in our survey rated unions somewhere in the middle, between 4 and 7.

Here is where this book adds clarity to the issue. If Americans oppose racial preferences, as described in Chapter 1, favor rigorous academics and the teaching of virtue (Chapters 2 and 3), and oppose giving boys access to girls' private spaces and male participation in girls' sports, then they oppose the policy positions of the teacher unions. Teacher unions advocate for racial preferences, want topics such as "white privilege" taught in schools at the expense of civics, oppose the use of phonics in California, and lobby in favor of the "transgender" movement.[67] And these unions use taxpayer money to do so. In some states, teacher union members can take paid leave to lobby state legislatures for their radical causes.[68]

Teachers unions were the leading organizations lobbying to keep public schools closed to in-person learning for as long as possible during the COVID-19 pandemic. That decision put a burden on parents who were trying to get back to work and resulted in significant student learning losses.[69]

★ ★ ★

We should not expect, nor do I recommend, that lawmakers design laws and rules exclusively around public opinion. Every American cannot be an expert on every issue. For example, I was surprised at the inconclusive responses to questions about effective reading strategies and the benefits or harms that come from teacher unions. Using phonics to teach children to read has substantial research supporting it that dates back at least a century, yet our survey was inconclusive on this question.

Americans are also split on how they feel about K–12 education in the U.S., a finding that matches the results from other reliable polls. This division helps to explain why parents and school board members seem to be on opposite sides of some tough issues today (and why school board elections have attracted so much attention since the pandemic). While successful public schools operate around the country, parents should be able to choose how and where their children learn, particularly when local schools are teaching content that does not align with a family's deeply held beliefs.

Parents should have other learning options available to them when schools teach gender ideology to kindergarten and elementary children, for example (my survey and others find widespread opposition to the teaching of "gender" to young children). Despite biological evidence that we are born to produce either sperm (male) or eggs (female), some schools are ignoring scientific facts, as well as parental beliefs, and are teaching these lessons anyway.[70]

My survey found mixed results when respondents were asked about critical race theory, with a sizeable portion of our respondents saying they were neutral on the topic. I explore this issue and find that Americans are not really undecided on the issue of race—they just do not always connect the dots between their understanding of racial issues today and the term "critical race theory." The responses to this question in the survey have significance for still other questions I asked, such as the questions dealing with DEI, how teachers discipline students in school, and teachers unions.

During the COVID-19 pandemic in 2020–2022, public schools simply lost track of tens of thousands of students nationwide.[71] Enrollment dropped by more than one million students, while the number of students being homeschooled and attending private school increased.[72] We should all be concerned about the plummeting reading and math scores and the coinciding declining measures of mental health among young people in public schools.[73] But we are also concerned about the cultural issues that are driving parents to speak out at board meetings and to oppose the way many schools are teaching about race, gender, and sex.

Given this information, I would have expected more respondents to be skeptical of K–12 schooling today on the questions pertaining to schools and satisfaction. The divided results, though, suggest that while, on average, education is in poor shape nationwide, satisfaction in K–12 schooling varies across partisan lines.

Surveys and Building Public Trust

The survey for this book and others that returned similar findings should give neighbors, co-workers, friends, and relatives the confidence to take positions unpopular with the mainstream media and radical left. The strongest support for DEI and "transgenderism" falls largely on the far left side of the ideological divide, and that support in results is outweighed in the poll results by those who support the idea that sex is immutable. In general, Americans do not want children taught that they can change their "gender." This position is backed by research, along with a growing number of stories of detransitioners warning others about the dangers of the drugs and surgeries that change vital human functions.

Americans can also be confident that racial discrimination is unpopular. For these issues around sex and race and the other topics on which the survey found agreement, citizens should speak up before elected boards and with their state and federal officials and can confidently say there are others with them.

For lawmakers, I explain in the concluding chapters how to design policies that are supported by polling—and research—and that make children safer, uphold civil rights laws, and protect individual liberty.

There will never be agreement on every issue, of course. Our representative system was created to protect the freedom of individuals and enable groups to defend their own interests. I do not argue that there are no differences between Americans, nor are our differences necessarily unhealthy for a society. The survey does, however, offer evidence that Americans are united on some very important questions that are driving debates in statehouses, schoolhouses, and even your house.

Americans are not polarized on key issues affecting our daily lives. Let's have a look at what these issues are and why the agreement matters.

CHAPTER ONE

DEI

While I am painfully aware of the social and economic ravages which have befallen my race and all who suffer discrimination, I hold out enduring hope that this country will live up to its principles so clearly enunciated in the Declaration of Independence and the Constitution of the United States: That all men are created equal, are equal citizens, and must be treated equally before the law.

—U.S. Supreme Court Justice Clarence Thomas[1]

Chad Ellis is a scientist—a chemist, to be exact. Exactness is something he appreciates. "If I'm exposed to a chemical spill, I deserve to know what's in that. If I'm exposed to something…I deserve to know where it's coming from and who stands behind it," he said in our interview.[2]

So when he was required to attend a DEI training program called "Here and Heard" as part of his job at Chevron Phillips, which develops chemicals and plastics, he wanted to know what he was being taught and where it came from. Why was he being told George Washington's teeth were "pulled from the mouths of enslaved persons" and that America is beset by systemic racism—and what do these things have to do with designing plastic materials?[3]

The DEI training not only took aim at America's foundational civil rights laws but was also meant to cause anxiety among the trainees. Ellis said the DEI trainer, who was a real estate agent, not a Ph.D. in counseling or with any identifiable academic background in race relations, told the Chevron employees that "people are going to leave [the training] angry."[4] The goal of the training was not to promote racial harmony but to create distress in the attendees' minds. The DEI videos used in the sessions were "purposefully designed to create visceral reactions," according to the trainer.[5]

Provoking people with claims of systemic racism is not inclusive; it does more to create suspicion than to foster a healthy workplace. Ellis asked the Oklahoma State Board of Examiners of Psychologists, which is responsible for ensuring that "only properly qualified psychologists practice psychology in the state," to review "Here and Heard." He wanted to know if the board thought the lessons and videos were attempts at psychological manipulation, not professional development. Ellis's complaint to the board of examiners alleged that he had "received confirmed mental health damage" to his person from the "coerced, mandatory workplace attendance" at the DEI sessions.[6]

While this board refused to make a ruling, Ellis and his attorney showed the trainings to Susan Brandon, a psychologist who worked as Research Chief at the Defense Intelligence Agency, an office in the U.S. Department of Defense. Brandon has an impressive background, having served on the High-Value Detainee Interrogation Group, a program involving the Federal Bureau of Investigation, Central Intelligence Agency, and Department of Defense.[7]

In a letter Ellis later used in court filings, Brandon stressed that she is not an expert on DEI trainings, but she said that her experience allowed her to determine that the videos resembled the psychological coercion used in military interrogations. Writing to Ellis, Brandon said, "What my conversations with you have reminded me is that these [DEI] programs may not only not change hearts and minds in ways that are beneficial, but that they can cause real harm and distress."[8]

"What I know of interview and interrogation methods whose goal is cooperation in order to elicit useful and valid information, is that attacking an individual's 'loyalty, intelligence, abilities, leadership qualities...[or] appearance' is counter-productive and is likely to make that individual less cooperative rather than more cooperative," Brandon said.[9]

She continued: "The Here and Heard video series...challenges the viewer to question their values as Americans....Such challenges can be understood not only as not affirming but as attacking the viewers' loyalties and intelligence."[10]

Brandon is describing the very essence of DEI. As the examples in this chapter will demonstrate, DEI questions American values. DEI training causes distress—not toleration and unity. And employees at companies around the country are being forced to undergo such trainings, even though the sessions have nothing to do with their actual job responsibilities. Still, for many years, *Fortune* 500 companies offered or required DEI sessions even as the sessions had nothing to do with the services or products a company provides or produces.[11] As of 2024, nearly every *Fortune* 500 company had a DEI statement on its website—though this began to change as 2024 rolled into 2025.[12]

Company officials first began changing their position on DEI after state attorneys general warned companies that their DEI practices, including the addition of race-based ratios to corporate hiring goals, may violate state and federal civil rights laws. For example, in 2024, Florida Attorney General Ashley Moody asked the state's Commission on Human Relations to investigate Starbucks for using such ratios.[13] One year earlier, the state attorneys general from thirteen states wrote a joint letter to *Fortune* 100 companies on the issue of using "race-based" employment practices.[14]

By connecting DEI to violations of civil rights laws, these state officials are removing doubts that DEI is merely an exercise in tolerance. DEI is nothing short of racist. The second Trump administration also issued two executive orders specifically condemning DEI, one pertaining to education and the other dealing with the federal workforce.[15]

Public pressure also helped convince companies to rescind their racist DEI policies. Advocates such as Christopher Rufo of the Manhattan Institute and documentarian and activist Robby Starbuck revealed companies' discriminatory policies on social media, causing several *Fortune* 500 companies, including John Deere and Tractor Supply, to withdraw their policies requiring DEI training and race-based hiring.[16]

But it gets worse: DEI has not only been inescapable in the workplace; it has saturated education. For all of these reasons, governors, state lawmakers, and the Trump administration have made the elimination of DEI a priority.

DEI in Education

Ellis, Rufo, and Starbuck are not the only ones documenting the harms of DEI. Vincent Lloyd is a professor at Villanova, an author, and a DEI trainer. But he questioned the way DEI has changed the way Americans talk about race. "Pushing anti-racism to its limits, what we reach isn't just hollow doctrine, but abuse: Pathological relationships that cut us off from the world, from the give-and-take of reasons and feelings unfolding over time that makes up life in the world," Lloyd wrote in the online magazine *Compact* in February 2023.

Lloyd teaches in the Africana Studies program at Villanova, and for many years he led seminars for students in which he would teach DEI concepts. "I am a black professor, I directed my university's black-studies program, I lead anti-racism and transformative justice workshops, and I have published books on anti-black racism and prison abolition," Lloyd wrote in *Compact*.

Yet when a summer seminar for high school students that he was teaching on "anti-racism" devolved into hostile struggle sessions under the influence of a newly minted Ivy League graduate who was assisting him, even Lloyd became disillusioned with anti-racism and the inescapable discrimination that DEI perpetuates.[17]

Some organizations describe DEI as a set of "values" concerned with "working to be supportive of different groups of individuals" (diversity), "fair treatment for all people" (equity), and "the degree to which organizations embrace all employees and enable them to make meaningful contributions" (inclusion).[18] In truth, DEI is an application of the philosophy known as critical race theory (CRT), a worldview that expands the Marxist idea of conflicts between economic classes to racial conflicts. CRT considers everything in public and private life in terms of racial differences—every event has a racist undertone (or overtone). Critical race theorists criticize civil rights laws and advocate for more racial discrimination, not less, in a quest for power, not tolerance.

There is more to say about critical race theory, but one of the challenges to understanding DEI is that the concept is difficult to define. Consistent definitions are hard to locate. In a survey of human resource managers who work in private businesses, 71 percent of respondents said their company did not have "an official definition" of DEI.[19] In a more recent report from the Iowa Board of Regents, which governs Iowa's public universities and directed a study group to research DEI, the regents wrote that "the phrase 'diversity, equity, and inclusion'…does not have a standardized definition within the context of higher education supports and services." According to the regents, what "descriptions" they could find "generally align with the federal protected class definitions and Iowa civil rights law."[20]

That means that DEI is supposed to have something to do with asking people to treat others the same without regard for race, ethnicity, country of origin, or sex. Yet, as the experiences of Ellis and Lloyd demonstrate, the teaching of DEI results in something very different from racial tolerance. Despite the different definitions for DEI, one report found that 67 percent of universities require DEI offices or programs on campus.[21] This means universities and businesses have ploughed ahead with DEI trainings without a consistent definition for the ideas they were propagating.

The offices that apply DEI on college campuses and in corporate America clearly do not defend civil rights laws. To wit, in Lloyd's case, the Ivy League grad assistant who led some of the sessions in his DEI summer workshop told "non-black students" that they needed to "shut up." Students were taught that "objective facts are a tool of white supremacy," and the assistant told Lloyd that he was not radical enough about "anti-blackness." He had "made the [classroom] space unsafe for black students" because he had dared to suggest alternatives to the antiracist narrative, the assistant said. Ultimately, the seminar collapsed—some students were expelled while others refused to participate. The Ivy League grad accused Lloyd of racism, and the accusation was enough to destroy any hope of the students learning anything.[22]

DEI does not respect or tolerate someone's skin color or ethnicity—DEI says your color defines you, the opposite of civil rights laws that protect Americans from being treated differently based on race or ethnicity.

★　★　★

Ibram X. Kendi was, at one time, the nation's best-known DEI trainer. His book *How to Be an Antiracist* was a *New York Times* bestseller, and he has lectured around the country on DEI and antiracism. According to Kendi's now-infamous quote from *How to Be an Antiracist*, antiracism requires discrimination in the present to correct for past discrimination and calls for future discrimination to pay for present discrimination. Kendi says favoring racial discrimination in this way is "antiracist," though Kendi has changed the way he talks about this term after mounting criticism, even editing the text of his *Antiracist* book since its publication in 2019 for future printings.[23]

As for DEI, diversity occurs when "antiracist power predominates," Kendi says.[24] Kendi calls for "resource equity," a suspiciously Marxist idea that favors redistributing resources to people regardless of what someone has earned. Considering his definition of antiracism, however, it hardly seems as though he really wants everyone to have the same things. More accurately, Kendi and the Ivy League graduate who assisted in Lloyd's course would rather that certain ethnic minorities benefited more from public policies than others. Extra points on a college application, for example, or a spot on the corporate committee in charge of employee hiring decisions just because they are an ethnic minority.

Make no mistake, then: DEI discriminates. DEI treats people differently based on race, which violates federal and state civil rights laws, along with the U.S. Constitution, and should violate the consciences of millions of Americans who do not want to be judged based on the way they look or what family they come from.

Discrimination is, by definition, the process of acting with racial preferences. Some people are preferred—given benefits or better access to things—because of the color of their skin. Kendi and other DEI advocates have tried and are trying to inject racial preferences into every corner of society. Not only do Kendi and other DEI supporters favor discrimination, they also oppose federal civil rights laws that outlaw discrimination. Kendi has publicly criticized the Civil Rights Act of 1964. Other critical race theorists have argued that civil rights only advanced in American law because White individuals thought they would stall racial unrest domestically and gain favor from other countries if they advanced racial equality (critical race theorist Richard Delgado calls this "interest convergence").[25] According to critical race theorists, civil rights progressed in the U.S. not due to ethical or legal reasons tied to America's founding ideals but because of White individuals' selfish goals and personal benefits.[26]

You read that right: Those who support DEI are highly critical of and even oppose, in some cases, the very laws that prohibit racism and that civil rights activists in the 1960s and 1970s risked their lives to promote and defend.

The Ellis and Lloyd examples are neither unique nor isolated. In fact, they may be representative of the culture DEI has created everywhere its ideas are applied. Just one month after Lloyd's article appeared in *Compact*, the magazine ran yet another story about a professor engaged in DEI training, Tabia Lee. She was fired from her position in the Office of Equity, Social Justice, and Multicultural Education at De Anza Community College in Cupertino, California, because she valued "open dialogue and viewpoint diversity." In other words, she wasn't radical enough. Her perspective "wasn't welcome," Lee says (she is now suing the university).[27]

In 2023, Kendi's Center for Antiracist Research at Boston University laid off half of its staff. University officials opened an investigation into Kendi's center over "a number of complaints from faculty and staff" and a lack of productivity from the office after receiving millions in grants and donations following the riots related to George Floyd in 2020.[28] This should come as little surprise because research has consistently found that DEI trainings are ineffective at changing individual behavior.[29] A recent study from the Network Contagion Research Institute and Rutgers University found that

DEI actually creates bias.[30] In 2025, Kendi left Boston University for Howard University, and his Center for Antiracist Research at Boston closed.[31]

Considering these events and the research on race relations in the U.S., I included questions about CRT, DEI, and racial preferences in the survey.

Americans Oppose Racial Preferences

My survey and others have found that Americans oppose the use of racial preferences. Consider college admissions, for example. One of the oldest applications of what we now call DEI is "affirmative action," better described as racial preferences, which is the term used in this book. In 2019, a Pew Research survey found that 73 percent of respondents, including 62 percent of Black respondents and 65 percent of Hispanic respondents, opposed college officials' consideration of race or ethnicity in university admissions.[32] Pew found similar responses (74 percent were opposed to using race, including 62 percent of registered Democrats) in another survey in 2022. In this second survey, 61 percent of respondents said high school grades should be a major factor in college admissions, and nearly 40 percent said standardized test scores should be a major factor.[33]

And then in 2023, just before the U.S. Supreme Court ruled against the use of racial preferences in the *Students for Fair Admissions* decision, Pew again found widespread opposition in yet another survey. Eighty-two percent of adults opposed college officials' use of racial preferences in admissions in this survey, while only 17 percent said colleges should consider race.[34]

Racial preferences in college admissions are one of the ways that DEI offices and training programs operationalize critical race theory—DEI puts CRT into practice. DEI advocates argue that people should exercise preferences between individuals in college admissions, hiring and job promotions, and more, based on race and/or ethnicity. DEI, racial preferences, and critical race theory are all part of the same worldview. Radicals also use other terms for them—critical race theory is often called "cultural competency," for example, or "social justice"—but the ideas are indelibly linked.

In fact, the founders of critical race theory devote a section in one of their key volumes, *Critical Race Theory: The Key Writings that Formed the Movement*, to racial preferences (again, calling it "affirmative action").[35] DEI offices on college campuses strongly stated their support for racial preferences before and after the Supreme Court ruling in *Students for Fair Admissions v. Harvard*.[36]

Consistent with the Pew Research results, my survey found that a majority of respondents were opposed to the use of racial preferences in college admissions, across two of our three sample groups. Nearly 52 percent of respondents from the general public opposed the use of racial preferences, while 23 percent were in favor. Fifty-one percent of parents were opposed to racial preferences, while 26 percent were in favor.

Curiously, school board members were split on the issue, with 45 percent in favor and 42 percent opposed.[37] But responses from this subsample varied across age ranges. That is, older board members were more likely to be opposed, and strongly so, compared with younger members. A majority of the sample of members aged forty-five or above were opposed to the use of racial preferences, including nearly 67 percent of respondents in the fifty-five-to-sixty-four age category.

Figure 1.1 **Should colleges use racial preferences in their admissions policies?**

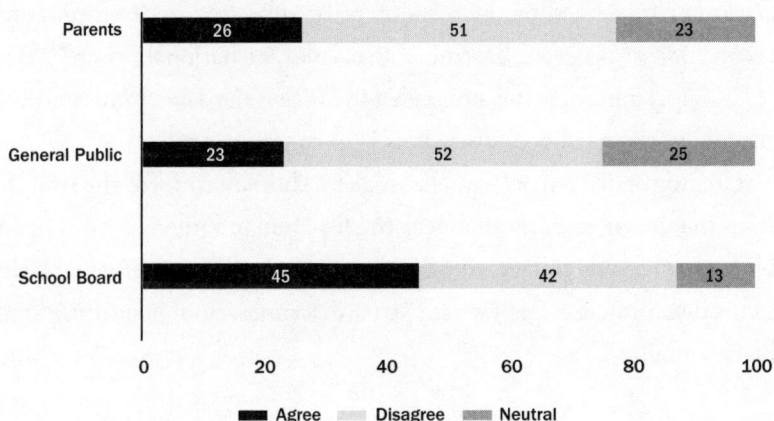

Figure 1.2 **School board members agree vs. disagree with the use of racial preferences in college admissions, by age**

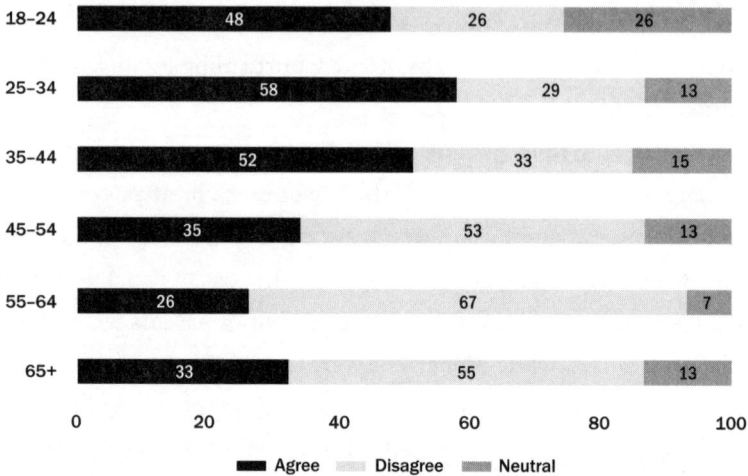

This is an example of when policymakers should "lean against" school board members' opinions (using Dionne and Mann's terms discussed in the Introduction) because school board members' preferred policies would violate civil rights laws. Remember, the Civil Rights Act of 1964, the seminal civil rights law in U.S. Code, says that no one can be "excluded from participation in, be denied the benefits of, or be subjected to discrimination" in a government program based on "race, color, or national origin."[38] And the U.S. Supreme Court has now ruled in *Students for Fair Admissions* that prioritizing race in college admissions is unconstitutional.

State university officials and lawmakers should reinforce the prohibition on the use of racial preferences in all public programs—from hiring public employees to college admissions, and anything in between. Using "present discrimination" to remedy "past discrimination" is nothing short of racist and illegal.

★ ★ ★

"We had a different set of problems in the 1950s and 1960s around race in the United States than we do today," said Wayne Lewis, the first Black president of Houghton University, a Christian college in central New York, in my interview with him.[39] Lewis taught at a K–12 school in North Carolina and was the commissioner of education for the state of Kentucky from 2018 to 2019.

"Is this to suggest that the United States is in a post-racial and ethnic utopia where we don't continue to have challenges? Of course not," Lewis answers.[40]

"We still have challenges," he says, "but this is not the United States of the 1950s and 1960s. We have to acknowledge that."[41]

Lewis has attracted attention for taking bold positions on race and "gender," speaking out against DEI, and opposing the idea that men should compete in women's sports. He was a guest of U.S. House Speaker Mike Johnson at the 2024 State of the Union address and has been featured on Fox News and the Christian Broadcast Network.

His position in favor of treating people equally under the law, regardless of race, makes him unique among university officials. As our survey demonstrates, though, he is not unique among Americans in general.

"What's important to me is that there is not discrimination," Lewis says. "We have to ensure that in our current practice, and moving forward, every young person…who wants to pursue a college education is not discriminated against based on their race and ethnicity, and that includes not having preference because of your race and ethnicity and not having opportunities taken away from you based on your race."[42]

Yet as Lloyd's experience and Kendi's ideas demonstrate, some on the radical left hold fast to the idea that racism is the defining feature of America and should be met with still more racism. This belief is having disastrous effects on young people because, at best, they are getting mixed messages about the meaning of their race and ethnicity, and at worst, they are being taught that discrimination is appropriate and skin color is more important than hard work and personal merit.

★ ★ ★

When the survey for this book asked our respondents what they think should be the most important factor to consider in college admissions, a student's race was never one of the top answers. This was true even for school board members, who, again, were the only group in our survey to have more respondents in favor of racial preferences than opposed. Forty-two percent of school board members said college admissions tests should be the most important factor in admissions, while just 2 percent said race should be the most important factor.

Parents and the general public strongly endorsed college admissions tests and high school grades as the most important factors in college admissions. Among the general public, 52 percent of respondents said college admissions tests should be the most important factor in the admissions process. One-third of respondents said a student's high school GPA should be the most important factor. Just 1.6 percent of respondents said race should be the most important factor, with 1 percent of respondents saying sex should be the most important factor. Even among respondents who identified as Democrats, only 2 percent said race should be the most important factor and less than 1 percent said sex should be the most important factor. School board responses were similar to those from the

Figure 1.3 **What should be the most important factor in college admissions?**

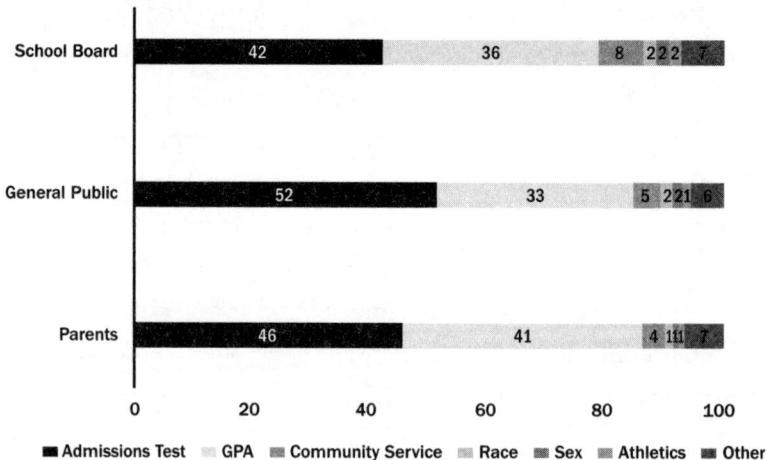

general public, with 36 percent saying high school GPA should be the most important factor and, as we have seen, 42 percent saying college admissions tests should be the most important consideration.

The share of parents saying race should be the most important factor was also around 1 percent. Forty-six percent of parents listed standardized tests as the most important factor, but more parents favored the use of a student's GPA as the determining factor (41 percent) than did school board members or the general public.[43]

In none of our respondent groups did a majority say that race should be the most important factor in college admissions. Even school board members, who said it is appropriate for college admissions officers to use racial preferences, still said these preferences should not be the most important factor in a student's application.

★ ★ ★

So why are college officials going to such great lengths to defend something that is racially discriminatory, that violates civil rights laws, and that the U.S. Supreme Court has ruled unconstitutional?

Following the court's decision in the *Students for Fair Admissions* case, officials at colleges across the country expressed their opposition to the court's decision. Washington University of St. Louis administrators issued a statement complaining that the ruling would "prevent higher education institutions from considering race as a factor in admissions."[44] Chief Justice John Roberts had written in the majority opinion that schools could take into consideration the experiences of a student who is an ethnic minority if they faced discrimination in their life. The decision explicitly said there are narrow, specific ways that colleges can consider whether someone has been the victim of racist actions.[45] Yet Washington University of St. Louis's chancellor called the ruling "personally painful."[46]

Considering the polling that opposes racial preferences, Americans should be shocked to learn that a college administrator finds it "painful" to follow civil rights laws.

Davidson College's admissions team released a statement practically admitting that they had used racial preferences to discriminate between applicants, saying, "The decision today by the United States Supreme Court hinders our ability, and that of other colleges and universities, to fully evaluate applicants. It is not the outcome we desired."[47] Other universities announced they were "disappointed," "deeply disheartened," and "deeply saddened" by the decision.[48]

Lewis, the Houghton University president, has said, "That's what I hear in every meeting that I go to. Every higher education meeting, every college presidents meeting."

"That's the dominant narrative. It seems to be the only acceptable public thing to say at this point," Lewis says.[49]

Does this mean the schools are also disappointed and disheartened by the U.S. Civil Rights Act that prohibits racism in workplace hiring, K–12 education, and other parts of American life? Few, if any, of the college leaders "disappointed" in the *Students for Fair Admissions* decision have made the effort to explain that their opposition to the decision means they also oppose federal civil rights laws.

"I've not heard anyone give a plausible answer for how you can justify or reasonably operationalize a system where you discriminate sometimes, and then other times you don't," Lewis says. "In the widespread, mainstream media this [color-blind admissions] is talked about like this is a white supremacist movement that is moving against minority students."[50]

The inconsistencies between DEI and the Civil Rights Act of 1964, which prohibits discrimination "on ground of race, color, or national origin,"[51] are unmistakable. Fortunately, state lawmakers are taking the necessary steps to protect civil rights for all Americans: Between 2023 and 2024, policymakers in ten states rejected DEI and related activities, some prohibiting the use of taxpayer spending on DEI programs. In November 2023, the Iowa Board of Regents called on state universities to "eliminate any DEI functions that are not necessary for compliance or accreditation," including DEI positions.[52] The regents said any services provided by DEI offices must be "available to all students."[53]

The regents also abolished another discriminatory practice enforced by DEI offices: requirements that job applicants complete a "DEI statement" as a condition of applying.[54] One year later, Iowa governor Kim Reynolds signed legislation abolishing DEI operations on college campuses. Texas lawmakers passed legislation saying public colleges and universities may not "establish or maintain" DEI offices on campus and school personnel may not promote "differential treatment of" or provide "special benefits to" individuals based on "race, color or ethnicity."[55] Ron DeSantis, the Republican governor of Florida, also signed legislation abolishing DEI offices and stating that taxpayer money may not be used in higher education to "advocate for diversity, equity, and inclusion, or promote or engage in political or social activism."[56]

In 2024, Kansas lawmakers adopted similar policies, along with policymakers in Alabama. In 2025, still more state officials adopted these policies, including those in Ohio, Indiana, and Mississippi, and more.[57]

So-called DEI statements or "loyalty oaths" are found in university hiring practices around the country, including in the University of California system and public colleges in Arizona. Investigations conducted by the Reason Foundation and the Pacific Legal Foundation found evidence that University of California officials made these "loyalty oaths" to DEI a condition of hiring. University of California Berkeley officials "rejected 76 percent of qualified applications" for an insufficient commitment to diversity "without even considering their teaching skills," according to Pacific Legal.[58]

In Arizona, the Goldwater Institute found that public university administrators "mandate diversity statements from applicants in over a quarter (28 percent) of job postings at the University of Arizona, nearly three-quarters (73 percent) of job postings at Northern Arizona University, and in more than four of five (81 percent) job postings at Arizona State University" (I wrote the foreword to this Goldwater report).[59] Even after ASU administrators made an official statement saying they no longer would require loyalty oaths, watchdogs still uncovered requirements in job postings.[60]

The cases of college admissions, loyalty oaths, and DEI demonstrate the confusion created by Kendi and other DEI advocates on the issue of race.

They say they support diversity and inclusion, but they are "saddened" by a Supreme Court decision that defends civil rights, and they feel it necessary to require people to pledge allegiance to DEI as a condition of hiring or promotion. They are clearly substituting racial favoritism for civil rights.

Connecting CRT, DEI, and Racial Preferences

While respondents to our survey were largely opposed to the use of racial preferences and want students to be judged based on their results in the classroom, our questions specifically using the term "DEI" solicited mixed responses. In our sample from the general population, respondents were split almost evenly on the question of whether college officials should use taxpayer funds and student tuition to pay for DEI departments and staff. Thirty-four percent were in favor, while 36 percent were opposed, with 30 percent neutral on the issue.

Here we find a split, which likely is a signal that Americans do not have fully formed views on the topic. Ambiguity is not uncommon in survey results. While Americans may have been undecided *on average*, groups that seemed evenly divided began to coalesce into more decisive positions once we disaggregated the data by political affiliation.

Among Democrats in our general-population sample, 54 percent were in favor, compared with just 17 percent of Republicans. Unsurprisingly, these figures were the reverse among those who said they were opposed (63 percent of Republicans opposed, compared to 16 percent of Democrats).

Notably, our survey was conducted just a few months before the revelation that former Harvard president Claudine Gay, a central figure in Harvard's DEI bureaucracy for many years, is a serial plagiarist. That should have been reason enough for the university's board to relieve her of her position. But she was also unable to explain the school's position on whether it is acceptable to call for the genocide of Jews, and she remained a vocal supporter of DEI. She resigned in early 2024.

Gay's case elevated the profile of DEI even more. In October 2023, the same month that she was called to testify before Congress about the

Figure 1.4 **Should taxpayer money and student tuition be used to pay for DEI on college campuses?**

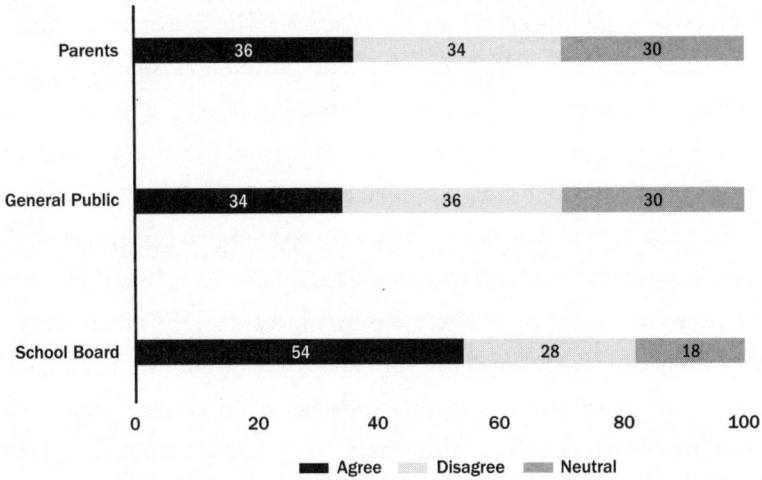

Group	Agree	Disagree	Neutral
Parents	36	34	30
General Public	34	36	30
School Board	54	28	18

■ Agree　░ Disagree　▨ Neutral

Figure 1.5 **Should taxpayer money and student tuition payments pay for DEI offices on public college campuses? (Results by respondent group and political party)**

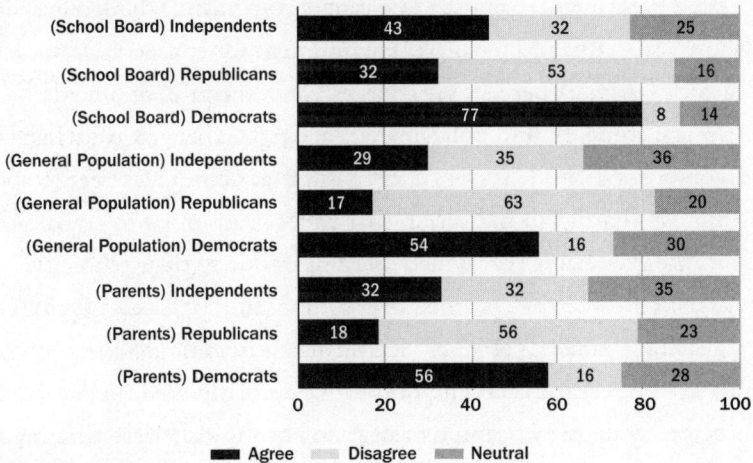

Group	Agree	Disagree	Neutral
(School Board) Independents	43	32	25
(School Board) Republicans	32	53	16
(School Board) Democrats	77	8	14
(General Population) Independents	29	35	36
(General Population) Republicans	17	63	20
(General Population) Democrats	54	16	30
(Parents) Independents	32	32	35
(Parents) Republicans	18	56	23
(Parents) Democrats	56	16	28

■ Agree　░ Disagree　▨ Neutral

way Harvard officials were dealing with antisemitic incidents on campus, Oklahoma Governor Kevin Stitt issued an executive order that prohibited the use of taxpayer funding on DEI on college campuses. (Oklahoma is one of the states, mentioned above, where public officials have restricted or prohibited DEI's discriminatory activities.) There are more offices to be closed: DEI offices have been nearly ubiquitous on college campuses for at least two decades. Research finds that taxpayers are funding nearly $500 million spent on DEI courses every year, and in its first months the second Trump administration moved to cancel some $600 million in grants to K–12 educational institutions that were engaging in DEI practices.[61]

Again, while DEI is hard to define, DEI offices claim that they are trying to promote tolerance and acceptance. Harvard's DEI office says they want to "fully embrace individuals from varied backgrounds, cultures, races, identities, life experiences, perspectives, beliefs, and values."[62] Statements like this are common among DEI offices.

But students do not feel safe or accepted. They are more afraid to speak their minds today than a decade ago. The share of students who feel their "freedom of speech is secure" has dropped 30 percentage points since 2016, according to a longitudinal survey conducted by the Knight Foundation.[63] A survey conducted in October 2023 by the University of Chicago and the Associated Press found that just 27 percent of respondents think universities provide a "respectful and inclusive" environment for conservative students and faculty. Forty-six percent say colleges are "respectful" of liberals.[64]

Parents, students, and policymakers are right, then, to ask what DEI has accomplished. Students on college campuses do not feel freer to speak their minds—hardly an indication that colleges are more tolerant. Some students are even being threatened on campus due to their ethnicity.

After Hamas terrorists killed over a thousand Israelis on October 7, 2023, including hundreds of innocent civilians, antisemitic incidents occurred on campuses across the U.S., and riots broke out nationwide in April 2024. Even before widespread campus riots, violent radicals were threatening Jewish students at some colleges. Jewish students had to hide in the attic of the Cooper Union college library in October 2023, which should send chills down the spine of anyone who knows the story of Anne Frank.[65]

The DEI officers who were supposed to promote acceptance were strangely silent.

Months later, in February 2024, Jewish students were still facing violent attacks, such as when a mob shut down a Jewish student event at the University of California, Berkeley.[66] We will return to the subject of the 2024 campus riots, but if DEI offices are really interested in respect and inclusivity, they are clearly failing to promote those ideas by any measure.

★ ★ ★

While the survey respondents opposed the use of racial preferences in college admissions, and while DEI clearly stands for racial preferences and against the Civil Rights Act, our survey found mixed results when I asked about DEI specifically. These responses seemed inconsistent.

The results showed that the share of respondents who said they were "neutral" on the issue of DEI was higher than those who said they were neutral on racial preferences. Perhaps this means that people are unsure about exactly what DEI is, and do not realize that DEI promotes racial bias. Given the ambiguous definitions of DEI provided earlier from the literature, this uncertainty is not surprising. Too many people have been taking DEI mission statements at face value and not looking at what is really happening in the workplaces and college campuses where DEI is embedded.

In addition to violating civil rights laws, DEI is too expensive for Americans to simply be neutral or uninformed about. Kendi, for one, is known for charging tens of thousands of dollars to speak on DEI before K–12 public school districts.[67] My prior research has found that as of 2017, companies were spending some $8 billion on DEI trainings annually.[68] Since that time, still more data has been unearthed about DEI spending in the public sector. The advocacy group Parents Defending Education (PDE) found that the U.S. Department of Education spent $1 billion on DEI initiatives between 2021 and 2024.[69]

The numbers are similar in higher education. A Goldwater Institute report found that public universities in thirty states have DEI requirements for undergraduates, which means taxpayers are funding these programs. Matt Beienburg, who wrote the report, estimates that taxpayers and students fund at least $1.8 billion of spending every four years on these DEI requirements.[70]

These are startling figures for programs about which Americans say they are either neutral or uninformed. In a 2025 survey conducted by *Axios*, half—or more—of the different groups polled said DEI had no impact on their career. Fifty-one percent of Democrats and 53 percent of Republicans said DEI had no impact. Fifty-two percent of Black respondents and 62 percent of White respondents said DEI had no impact.[71] These results are consistent with other survey research dating back decades that has found DEI does not change the attitudes and behaviors of program participants.[72]

If these programs have no impact on participants—and violate civil rights laws by calling for racial favoritism—then corporations should not be investing in these trainings. Nor should colleges and universities operate DEI offices and maintain DEI staff.

In the survey for this book, a higher share of respondents were neutral when asked about critical race theory than were neutral on the issue of racial preferences. In an attempt to word the question on critical race theory fairly, I used language from critical race theorists themselves to describe their theory. In *Critical Race Theory: An Introduction*, professors Richard Delgado and Jean Stefancic explain the theory in this way:

Unlike traditional civil rights, which embraces incrementalism and step-by-step progress, critical race theory questions the very foundations of the liberal order, including equality theory, legal reasoning, Enlightenment rationalism, and neutral principles of constitutional law.[73]

Our question provided this definition, then asked respondents if they had a positive, negative, or neutral opinion on the theory.

Here again, as with DEI, a nontrivial segment of our survey respondents said they had a neutral perspective. Among school board members, 19 percent of respondents were neutral, while among the general public 38 percent were neutral (a larger share than those reporting being in favor or opposed) and among parents, 36 percent were neutral (almost the same share who reported having a positive opinion). The group of respondents who had the largest segment with positive opinions of the theory were school board members. Almost 54 percent of board members had positive opinions about critical race theory, while nearly 27 percent had negative opinions and 19 percent were neutral.

A reasonable interpretation of the results here is that a significant share of the respondents who were parents or from the general public sample do not know what critical race theory is. Other polling also finds that Americans do not know much about the CRT worldview. A CBS survey in 2022 found that 65 percent of respondents knew little or nothing about critical race theory.[74] Another poll, conducted by researchers at Northeastern,

Figure 1.6 **Do you have a mostly positive, negative, or neutral opinion about critical race theory?**

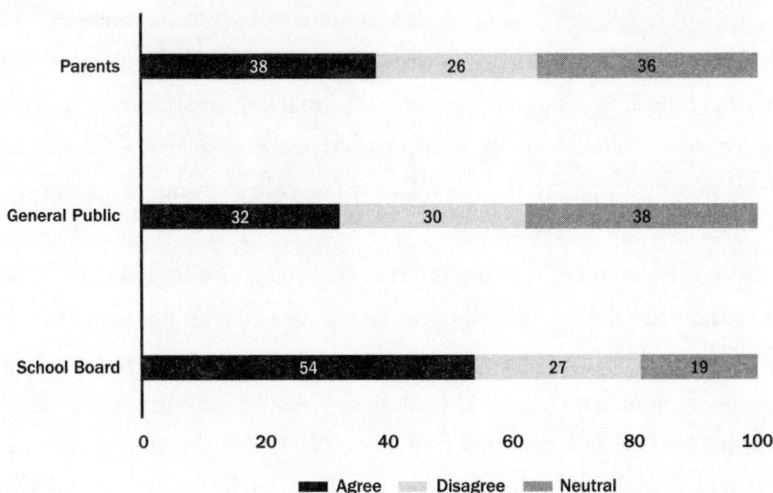

Harvard, Northwestern, and Rutgers Universities, found that 7 out of 10 respondents had "a hard time articulating what CRT is."[75]

In recent years, critical race theory has become a hotly debated topic and the subject of several books. "Critical theory" and its philosophical kin, (critical legal theory, critical gender studies, and critical race theory) are elaborate, complex ideas rooted in Marxism—and critical race theorists readily admit this.

One of critical race theory's founders, Kimberlé Crenshaw, now a law professor at UCLA Law and Columbia Law School, says the theory was created when a group of "neo-Marxist intellectuals, former New Left activists, ex-counter-culturalists, and other varieties of oppositionists" organized and expanded Karl Marx's philosophy that society is riven by conflicts between the rich and poor.[76] Critical race theorists argue that society has irreparable class *and* racial conflicts. Mostly law professors, these self-described Marxists were "committed to expositing and challenging the ways American law served to legitimize an oppressive social order."[77]

According to critical race theorists, everything in life must be considered from the perspective of racism, and so activists must force change to occur. Crenshaw says, "There is no exit—no scholarly perch outside the social dynamics of racial power from which to merely observe and analyze."[78] In sum, critical race theorists developed their ideas out of Marxism, oppose America's founding ideals such as constitutional law, and believe civil rights laws are a sham. DEI is an application of critical race theory: DEI trainers who frequent workplaces and the DEI staff on college campuses put critical race theory's ideas into practice.

Both DEI "trainers" and critical race theorists oppose civil rights laws. In fact, theorists claim that civil rights laws in the U.S. only advanced in the 1960s because White people wanted to preserve their power, a radical—and cynical—view of American life (this is the idea of "interest convergence" described earlier, as developed by Derrick Bell and the aforementioned Richard Delgado).[79] Kendi has written that the Civil Rights Act of 1984 was "intended to dismantle racism [but] also spurred *racist* progress" [emphasis in the original].[80]

While a notable share of responses from our survey of the general public and parents on the CRT question were neutral, once the groups are separated by political affiliation, the divides become clearer, just as we found in the responses to our question about DEI. Among parents who said they were Republican, almost half—48 percent—view the theory negatively, while just 24 percent had a positive opinion. Fifty-eight percent of parents who were Democrats had a positive view. Likewise, among the general public, 52 percent of Democrats had a positive view, and 56 percent of Republicans had a negative view. School board respondents showed a similar divide.

The responses to this question, as well as to the question about DEI, reflect the commonsense understanding of how polling works. Not every American follows every issue closely, and unfamiliarity sometimes looks like ambivalence in survey results. Yet when the results from questions regarding race are disaggregated, the surveys find that those who identify themselves with one side of the aisle or another were more likely to provide responses that were consistent with the political positions of their party. While not conclusive, this suggests that those who are more politically motivated do have opinions.

Figure 1.7 **Positive/Negative/Neutral view of Critical Race Theory, by party identification**

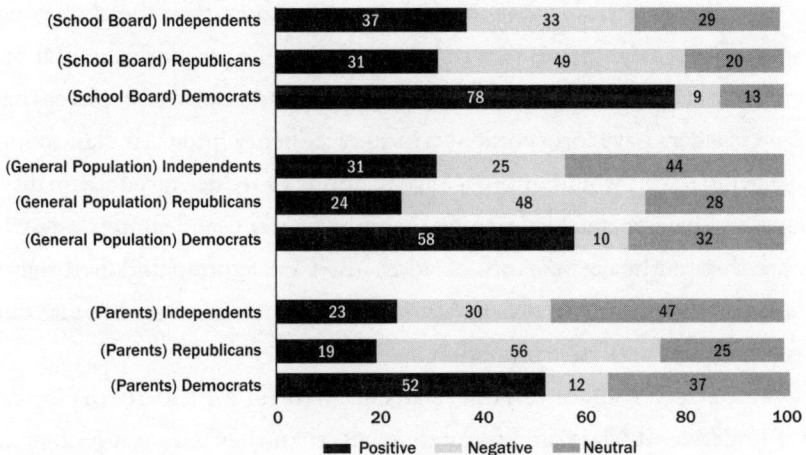

Critics may argue that I cannot prove that the reason too few Americans oppose critical race theory is that not enough people understand it. But other surveys asking similar questions have found high levels of opposition to the theory. Surveys conducted by Parents Defending Education have found that respondents have negative opinions about the ideas CRT promotes. In a poll conducted in 2021, 70 percent of voters said it was not important or not at all important to "teach students that their race is the most important thing about them."[81] An Economist/YouGov survey from 2021 found that 58 percent of respondents had a negative view of critical race theory.[82] In a survey I helped design in 2021, 50 percent of a nationally representative sample of parents said they did not want their children taught that slavery is the "center of our national narrative," a claim of *The New York Times*'s "1619 Project," which argued that America is defined by slavery. Only 42 percent said they did want this taught. Seventy percent of parents wanted children taught that "slavery was a tragedy that harmed the nation, but our freedom and prosperity represent who we are as a nation, offering a beacon to those wanting to immigrate here."[83]

Given the survey evidence from the poll for this book and others, Americans oppose the "critical" worldview once they recognize the discrimination caused by the philosophy. CRT intentionally divides Americans by immutable characteristics. CRT's racial obsession drives a wedge between us by telling Americans that skin color matters more than the choices we make. This is a dangerous idea to be teaching young people. Joshua Dunn, professor at the University of Colorado at Colorado Springs, explains that some teachers have incorporated critical race theory into their classrooms "believing that it would improve race relations or reduce racial inequality; however, they are quickly learning that many parents and students do not share their enthusiasm." And, he adds, "the Constitution and civil rights statutes could be an obstacle to [critical race theorists'] goals" because our laws prohibit racial discrimination.[84]

If a sizeable share of Americans are neutral on this theory or do not understand Marxism's ultimate goals, then they may not recognize racial segregation until it is too late. For example, public school officials in areas such as Newton, Massachusetts, and Westchester County, New York, created "affinity groups" that segregate students according to race for certain school activities.[85] While an "affinity group" sounds benign, prohibiting students from associating with other students based on skin color is...racist. Furthermore, according to research on racial segregation in schools—which violates any number of state and federal laws—students feel more like victims and are more likely to report feeling left out in affinity group settings.[86]

Advocacy groups such as Parents Defending Education (PDE), the group mentioned earlier that has surveyed parents about their feelings on critical race theory and radical gender ideology, have sued school districts over their affinity-group activities and won. In Wellesley, Massachusetts, the school district settled with PDE and ended their affinity-group program after the challenge.[87]

Yet if Americans do not know that critical race theory promotes more racial segregation and opposes civil rights laws, they will have difficulty connecting events featured in news headlines about radical activity in K–12 schools with the theory. If Americans oppose racial preferences, which they did in our survey as well as surveys conducted by Pew Research and others, then they oppose critical race theory and DEI too.

Ending the Racial Obsession

More Americans must recognize the connection between DEI, CRT, racial preferences, and discrimination. The survey results on DEI and CRT and the political divides indicate polarization (or at least ambiguity) on these topics. But the strong results opposing racial preferences and in favor of meritocracy in college admissions indicate that the majority of Americans favor colorblind policies and equality under the law. CRT and its application through DEI constitute a worldview that rejects meritocracy and colorblindness in favor of "affirmative action" and race essentialism.

Not only do CRT and racial favoritism conflict with civil rights, but the critical philosophy distracts policymakers from finding solutions to the problems that plague voters and taxpayers, such as low-performing schools.

"We continue to have a challenge around ensuring young people have appropriate opportunities to get a college education, but I don't think we have acknowledged the root of where most of that challenge lies," Houghton President Lewis said in our interview. He continued later: "The root of that is as clear as day: We're not preparing young people appropriately at the elementary, middle, and high school level academically to gain acceptance to college or to be successful in college."

And in our conversation, Lewis emphasized the importance of preparing students for postsecondary work.

> As long as we continue to push kids through school, graduate kids who can't read or who can barely read, can't do basic mathematics, meet minimum standards for high school graduation—this conversation about racial preferences in college admissions, it serves to deflect attention from the real issue, which is that there are way too many kids graduating, disproportionately kids of color and from low-income backgrounds who haven't gotten the skills that they should have gotten in elementary, middle, and high school. That, I think, is primarily where our attention needs to be.[88]

And this is where we turn next. What do Americans think about schools in the U.S.? And what do these opinions say about this book's claim that Americans are not polarized on the issues? To answer this question, I asked the general public, parents, and school board members for their opinions on K–12 classrooms.

CHAPTER TWO

COVID, STUDENT ACHIEVEMENT, AND THE READING WARS

He who is to be good must have been brought up and habituated well, and then live accordingly under good institutions, and never do what is low and mean, either against or with his will.

—Aristotle, *Nicomachean Ethics*[1]

During the COVID-19 pandemic in 2020 and 2021, Melissa Jackson discovered there was a lot she did not know about what her children were learning in school.[2] "It was actually a learning opportunity for me as a parent," she said in our phone interview. In particular, the radical political slant of much of the classroom material shocked her.

"My son had a debate class and the teacher decided to have an assignment on BLM," as in Black Lives Matter, the radical group that advocated for defunding police. BLM also promotes radical ideas on gender such as "hold[ing] space for our siblings who are agender, intersex, transgender, and gender expansive to participate and lead," which were not ideas Jackson wanted her children exposed to, especially without a alternative perspective.[3]

"The assignment that the debate teacher offered in sixth grade for BLM was more of a reading comprehension assignment. It was an article with a positive spin on BLM," without an opposing perspective that discussed the damage being done to private property and small business owners during the riots of summer 2020 that involved many BLM members and their allies, Jackson explained.

No mention was made of how the founders of BLM were trained as Marxists.

No mention was made of their radical connections, or of the fact that they described themselves as students and allies of Angela Davis, who twice ran for vice president as a member of the Communist Party of the United States.[4]

The BLM Global Network Foundation, an organization that raises money for the BLM grassroots organization founded by Patrisse Cullors (who led the foundation), Alicia Garza, and Opal Tometi, was accused of fraud in 2022.[5] Revelations of the purchase of a $6 million luxury house in Southern California, among other extravagant purchases, roused suspicions. By 2023, public support for BLM as a movement had fallen from 55 percent to 51 percent, while opposition had increased from 34 percent to 46 percent.[6] By March 2025, construction crews were removing the giant letters that spelled out "BLACK LIVES MATTER" on a Washington, D.C., street just one block from the White House.

But all of this was still to come. As for her daughter's school in 2020, Jackson continued, "I waited a few days thinking [the teacher] would provide an opposing opinion, and she didn't. I approached her with what BLM really was, and she said I didn't understand BLM."[7]

Jackson's story is hardly unique. Beanie Geoghegan, co-founder with Jackson of Freedom in Education, a group led by parents advocating for high quality K–12 content, says, "A lot of our stories sound alike" in their discovery of ideologically skewed topics seeping into classrooms.

Geoghegan has served on parent-teacher associations at her children's school and worked as a substitute teacher, but even she was startled by what her children were doing—or not doing—in class during the pandemic.

Her daughter's high school was one of the best in her state, but Geoghegan says that after March 2020, "The rest of the year was a waste." She says her daughter was only required to read one book as part of her coursework for the entire school year.

Public Opinion on Education in the U.S.

Geoghegan says she heard many similar reports when she talked to the parents of her children's friends during the COVID-19 pandemic.[8] Gallup polling, which has tracked national satisfaction with education for nearly twenty-five years, found that after 2020, the public perception of K–12 schools dropped sharply.

When Gallup asked how satisfied Americans were with education in 2024, 55 percent of respondents reported some level of dissatisfaction, while 43 percent reported some level of satisfaction. The responses had been evenly divided just five years earlier, between 2018 and 2019. Then, in 2020, the lines split like a pair of scissors and satisfaction levels moved in opposite directions, with fewer respondents reporting being satisfied with K–12 education in the U.S.[9]

In a different survey, released in February 2025, a poll dealing with Americans' views of the "state of the nation," Gallup found that 73 percent of Americans were "dissatisfied" with "the quality of public education in the nation."[10]

Some polling during the pandemic had hinted that this change in

Figure 2.1 **Gallup Polling on K–12 Satisfaction 2018–2024**

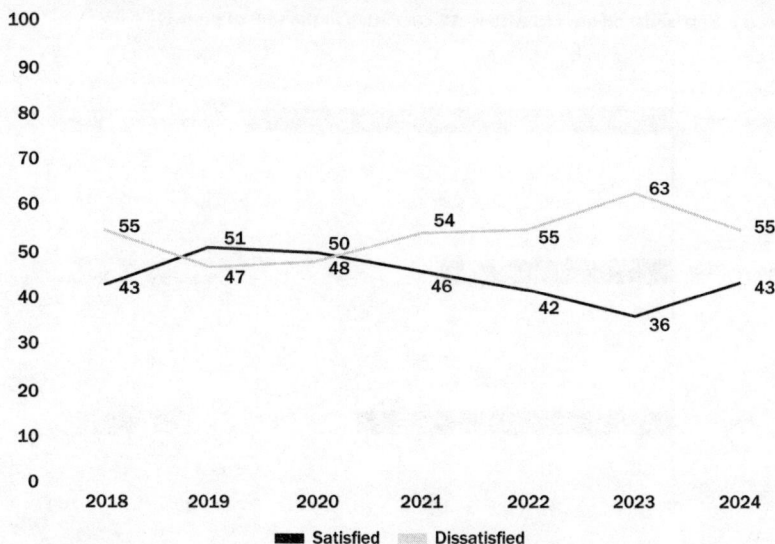

Source: Megan Brenan, "Americans' View of K–12 Education Improves from 2023 Low," Gallup, August 28, 2024, https://news.gallup.com/poll/649385/americans-view-education-improves-2023-low.aspx.

public perception was coming. *Education Next*, a journal edited by education researchers at Harvard and Stanford, found that parents of children receiving hybrid or remote instruction during 2020 were less satisfied than parents of students attending class in person. More public schools were closed to in-person learning than private schools.[11] The survey conducted for this book offers some more detailed responses on this issue of schooling satisfaction—responses that begin to uncover the lines that divide Americans on education and reveal those areas on which there is agreement.

In the survey described in these pages, the group most satisfied with K–12 education in the U.S. was the subgroup of school board members. Overall, nearly 70 percent of school board members reported some level of satisfaction, and only 18.5 percent reported some level of dissatisfaction. Very few reported being neutral on the question.

Slightly more than half of parents reported being satisfied, while members of the general public were largely split on the issue. More people are satisfied with their child's school, even as the satisfaction levels are lower for

Figure 2.2 **How satisfied are you with K–12 education in the United States?**

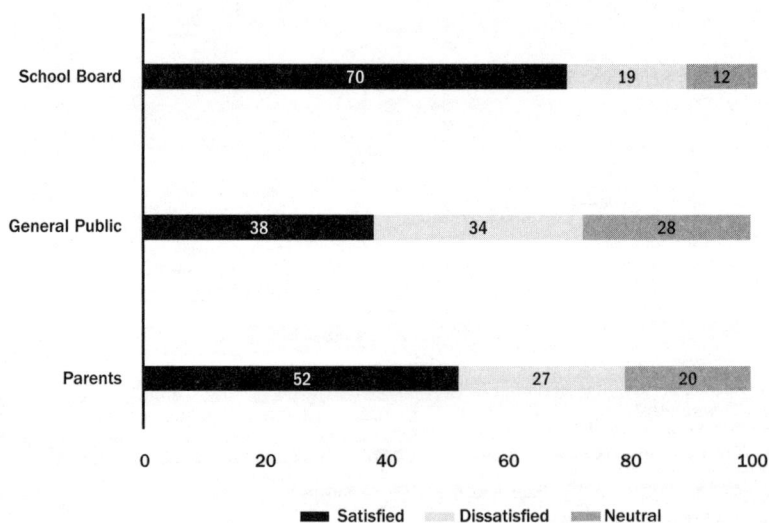

education in the U.S. in general. Seventy-four percent of parents reported some level of satisfaction with their child's school ("extremely" or "somewhat"), while 72 percent of the general public also said they had some level of satisfaction (Figure 2.3). Unsurprisingly, 82 percent of board members who were parents reported some level of satisfaction.

Education Next's survey, which has been conducted annually since 2007, found similar results. Fifty to sixty percent of respondents in the latest poll have said they would give their local public schools an "A" or "B."[12] Though their respondents report high levels of dissatisfaction for the public school system *overall* today, 76 percent of the parents of K–12 students are satisfied with their oldest child's education.[13]

What the Data Tells Us

First, more people are dissatisfied or neutral on K–12 schools in the U.S. today than in prior years. Public opinion has shifted on this question. Second, people still like their local school or the schools their children are attending. Some of this satisfaction may be driven by selection bias (you

Figure 2.3 **How satisfied are you with your child's school?**

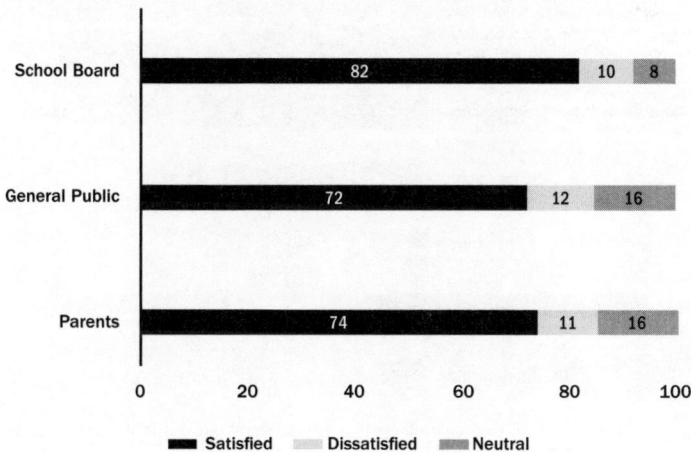

choose your child's school, either directly or indirectly by where you decide to live). High schools have long been the centers of many communities, and many people naturally feel an allegiance to their local school.

In fact, considering the increasing share of parents and families who are choosing schools today, we asked our respondents what they are looking for when they consider a school. Between 2012 and 2019, public school enrollment increased by 2 percent (one million students), but in 2020, the first year of the COVID-19 pandemic, enrollment dropped by 3 percent.[14] These data could be a reflection of demographic trends, but more parents are choosing where and how their children learn by selecting charter schools (public schools of choice), homeschooling, and other alternatives to assigned schools.[15]

Echoing Latasha Field's comments from this book's introduction, a healthy share (nearly one-third) of our respondents said they consider a school's record of academic achievement to be most important to them. Yet nearly an identical share said they were interested in a school's "values and culture." Thus the stories from Jackson and Geoghegan about their

Figure 2.4 **What is the most important outcome/factor you consider when choosing a school for your child (parent sample)?**

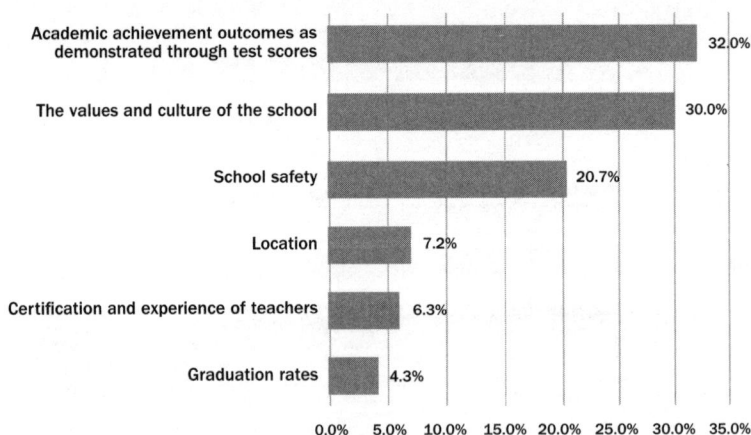

children's schools and instructional practices during the pandemic exemplify what many parents were feeling during and after COVID-19.

★ ★ ★

"My daughter, among many other things, was talking about internalized misogyny" after she had been taught radical ideas in class, Geoghegan says. "I know I want them back in school [after the pandemic], but do I want them back in school the way they were in back in school before?" Geoghegan asks. "I was walking around in this fit of rage," she says.[16]

In April 2024, Geoghegan, now a visiting fellow with the Independent Women's Forum, a conservative advocacy group for women's rights, testified before a Congressional subcommittee on the effects that COVID-19 school closures had on schoolchildren.

"If I were to summarize the effect school closures had on my youngest son...in a word, I would say it delegitimized school for him," Geoghegan wrote in her testimony.[17] Not only were students not given enough work to do when classrooms were closed to in-person learning, but, Geoghegan says, "Instead of capitalizing on all of the free time students had to read great books in his English class, his teacher focused on intersectionality [an idea that is part of critical race theory] and identity."[18] Many parents around the country can relate to Geoghegan and Jackson's frustrations.

It's not clear what was worse: for students to attend school and not be remotely challenged or to find that thousands upon thousands of students were simply absent from classrooms. In March 2024, a *New York Times* headline read, "Why School Absences Have 'Exploded' Almost Everywhere," citing research from the American Enterprise Institute and C2i that found the share of students who were chronically absent (missing at least 10 percent of a school year) had increased 15 percentage points since before the pandemic (13 percent to 28 percent).[19] A study from the Manhattan Institute, a research organization based in New York City, found that the rate of chronic absenteeism in this city jumped from 26.5 percent in the 2018–2019 school year to 34.8 percent in the 2023–2024 school year.[20]

These numbers are larger than the national average reported by *The New York Times*, but the increase is significant because New York City is the largest school district in the U.S.[21]

The *New York Times*'s report quoted Duke University professor Katie Rosanbalm as saying, "Our relationship with school became optional" during and after COVID-19.[22]

★ ★ ★

As the survey results described in the next chapter will explain, while there are divides over school satisfaction, Americans have shown agreement across surveys on what they want from a school: we want schools to challenge students academically and emphasize civics and character and virtue. So considering the consistently poor performance among U.S. students on national comparisons and international tests, we should be looking for improvement.[23] In math, U.S. fifteen-year-old students score the same as the global average score according to one leading measure, but the average U.S. score is below the average in 21 other countries, out of the 36 that participate in this assessment.[24] U.S. students fare better in reading and science on international comparisons, but back home, on state-level evaluations, reading scores among 4th and 8th graders have trended downward since 2015 and 2013, respectively.[25] In other subjects, American children are struggling to post proficient scores on the most reliable indicators of achievement: civics, geography, history—the story is the same across these subjects.[26]

Our survey and others found that Americans are not polarized on the ways in which they want schools to change and the subjects they want emphasized more.[27] Surveys reveal that Americans want schools to focus more on civics instruction and do more to teach about traditional values such as personal responsibility (Chapter 3).[28]

We have to pause, though, before we can even discuss how to improve civics instruction or decide which virtues schools should teach. Americans must grapple with a far more basic problem: reading.

The Reading Wars

"I finally feel understood," wrote a relieved parent to Emily Hanford, senior producer and correspondent for American Public Media.[29] Hanford's groundbreaking reporting on the widespread failure of what is called the "cueing" method of reading instruction in elementary schools has rekindled a longstanding debate over how educators teach students to read.[30] The parent's message to Hanford is worth quoting at length because it echoes thousands, if not millions of parents who—*across generations*—have been frustrated and angry about the condition of literacy in K–12 schools:

> My son is a second grader. He has been struggling with reading and writing. This has been so heartbreaking for me. Reading and writing are priorities in our home, yet I feel utterly hopeless.... Parents don't talk about this with other parents. When you admit your kid is behind, does that mean you've failed as a parent? Then I wonder about the poor families (I grew up with a teenage single- mother-immigrant [*sic*]) who don't know. –Jenny, from New Jersey[31]

Hanford's podcast *Sold a Story* explained that educators' use of cueing has persisted despite repeated studies finding that cueing is, at best, an incomplete method of teaching reading and, at worst, utterly ineffective at preparing students for a life of reading.[32] For decades, researchers have documented the weaknesses of cueing and the faults of a related precursor method, but cueing has persistent defenders who have helped it maintain a prominent place in American education.[33]

Some definitions are in order. The most widely practiced and hotly debated methods of reading instruction in K–12 schools can be summarized as falling into the categories of "phonics" and the "look-say" methods.[34] "Look-say" eventually developed into "whole word" and "cueing," while "whole language" uses a combination of phonics and look-say, with a heavier dose of the latter.[35]

Today, the cueing method is almost indistinguishable from the whole word, which itself is derived from look-say techniques. One veteran teacher told me via email that she uses both phonics and cueing to teach reading—phonics in the younger grades and cueing to help students understand new words.[36]

Phonics is unique on this list of reading methods because it is focused on teaching students to sound out letters and recognize letter patterns.[37] There are differences between the three look-say methods—cueing, whole word, and whole language—but the key to distinguishing among these approaches and phonics is that the look-say methods involve prompting students with some form of context clue (usually a picture).[38]

While different methods for reading instruction have different strategies, the essence of the cueing, whole word, and whole language methods is to pair a picture with a word or sentence to help students connect the letters and the visual. With cueing, students can be shown a picture of a fish, for example, as a context clue, and then the letters "f-i-s-h" are provided below the picture on the page.[39] Students connect the picture to the assembly of letters beneath it and are supposed to identify the word or even a set of words in this way.

Over the years, some widely used teacher manuals that guided instructors to use cueing even coached teachers to reduce their emphasis on phonics, which is crucial to explaining the reading wars and American students' struggles learning to read.[40] Teaching materials that employ the cueing method often do not combine context clues with phonics-based instruction.

Lawmakers, parents, and educators have waged what have been called "the reading wars" over how to teach reading since the early 20th century, with many pointing fingers at each other over who is to blame or which method of reading instruction is at fault for poor results.[41] My survey asked respondents how they felt about different approaches to teaching reading. There are curious divides over how much Americans know about reading instruction, particularly the efficacy of phonics verses the look-say method and its modern counterpart, cueing.

Over the last 50 years, the cueing/whole word methods were among the most widely used methods to teach reading in the U.S., especially in the 1980s and early 1990s.[42] By 2000, Hanford says phonics and cueing were really the only competing approaches to teaching reading.[43] Lucy Calkins, the former director of the Reading and Writing Project at Columbia's Teachers College, was one of the leading figures behind the cueing method, and her curriculum was, at one time, the third-most frequently used in the country.[44]

★ ★ ★

To understand the past and present of reading instruction in the U.S., three ideas are essential to the story. First, education research consistently demonstrates the effectiveness of teaching phonics.[45] Second, the look-say method and its progeny are part of the progressive movement that drastically shifted K–12 instruction away from memorization and order to "student-focused" teaching throughout the early 20th century.[46] Reviews of look-say and cueing found that some proponents of the methods allow students to be imprecise and even wrong in their identification of letter combinations—a startling lack of rigor.[47] Third, an increasing number of state officials in recent years have called for a return to phonics, to great effect for young children.[48]

Cueing, on its own, has proved inadequate to teach students to read, yet teachers around the U.S. have used materials that rely on cueing almost exclusively.[49] As a result, students have not been learning to read—or at least not been learning well enough to read material consistent with their grade level.[50]

Nationwide, reading scores have been trending lower for nearly a decade, with comparatively steep declines after the pandemic years of 2020–2022.[51] In 2024, results from the Nation's Report Card found that, on average, 8th graders were scoring lower in reading than at any point in the last twenty years. Achievement gaps have increased between students at the top and bottom of the achievement scale.[52]

It is important for parents, teachers, and lawmakers to agree on reading because it is an essential skill—which sounds obvious until we recognize what happens if someone does not learn to read well or at all. An illiterate person cannot complete a job application, apply for a driver's license, or fill out a loan application.

"The level of one's reading ability (as reflected in the vocabulary items and passage types on a reading test) predicts the level of one's ability to learn new things," explains E. D. Hirsch, Jr., an education historian and creator of the Core Knowledge curriculum.[53] The Core Knowledge Foundation lists hundreds of schools around the U.S. using their curriculum, which puts a special focus on creating a shared set of knowledge among students to foster better understanding among Americans.[54] Core Knowledge and what are known as "classical" schools share a focus on reading content that transmits the core ideas of Western Civilization—books that have stood the test of time, concepts such as democracy, and what we now consider American traditions such as individual rights and representative government.[55]

If a person does not learn the essential skill of reading, they cannot share the ideas that help create a sense of national identity. At a more basic level, they will also struggle to earn a living and establish "good social relationships" and even turn to crime.[56]

Hirsch writes, "Scores on reading tests predict job performance. Obviously, reading scores do not predict whether somebody can fix your car's engine. But, according to studies conducted by the armed services, reading scores do predict how readily and well a person will learn to fix your car's engine."[57]

Fix your car's engine or learn other valuable skills that give individuals better options than crime. The National Assessment of Adult Literacy finds that two-thirds of students who cannot read by the end of 4th grade will be incarcerated later in life or will be living in poverty as adults.[58] The overall illiteracy rate for incarcerated adults is estimated to be 75 percent.[59] Nearly two out of every three prisoners, state and federal (61.7 percent), did not have a high school diploma at the time they entered prison.[60] Unsurprisingly, then, 29 percent of inmates score below level 2 (out of 5) on the U.S. Department of Education's literacy scale—making them functionally illiterate.[61] Furthermore, "85 percent of all juveniles who interface with the juvenile court system are functionally low literate."[62]

If you cannot read, you are unlikely to finish school (or if you do finish, you likely did not learn the skills needed to be successful in the workplace or college), making it more difficult to earn a living after you graduate. Sure enough, as of 2014, 51 percent of inmates were not employed full-time before they were incarcerated, and 19 percent were unemployed.[63]

For some ethnic subgroups, the statistics are particularly dire: In 2000 and 2010, working-age Black men ages 20 to 24 without a high school diploma were more likely to be in prison than employed.[64]

Latasha Fields, whose inspiring story begins this book, bemoaned the dismal reading scores in her home state of Illinois and the city of Chicago, a majority-minority school district. Black 4th graders in Chicago public schools score nearly 50 points below their White peers, on average.[65]

"You can't ignore that," Fields told me. She pointed to Illinois' $11 billion education budget, much of which (over $8 billion) goes to Chicago.[66] "Clearly money is not being allocated properly," she said.

Put simply, if teachers and lawmakers and parents can find agreement on how to improve the quality of reading instruction, more people will have the skills needed to be productive, giving them less reason to resort to crime. Parents and policymakers should have higher goals for young people than avoiding prison, but reading scores are so low, and the incarceration rates of those who cannot read are so high, that we have no choice but to start with the very basic goal of improving literacy for the benefits it can have on everyone, including the nation's jail and prison populations.

★ ★ ★

"In many ways, the history of the reading wars might aptly be characterized as an 'epic of progress' and a 'tale of conflict,'" says Harvard education professor James S. Kim.[67] The "progress" is not referring to better reading scores but to brief periods of agreement between lawmakers and researchers over the last 130 years on what makes for good reading instruction, with prolonged periods of debate in between. The war's casualties are millions of students and parents who have watched their children fail at reading after using the cueing method.

Phonics was a common way to teach reading and spelling in the U.S. at the time of the nation's founding.[68] The *New England Primer*, widely used in one-room schoolhouses in the colonies and young states, emphasized letters and sounds.[69] Benjamin Franklin and Daniel Webster both developed ways to teach phonics to foster consistency across the way English was spoken and written in our nation's early days.[70]

Unfortunately, K–12 education is susceptible to fads, and look-say had powerful advocates who pushed educators to use this method at the exclusion of other approaches, such as phonics. Prominent educators began discouraging the use of phonics in the late 19th and early 20th centuries.

For example, in the 19th century, Horace Mann, considered the father of common schools and onetime commissioner of education in Massachusetts, criticized the practice of sounding out letters in favor of teaching students whole words.[71] "Letters and words present superficial form only," Mann wrote in 1841.[72] "The alphabetic column presents an utter blank" and letters are "skeleton-shaped, bloodless, ghostly apparitions," he said.[73]

The field of education became more progressive in the 20th century— moving away from the traditional approaches of using memorization and structured, teacher-led instruction.[74] The ideas of John Dewey, who favored look-say, criticized teaching that used repetition and structure. "Progressive educators continued to abhor any instructional strategy that called for drills, worksheets, or highly structured, teacher-directed lessons," writes the late Andrew Coulson, a policy analyst and education historian at the Cato Institute.[75]

As described above, research demonstrated that phonics was more effective than other instructional approaches, but debates ensued for decades among researchers and practitioners. Researcher William S. Gray famously wrote *On Their Own Reading* in 1948, which argued in favor of the whole word method. Rudolph Flesch answered Gray in 1955 with *Why Johnny Can't Read* and argued in favor of phonics (Gray went on to publish *Why Johnny Still Can't Read* in 1981).[76]

At the height of the reading wars in 1967, Harvard professor Jeanne Chall reviewed the leading research and found that 27 out of 30 studies comparing phonics with "look-say" methods demonstrated that phonics-based methods helped students learn to read faster and more accurately.[77]

Case closed, right? Nope. As Harvard reading historian Kim explains, some educators criticized the studies Chall included in her report as not being rigorous in their methodology, and Chall decided that more research was needed.

Cato's Coulson writes,

> A funny thing happened as a result of all these research findings on the advantages of phonics over look-say, and of synthetic phonics over analytic phonics: Nothing. The story of reading instruction from the turn of the century to the 1950s was one of the increasing entrenchment of the look-say method. By the late fifties, phonics was almost entirely absent from reading instruction texts.[78]

Another education historian wrote in 1968 that "phonics has a way of disappearing and returning to reading programs," as researchers continued to review the results from different reports, creating no end of confusion for parents and lawmakers and even educators.[79] Look-say and its progeny were favored by "experts" and had to be taught with certain techniques and in a specific order, making it difficult for parents to intercede and help children with the methods.[80]

Research in favor of phonics continued to stack up, though. Another report backing phonics was released in 1985 by the Commission on Reading, entitled *Becoming a Nation of Readers*.[81] Federal education officials appointed the commission to survey the research on reading instruction and report their findings.[82]

"We now know that learning efficient word recognition and grasping meaning are companion skills from the time a child first reads," said the report, authored by a group of professors and a 1st grade teacher.[83] Children who are taught using phonics along with word-recognition techniques learn to read faster than children not taught phonics—they can identify words better, and they perform better on assessments of sentence and story comprehension.[84]

Hanford's podcast is far from the first project to argue that phonics-based instruction is superior to cueing, but her timing and use of new research make her argument compelling. Her investigative reporting provides a hit parade of still more academic studies documenting the problems with the cueing method and the benefits from phonics instruction.[85] The research on cueing consistently finds that this method does not teach students to assemble words quickly from letters, and "the ability to read words in isolation quickly and accurately is the hallmark of being a skilled reader."[86] Skilled readers are adept at recognizing words as a sequence of letters, Hanford says in her summary, not simply depending on pictures as cues.[87]

Research released around the same time as Hanford's reporting added still more evidence that teachers' predominant use of cueing in American classrooms has been misguided. In 2020, Student Achievement Partners (SAP) released a paper explaining—again—that the U.S. has a literacy crisis in K–12 schools.[88] The researchers reviewed a prominent set of cueing/whole word teacher instructional materials developed by Calkins, the former Columbia professor who supported cueing, called *Units of Study*. SAP asked seven professors who specialize in reading research to determine whether *Units of Study* employed methods that would make for successful readers.

The SAP report explains that Calkins' materials undermined phonics instruction, and it quoted from *Units of Study's* teacher guides, which say,

"Every minute you spend teaching phonics...is less time spent teaching other things," while recommending the cueing method. This is an example of the way in which look-say and cueing advocates marginalized the use of phonics instruction. The SAP report, which points to the research showing the efficacy of using phonics instruction, says the critique of phonics and promotion of cueing in *Units of Study* "is in direct opposition to an enormous body of settled research and even runs contrary to the *Units of Study* foundational skills materials that support the teaching of phonics."[89] The SAP report says "systematic phonics—defined as explicit teaching of phonics patterns following a scope and sequence—is essential, and abundant research...supports this."[90]

Essential, even if not sufficient on its own. The reviewers said "phonological awareness, phonics, and word recognition" were "foundational skills," and researchers who study reading instruction explain that these skills comprise what is now called the "science of reading."[91] The term "science of reading" is widely used today to describe the research that supports a combination of effective instructional practices, with the notable inclusion of phonics-based instruction.[92] The science of reading is not a curriculum, exactly, and the method is described as a collection of teaching practices that includes phonics—contrary to the cueing/whole language essentialists that dominated reading instruction for many years.

Hanford explains that the significance of the SAP report is that "it appears to be the first time a group of reading researchers have reviewed a curriculum [not just different teaching methods] and determined whether the lessons reflect more than 40 years of scientific research on how reading skill develops."[93]

I interviewed another veteran 1st grade teacher who specialized in reading instruction, and asked her about phonics and the science of reading. "It is important to understand that the beginning, essential component of reading instruction is phonological awareness," she said.[94] "There is a continuum of skills beginning with listening and moving into the more advanced skills of blending and then ending with phonemic awareness," she says.

She continues: "A child's ability to segment, blend, and manipulate sound is instrumental in learning to read. If a child is taught phonics, then they are given the knowledge necessary to unlock the code of reading."

In another interview, this one with a 3rd grade teacher, I asked about the phonics–cueing debate, and her answers pointed to the science of reading, with an emphasis on phonics.[95] "We need both methods to help students succeed in reading," she said. "Students need to have phonics in the young grades. Then as the students have a foundation of strategies, it will help them read all kinds of materials," she said.[96]

★ ★ ★

In addition to the harm that came from abandoning phonics, the progressive education movement's philosophy of moving away from memorization and structure meant losing a significant degree of accuracy. A recurring theme in the rise of progressive teaching methods through the 20th century, especially in reading, was the decline in precision.[97]

"The inventors of look-say reading thought that teaching children the sounds of letter combinations (phonics) required lots of drill and memorization, resulting in tedium," says a commonly used handbook for homeschooling and classical education, *The Well-Trained Mind* by Jesse Wise and Susan Wise Bauer.[98] *The Well-Trained Mind* explains how methods such as memorization can be used to good effect for children.

In the look-say and whole word methods, write Wise and Wise Bauer, "It doesn't matter if the meaning may not correspond to what's in front of [a student]."[99] Illiteracy "soars" in states where look-say methods are dominant, they write.[100] Cato's Coulson cited teacher manuals for reading instruction produced in the 1990s that focused on whole word methods and even trained teachers to allow for inaccuracies in word identification if the student's answer is still within the context of a passage.[101]

Wise and Wise Bauer write, "Whole-language teaching still encourages children to guess."[102]

Left-leaning politicians who shared a progressive worldview with progressive educators tried to address low reading scores more than thirty years ago through whole word. President Bill Clinton made reading a priority in his second campaign for president in 1996 and proposed nearly $3 billion in taxpayer resources be devoted to reading programs based on look-say methods.[103] Clinton and his education secretary, Richard Riley, favored the "Reading Recovery" program, which Hanford explains in *Sold a Story* was developed by one of Lucy Caldwell's predecessors and uses the cueing method.[104] And yet average 4th grade reading scores were the same in 2000 as they were in 1992.[105]

Clinton and Riley were simply following the education fad. Whole language had spread quickly across American education through the 1980s into the 1990s.[106] In 1989, a veteran teacher wrote in the *Elementary School Journal* that he has "witnessed many movements, fads, and panaceas" during his career, yet he says, "never have I witnessed anything like the rapid spread of the whole-language movement."[107] Harvard's Kim says that the cueing crowd had won over state lawmakers and educators, convincing state officials to purchase textbooks and curriculum, such as those created by Calkins, that used cueing methods.[108]

Textbooks are big business in the K–12 and postsecondary world. Hanford's reporting documents that 83 of the largest school districts in the U.S., such as Baltimore County, Chicago, and New York City, spent at least $215 million on cueing materials just between 2010 and 2020.[109] As part of her research, Hanford says she purchased one of the teaching kits created by whole-language gurus Irene Fountas and Gay Su Pinnel for $3,947—just for one kit.[110] Fountas and Pinnel "weren't saying no to phonics," Hanford explains, "but they were saying you can teach a child to read without phonics," which contradicts important research.[111]

Large states such as California and Texas tend to dominate the textbook market.[112] If one of these states with sizeable student enrollment figures adopts a certain book, curriculum creators anticipate other states will follow and produce more copies. So when California schools began using cueing-related materials in the late 1980s, this decision had a ripple effect nationwide.[113] Harvard's Kim reports that in 1992, a U.S. Department of Education survey found 69 percent of California teachers were putting a heavy emphasis on whole language, with 40 percent of instructors in other states doing the same.[114]

The early returns were dismal. In 1992, 52 percent of California 4th graders were scoring below the basic level on the Nation's Report Card.[115] Scores continued to fall in 1994. Former California state commissioner of education Bill Honig would later offer a damning assessment of the move to adopt methods akin to cueing instruction.[116] Kim says, "In retrospect, Bill Honig admitted that the 1987 language arts framework and whole-language practices were not based on proven strategies."[117]

Honig said, "It is the curse of all progressives…that we are anti-research and anti-science, and we never seem to grasp how irrational that attitude is. This is probably our deepest failure."[118]

Some in California are slow to change and still bear out Honig's critique of progressives: In 2024 and 2025, the California Teachers Union, which has a membership of 310,000 and reliably supports left-of-center causes, opposed legislative proposals that would have introduced more phonics instruction into state classrooms.[119] Today, the reading scores of 4th graders in California are nearly the same as the national average—which means the scores are not good, especially among Black and Hispanic students. Scores have improved only slightly since 1998, but nearly half of 4th graders in the state (44 percent) cannot read at what is considered a "basic" level.[120]

Polling on Phonics

My survey of the general population found that respondents were split on reading instruction: 46 percent were in favor of teachers using phonics in school while 47 percent favored the "whole word" method, the cueing method described earlier. When we asked parents, though, we found that half of parents prefer phonics, while 42 percent favored cueing and 7 percent were undecided. Given the complicated, back-and-forth battles over phonics and cueing that have taken place in the 18th, 19th, 20th and now 21st centuries, it is no surprise that people are divided on the issue.

School board members, on the other hand, were more in favor of phonics. Fifty-four percent favored of phonics compared to 39 percent choosing whole word.

Given the mixed results on our survey and the compelling evidence in favor of making phonics central to reading instruction, this is an issue that deserves more attention from families, school board members, and policy-makers. Just as many do not recognize the connections between racism and DEI and critical race theory described in Chapter 1, many Americans may not see the important distinctions between phonics and cueing.

The evidence on the effectiveness of phonics is significant—especially since those who have been deeply invested in the cueing method have changed their positions in recent years. In 2020, the reporter and podcaster Hanford reported that Calkins, the best-selling author and researcher whose work had dominated the field of reading instruction, and her team decided their work needed "rebalancing" as the evidence continues to mount in favor of phonics.[121]

Figure 2.5 **Do you believe teachers should teach students to read using phonics, whole word method, or other?**

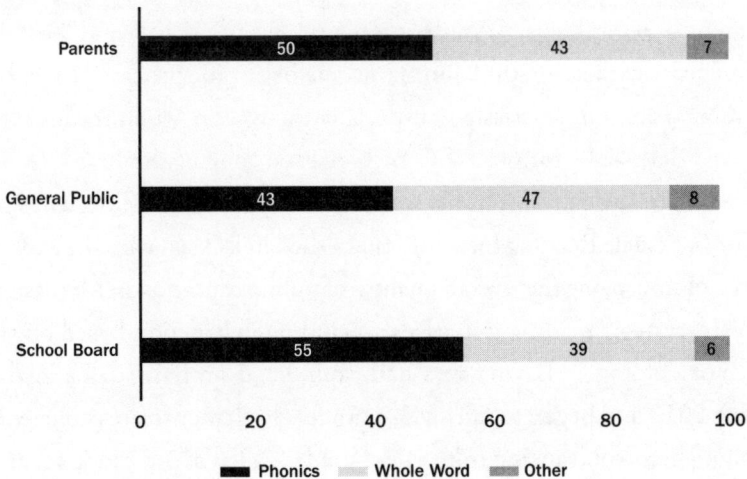

In September 2023, Columbia officials announced Calkins's Reading and Writing Project (which focused on cueing) at the school's Teachers College was closing.[122] Calkins said she was not denying the criticism against her method but would take time to "[try] to address the reading wars."[123]

★   ★   ★

Neither researchers nor policymakers have identified a policy or teaching technique that explains all of the reasons why student test scores increase or decrease. Education research is best described in terms of trends—large scale policy changes take time to have an effect. Every child is different and may respond differently to certain interventions.

When we do see a change in student results, especially a large change, analysts and the media are sure to notice and seek an explanation. The sharp change in reading scores among Mississippi students in recent years is one of those trends. In 2013, average reading scores among Mississippi 4th graders on the Nation's Report Card were ranked among the worst in the country.[124] Only the scores from New Mexico and Washington, D.C., ranked lower than those of Mississippi students.[125] Among education researchers, Mississippi gained a reputation for consistently being at the bottom of state rankings on student achievement.[126]

But years earlier, in 2000, Jim Barksdale began the process of turning education around in Mississippi, especially the way in which reading was taught.[127] Barksdale, former CEO of Netscape (one of the first internet browsers), was aware of his home state's poor record. He and his wife created the Barksdale Reading Institute, established in Jackson with the express purpose of improving the "overall quality" of public education in Mississippi "through strategic reading initiatives," including instruction based on the science of reading.[128] Lawmakers had capitalized on Barksdale's investment by 2013 and began requiring 3rd graders to demonstrate proficiency in reading before advancing to the next grade (called a "3rd grade reading retention" law).[129]

Lawmakers also passed a charter school law that year, allowing for the creation of independent public schools that could be closed for low performance, along with a new program to help preschool students.[130] Two years later, Mississippi lawmakers adopted an education savings account law that allows parents of children with special needs to choose how and where their children learn by customizing their education.[131] With an account, the state deposits a portion of a child's spending from the state education formula into a private account that parents use to buy education products and services for their children.[132] Parents can use an account to choose a private school, find a personal tutor for their student, pay for education therapy—which can be invaluable to children who are struggling in reading—and more.

The focus on education policy paid off: Mississippi 4th grade average reading scores have jumped 10 points since 2013—the largest increase in the country—and 19 points since 1992 (the second-largest increase).[133] In January 2024, researchers at Harvard and Stanford found that Mississippi was one of only three states where average reading scores for children in grades 3 through 8 had risen to pre-pandemic levels.[134]

Florida adopted a reading retention law in 2003, and while every education reform has its skeptics, few can argue with the progress: Florida 4th grade reading scores have increased 16 points since 1992, putting the state just behind Mississippi and Washington, D.C., in terms of growth over the last three decades.[135]

The student groups who have historically struggled the most in school saw dramatic progress in the state. The average 4th grade reading score for Hispanic students in Florida has jumped 12 points since 1992, and the average score for Black students has increased 19 points.[136] Research on Mississippi and Florida's reading retention laws has found a positive correlation between student achievement and policies that require 3rd grade students to demonstrate they can read before moving to 4th grade.[137]

Success such as this was bound to attract attention. Improvements to student achievement are typically measured in much smaller increments and are hard to come by. Among 17-year-olds, scores in math and reading on the

Nation's Report Card have not measurably changed since the 1970s.[138] The achievement gap between wealthy students and children from low income families has also remained largely unchanged over the last 50 years.[139]

So, again, state lawmakers nationwide have noticed the gains in Mississippi and Florida and are looking to adopt 3rd grade retention provisions, along with expansive private education choice laws. Colorado lawmakers now require school officials to use "evidence-based" reading techniques that include the "science of reading," which involves phonics and does not rely on cueing.[140] According to *Education Week*, as of 2022, lawmakers in 40 states had adopted proposals similar to those in Colorado and Mississippi or otherwise began to retrain reading instructors.[141] Legislators in Arizona, Arkansas, Louisiana, and Tennessee have also adopted 3rd grade reading retention laws.[142]

State lawmakers are also providing more ways for families to find private learning opportunities for their children to help with reading. Florida, in fact, has a scholarship program specifically for parents to use to help students with reading and math.[143] Florida has other K–12 private school scholarship options, and these private learning options are the largest in the country by the rate of students participating.[144] Today, all families in Alabama, Arizona, Arkansas, Florida, Idaho, Indiana, Iowa, Louisiana, Ohio, Oklahoma, New Hampshire, North Carolina, Tennessee, Texas, Utah, West Virginia, and Wyoming can apply for similar scholarships or education savings accounts in their state (more information on school choice laws across the states is provided in this book's concluding chapter).[145]

★ ★ ★

If we can agree that reading is an essential skill, and if researchers overwhelmingly find that phonics is effective and should be used in concert with other methods, this consensus may help the nation with the incarceration issue we introduced earlier.

The U.S. has higher violent crime rates than most other countries and incarcerates a larger share of our population than any other country in the world for which researchers have reliable data.[146] Crime statistics are tricky things, though. True, more than two million people are behind bars in either federal or state prisons or locally run jails, but most people sent to jail are sent for short periods (less than one year) while they await sentencing or a bail hearing.[147] Research finds that the vast majority of violent crimes go unsolved, which means there are likely more who should be incarcerated.[148]

The overlap between illiteracy and incarceration is striking. Illiteracy is not a criminal offense, of course, but research clearly links illiteracy to negative outcomes such as dropping out of school, unemployment, and crime.[149] And the corrections system is expensive, costing some $80 billion per year in federal, state, and local taxpayer money.[150] This means that the results of illiteracy are consequential not only for the illiterate, but for taxpayers as well.

Some on the left may disagree with this position and argue that there are inequalities in society that affect ethnic minority individuals and communities more than Whites.[151] Incarceration is high on their list. Lawyer and author Michelle Alexander's *The New Jim Crow* is a *New York Times* best-seller and garnered praise from many on the ideological left, including Cornel West, the NAACP, and Ibram X. Kendi.[152] Alexander argues that the disproportionate levels of incarceration ("mass incarceration" is the prevailing terminology) among Black men is a new form of the Jim Crow laws that were used to discriminate against Black Americans in the early 20th century.[153] BLM, the Marxist organization that Melissa Jackson's children were called to sympathize with by their teacher, has also used the term, "new Jim Crow," along with the ACLU.[154]

While radicals' claims of "mass incarceration" do not hold up to scrutiny, the incarceration rates among ethnic minority individuals are troubling, as are the underreporting of crimes that disproportionately affect ethnic minority communities. Most crimes committed against Blacks come at the hands of Black perpetrators.[155] Black Americans represent 13 percent of the general population but 37 percent of those who are incarcerated.[156] Nearly half of those serving life sentences are Black[157]—all data points that show that more-effective K–12 education policies could help millions of

Black Americans live their best lives and become pillars of their families and contributing members of their communities.

Policymakers must recognize the connection between providing young people with quality educational opportunities and reducing the prison population. Again, education and incarceration are inversely related: more education correlates with lower incarceration rates. So does improving the rates of literacy and education attainment, both of which produce positive outcomes for those who are already incarcerated.[158]

Gerard Robinson, who has led the state education agencies in Florida and Virginia and now teaches at the University of Virginia's School of Law, explains that expanding the education opportunities available to the incarcerated is crucial.

"Incarcerated people who participate in correctional education have a 43 percent lower likelihood of returning to prison than peers who did not participate in a program," Robinson wrote in *A Story to Tell* (not to be confused with Hanford's podcast, *Sold a Story*).[159] He says that incarcerated individuals who participate in some form of education are also more likely to find a job after release, and because these individuals are less likely to go back to prison, every dollar spent in a correctional education program results in a 4–5 dollar decrease in the overall cost of incarceration.[160]

The societal and individual benefits are greater if a person does not have to go to prison in the first place in order to learn how to read (or learn math skills, etc.). Robinson also found that nearly 60 percent of incarcerated adults do not participate in education programs while behind bars.[161] This means that getting education right the first time—reading especially—matters tremendously because not all who are incarcerated will take advantage of the options available to them while in jail or prison.

There is room for agreement on the issue of incarceration and education between those on the political right and left. Conservatives believe individual freedom is crucial to forming families, and that families are the binding agents of communities. Productive citizens make healthy families, which make healthy communities, which make a healthy nation. Those on the left say they want to reduce inequality and expect the government to provide resources at least to individuals in need.[162]

But the overlap between illiteracy and incarceration is obvious. We do not have to find consensus on ideological explanations such as "systemic racism" to agree that learning to read helps students finish school, and finishing high school helps individuals find jobs and makes them less likely to land in jail or prison.

And while federal lawmakers have tried without success to improve literacy rates, state lawmakers have seen success in recent years as more evidence has demonstrated the shortcomings of cueing. This is a significant victory for taxpayers, families, students—and individuals who, without learning to read, may have found themselves incarcerated later in life. Those on the right and left can agree that America would be better off if we had more adults who were employed and contributing to their communities than behind bars. Better reading instruction is a great place to start.

★ ★ ★

The quality and accuracy of *what* we choose to read matters greatly as we form a consensus about ideas, pursue truth, and sketch the boundaries of different debates. The Education Department's *Becoming a Nation of Readers* said as much in 1985, along with its emphasis on including phonics in reading instruction. "Text comprehension depends upon a reader's prior knowledge, experience, and attitudes; meaning is constructed as a reader links what he reads to what he knows," reads the report.[163]

True enough.

What do students need to know once they learn to read? Let's start with civics.

CHAPTER THREE

RECLAIMING CIVICS

It cannot be doubted that, in the United States, the instruction of the people powerfully contributes to the support of a democratic republic; and such must always be the case, I believe, where instruction which awakens the understanding is not separated from moral education which amends the heart.

—Alexis de Tocqueville, *Democracy in America*[1]

"For immigrants like me, I came here believing, and still do believe, that America is a bastion of freedom," said Suparna Dutta, an immigrant from India and onetime appointee to the Virginia Board of Education, in our interview.[2] Dutta is a mother of two and one of the founders of Coalition for TJ, a parent-led organization that objected to attempts to lower the academic standards at one of Virginia's best-achieving high schools, Thomas Jefferson High School for Science and Technology.[3]

Dutta believes the U.S. Constitution "is pretty remarkable."[4] This is why she was shocked at another board member's attempts to mar the Constitution and the Declaration of Independence in discussions on the state's academic standards, saying at a 2023 board meeting that the documents were guilty of "enshrining slavery."[5]

Like Latasha Fields, Wayne Lewis, and others with whom I spoke in writing this book, Dutta believes in the American Dream and fiercely opposes attempts to belittle our founding documents. As this chapter will explain, her brief tenure on the Virginia State Board of Education was marked by a conversation about the state's academic standards that turned into a political spectacle involving intrigue and religious bias—all over questions about how civics should be taught in school.

Hers is a local story, one of many like it happening on school boards around the U.S. It's an example of why an authentic appreciation of civic education is, and has always been, a crucial subject for students.

The New York Times has called civics "the latest education battleground."[6] But surveys and other research find that Americans largely agree about what they want in civics education, in terms of actual content, and who we have voted into office to determine how civics is taught. The mainstream media and vocal radical minority who are in favor of DEI, CRT, and "action civics" want us to think that those who disagree with them are out of step. On this issue, my survey found that the claims of polarization are a myth.

★ ★ ★

Parents know that children are like sponges, constantly absorbing ideas and imitating the things they see. Any mom or dad who has ever put a "swear jar" in the kitchen knows that shaping a child's habits is essential. The survey in this book found that Americans want children taught character and virtue in school as well as at home, which is a reflection of the belief that a young person's sense of right and wrong is constantly developing. Such lessons will certainly take more than a swear jar at the front of the classroom.

Virtue is essential to the academic subject of civics. Parents and educators could compose long lists of habits that they would call virtues, but for the sake of the discussion here, we can simply refer to basic decency and common sense, things like patience and kindness, close cousins of the cardinal virtues Plato identified in the *Republic* as wisdom, courage, moderation, and justice.[7] These virtues underpin civics, when well constructed.

The Bill of Rights Institute, a nonprofit educational organization that creates resources on civics and history, says,

> The maintenance of our republican government requires the people be vigilant, informed, and *virtuous*, ensuring that governing institutions are directed towards their right ends. Good habits, or *virtues*, promote self-government and help guarantee that communities orient themselves towards advancing the spirit of a common purpose [emphasis added].[8]

In the survey for this book, I found that Americans want such things to be emphasized more in K–12 schools.

Civics can be broadly defined as the study of the rights, responsibilities, and duties of individuals in a society.[9] As taught in K–12 schools today, civics is a combination of history, government, and philosophy, instruction on how our government works, why our Founding Fathers designed our institutions in a particular way, and how students can be productive citizens.[10]

Traditionally, civics has been considered as part of the overall project of forming citizens and teaching children the difference between right and wrong.[11] In 1912, a high school civics textbook by Samuel Eagle Forman defined civics by saying that "a lesson in civics is a lesson in ethics."[12] He writes,

> To equip a lad with a knowledge of the working of governments and the rights of citizens, without equipping him with a conscience that will constrain him to practice the virtues of citizenship, may be to prepare him for a more successful career as a public rogue.[13]

He praises the U.S. Constitution, an example of "a lesson in ethics" and a document that extols the "virtues of citizenship."[14] Civics instruction, then, at least a century ago, combined patriotism, traditional values such as honesty, and political participation.

Forman's textbook is typical if not representative of the books on history, civics, and related education topics of that time. Peggy Noonan, former speechwriter for President Ronald Reagan and now a columnist for *The Wall Street Journal*, highlighted the *Manual of Patriotism: For Use in the Public Schools of New York* in a column in May 2024, which includes much the same language as Forman's book.[15] Published in 1900, "the manual was written after the [New York] Legislature passed an 1898 law requiring public schools to display the American flag and 'encourage patriotic exercises,'" Noonan writes. The book was meant to "'awaken in the minds and hearts of the young' an 'appreciation' for 'the great deeds' of their nation," which sounds similar to Forman's text.

There is an important overlap between civics and virtue—and it is important to give students an appreciation for our nation's founding. Policymakers on both sides of the aisle agree that civics instruction is due for an overhaul, though they have long disagreed about what these changes should entail.[16] Forman's explanation gives us a good starting point. Civics should teach students to "learn to tolerate and respect the opinions of others, to recognize the worth of others, to express themselves with candor but not with violence and abuse, to abandon notions based upon ignorance and prejudice, to submit gracefully to defeat."[17] This sounds like a good explanation of character and virtue, but as you will see, these things are often not what schools are teaching today.

What Should We Teach?

Melissa Jackson and Beanie Geoghegan, the parents and advocates who were frustrated with public school responses to the COVID-19 pandemic, wanted to do something about their children's educations. In Geoghegan's testimony before Congress cited earlier, she said her son could not understand why schools were closed but liquor stores were open and considered "essential" businesses.[18] "In a word," Geoghegan said in her testimony, "they said [school] seemed optional," the same word used by the Duke professor quoted by *The New York Times* and cited in the last chapter. Her frustration with what she saw as an effort to deprioritize education moved her and Jackson to think about how to re-instill a sense of purpose for learning in their children.

"This is not going to be fixed by increasing funding to the very institutions that shut their doors to millions of students nationwide and left the parents to pick up the broken pieces of their children," Geoghegan said in her testimony.[19]

After March 2020, when schools closed down due to COVID, "the rest of the year was just a waste," Geoghegan said in our interview.[20] "I've never really been one to sit on the sidelines in my kids' education," she said. She explains that just as she has been active in her kids' schools, she expects her children to try to be part of the solution, instead of just complaining.

"If my kids kept coming to me to complain about something, [eventually] I would ask them what they could do about it," Geoghegan said.[21] On the topic of curriculum, though, Geoghegan and Jackson still saw work that parents could be a part of, and they wanted to practice what they were preaching to their children.

Geoghegan and Jackson formed Freedom in Education, an advocacy organization dedicated to helping "cultivate a civically virtuous society" through advancing quality K–12 curricular materials.[22]

"We started researching solutions" to the problems they saw in their children's educations, Geoghegan says. "What we discovered is there is a treasure trove of people and organizations who are working on solutions [to bring high-quality curriculum to schools]. A lot of time they do the heavy lifting of creating the solutions, but they have trouble promoting," she said.[23]

"We now want to be the catalyst to get these out into schools," Geoghegan says.

Freedom in Education prioritizes civics instruction that "clearly [teaches] why America was founded" and explains citizens' responsibilities.[24] Freedom in Education's mission statement reflects the ideas Geoghegan and Jackson told me in our interview. Their vision is for a nation of "engaged parents raising virtuous children equipped with core knowledge and an understanding of America's founding principles," a statement in stark contrast to the oppressor-versus-oppressed narrative described by critical race theorists and BLM activists.[25]

"People want [a] simple curriculum that is focused on facts and not driven by political ideologies," Jackson says of her organization's mission.[26]

She's not alone, and the survey for this book demonstrates that Americans are not polarized on this issue. The survey found that Americans want schools to teach about virtue and character. Seventy-eight percent of parents in our sample agreed that public schools should teach students about character and virtue. Just 5 percent disagreed. These responses were consistent across party lines, too, with both parents who identified as Democrats and those who called themselves Republicans responding favorably to character-related instruction. The respondents from the general population were also in favor by a wide margin, with 74 percent saying they wanted public schools to teach about character and virtue.

The segment of the survey respondents who were most in favor of schools teaching about character and virtue were the school board members. Eighty-five percent of board members were in favor, and, again, the responses were consistent across party lines.

All of these responses are consistent with a prior Heritage Foundation survey published in 2021 that asked a similar question.[27] In that survey, we asked a nationally representative sample of parents and a subsample of school board members, "Do you believe [your child's school/public schools] should engage with character and virtue?" and found that 83 percent of parents and 89 percent of school board members were in favor.[28]

Freedom in Education raises money to donate classic works of literature, fiction and nonfiction, to classrooms and to create lesson plans on civics for K–12 classrooms that teachers can use during Constitution Week each year (September 17–23) to help with civics, among other subjects.[29] In the survey for this book, 57 percent of parents said K–12

Figure 3.1 **Should schools teach about character and virtue?**

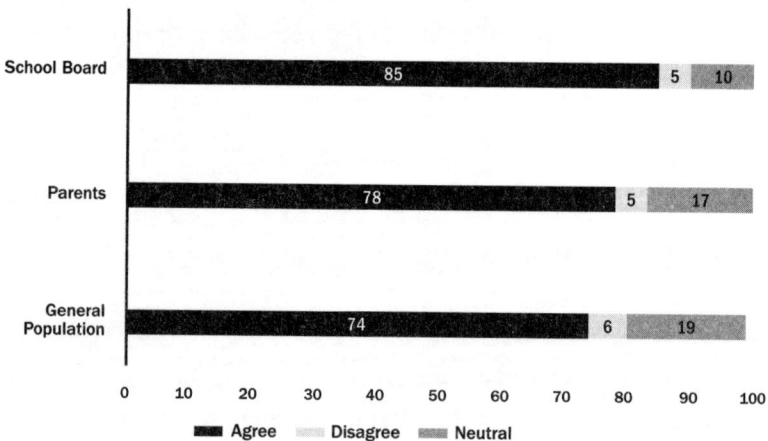

	Agree	Disagree	Neutral
School Board	85	5	10
Parents	78	5	17
General Population	74	6	19

schools should emphasize civics more. Half of Republican parents gave this response, and 68 percent of Democrats agreed. Among the general public, 57 percent said civics should be taught more, again with majorities agreeing on both sides of the political aisle. Sixty-nine percent of school board members said the same.

Civics is an area in need of attention. The U.S. Department of Education measures student progress in civics every four years as part of the Nation's Report Card, and U.S. students post consistently low scores on these tests. In the latest results from 2022, average scores on the civics assessment had fallen three points from 2018.[30] One-third of students scored at or below a basic level, as defined by the skills associated with their own grade level.

This is not a new problem—scores have been this poor since 1998.[31] In fact, lawmakers on the right and left have acknowledged the problem, with different solutions.[32] Just as the reading wars demonstrated, education has once again proved to be prone to fads: during President Barack Obama's administration, then-Education Secretary Arnie Duncan advocated for "action civics," which he hoped would replace traditional civics—instruction on the Founding Fathers' contributions to political philosophy, basic information

Figure 3.2 Do you believe the focus on civics in K–12 schools needs to be emphasized more, less, or stay about the same?

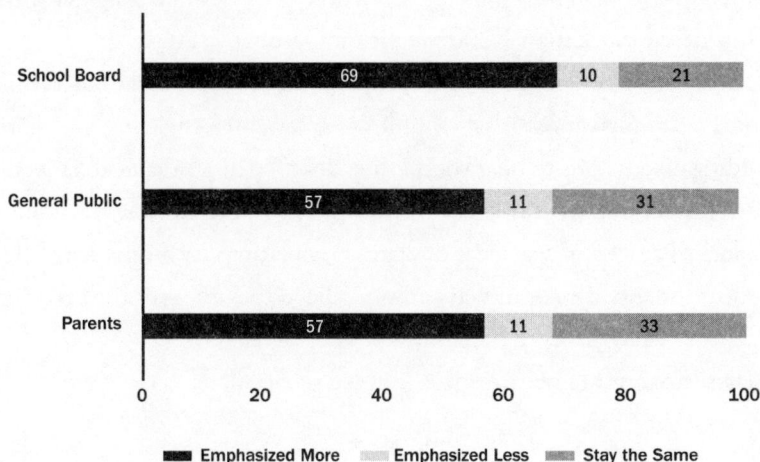

about voter participation, and key events in our nation's history of political activism—with political advocacy.[33]

Action civics is laden with progressive causes, teaching students to protest gun laws and advocate against "climate change" using school walkouts and other demonstrations.[34] Duncan's team said schools needed to "move beyond your 'grandmother's civics'" and deprioritize facts in favor of political action.[35] Just as more-sober-minded educators recognized the weaknesses in using cueing methods exclusively to teach reading, many saw the perils of training students to be activists. Action civics trains students to be protestors and politically engaged before they have the knowledge necessary to evaluate complex political and policy positions. By 2019, President Donald Trump's administration returned to the "phonics" of civics instruction and released a report reemphasizing America's founding ideals and rejecting action civics.[36]

Still, as this book goes to press, action civics remains in force in schools around the U.S.[37] And colleges are paying a price. The behavior of rioting college students who "encamped" themselves on college campuses in spring 2024 is remarkably similar to the action civics activities students learned in K–12 such as school walkouts. These encampments were widespread in 2024, from Columbia University to the University of Southern California, as students advocated for Hamas, the terrorist group dominating Gaza and that murdered more than 1,200 people on October 7, 2023.[38]

The students at Columbia who occupied and vandalized Hamilton Hall, one of the campus's most historic buildings, were not engaging in debates or holding discussions to hear competing ideas.[39] The students at Emerson in Boston were not inviting speakers representing both sides of the issue as they blocked a right-of-way near downtown, violating city ordinances.[40] The Stanford students who occupied and vandalized the offices of the president and provost were not even listening to opposing views.[41]

These actions are neither civic-minded nor civil.

★ ★ ★

State departments of education and state boards design and adopt academic standards, and these standards must be renewed periodically. As a result, debates over how to teach civics, history, and social studies recur about every four years in many states.[42] In Louisiana and South Dakota, for example, state lawmakers have adopted academic standards for social studies that, as Louisiana State Superintendent Cade Brumley says, "reflect the totality of events that have made America an exceptional nation, including our accomplishments and flaws."[43] Louisiana's standards include discussions of leading figures in U.S. history, with an emphasis on the Founding Fathers.[44] The standards also include values such as "responsibility," "respect," and "hard work," along with sections on local history, slavery, and the conflicts between America's early settlers.[45]

In an interview with me, Brumley explains that he knows of the competing ethnic studies and social studies textbooks and standards from other states and wanted to provide content that was strikingly different by offering an optimistic view of America.[46]

"It often felt as if I were standing between kids and Marxism or communism or radical ideology or all of those things. We just held the line," Brumley says.[47]

South Dakota's new social studies standards also place a heavy emphasis on the features of American's constitutional republic that are unique in world history.[48] The state department of education wrote that they designed the new standards to provide "honest, balanced, and complete accounts of historical events and debates that foster a love of country that, like any love, is not blind to its faults" and "history and civics instruction free from political agendas and activism."[49]

As though they already knew the findings from the survey for this book, state officials wrote, "We believe parents desire their children learn to be wise and virtuous."[50] Fittingly, then, "The state, echoing the American Founders, requires a citizenry that is wise and virtuous in order to sustain free self-government."[51] South Dakota's standards, like those in Louisiana, include instruction about our Founding Fathers and other key historical leaders, as well as lessons about local issues such as tribal lands and Native American history that are unique to South Dakota.[52]

Compare these standards to what is happening in California and Minnesota. In California, while the state has social studies standards, the state department of education has also produced ethnic studies academic standards that are already in use by districts such as Haywood Unified, near San Francisco, and Los Angeles Unified School District, the second-largest school district in the U.S.[53] In fact, state lawmakers adopted a provision requiring high school students to take an ethnic studies course before they graduate, a requirement that went into effect in 2025.[54]

The ethnic studies model curriculum developed by the California Department of Education is teaching opposite lessons about social cohesion and cultural norms from the standards in Louisiana and South Dakota. California officials dedicate an entire section of the ethnic studies model framework to intersectionality, which is academic Kimberlé Crenshaw's addition to critical race theory.[55] Intersectionality is rooted in identity politics and the idea that culture can only be explained as a battlefield on which ethnic groups and interest groups compete for power: "Intersectionality....recognizes that people have different overlapping identities, for example, a transgender Latina or a Jewish African American. These intersecting identities shape individuals' experiences of racism and bigotry."[56]

Gone are lessons about virtue and teaching students to aspire to emulate the sacrifices of the early colonists. Now, students have multiple supposedly oppressed identities, and therefore multiple ways to describe themselves as victims.

And while South Dakota's standards aim to inspire a love of country, even after acknowledging its faults, California's standards include readings from the radical Howard Zinn, whose *A People's History of the United States* serves to condemn America's triumphs and accuses our founders of being bigots.[57] Among the many problems with Zinn's work was that he did not include a single footnote in the entire book to support his claims—a poor example of scholarship from the onetime professor.[58] Zinn had no interest in advancing civics instruction, certainly not around the virtues outlined in this chapter. Rather, he wanted to "awaken a greater consciousness of class conflict, racial injustice, sexual inequality, and national arrogance."[59]

In Minnesota, policymakers adopted new social studies standards in 2024 with ethnic studies standards incorporated.[60] Legislators have required that students take a social studies course before they graduate and required that every school district offer a course in ethnic studies, which means that nearly every Minnesota K–12 student will encounter these standards before they graduate high school.[61]

Katherine Kersten, of the Center of the American Experiment, a research institution based in Minnesota, wrote in the *Minneapolis Star-Tribune* that the Minnesota Department of Education delayed the public release of the content that schools would be using in the standards (as this book goes to press, the content standards were still not available on the Minnesota Department of Education website).[62] The center was able to obtain the material through a public data request.

What the center found was content straight out of a Marxist handbook. History is described as a competition for military and political control, and students are told to describe how identity groups have "fought…against systemic and coordinated exercises of power." Students are taught to analyze "colonialism" and "dominant and non-dominant narratives," using the conflict between Israel and Palestine as an illustration.[63]

"These people just had an ideological agenda, and that is what they gave priority number one to as they put this together, not actual learning by students who need to understand who we are and where we came from," Kersten said in an interview for this book.[64]

The St. Paul Public School District illustrates how these radical ideas are put into practice. As in California's standards, the district's presentation of its ethnic studies content lists intersectionality, one of the core themes of critical race theory, as part of the coursework's main ideas.[65] The course description uses many of the words and ideas commonly found in critical race theory materials such as "identity," "power structures," and "forms of oppression." Students are to "actively question, challenge and expose the world's systems and operations in order to recognize and analyze systems of inequality," which sounds like a noble goal until we remember that they are pointing to America and encouraging students to dismantle American institutions.[66]

The content discussing Israel and Palestine takes on additional significance after October 7, 2023.[67] Again, as Israel went to war to defend itself and rescue hundreds of innocent people the terrorists took as hostages, protests and demonstrations broke out across colleges campuses and some high schools in the U.S.—demonstrations, in nearly every case, in favor of Palestine.[68] In the spring of 2024, Columbia University officials moved all classes online because they could not guarantee student safety after protesters created an encampment on campus, many wearing masks and threatening Jewish students.[69] Jewish students report fearing for their safety as videos posted on social media show antisemitic students circling Jewish students and hurling invectives at them. One anti-Israel protestor hit a Jewish student in the face at Columbia, while a Jewish student at Yale was stabbed in the eye with a flagpole during a similar violent outbreak.[70]

★ ★ ★

In her reporting on the standards, Kersten found that a group called Education Liberation Minnesota (EdLib MN) helped draft the ethnic studies materials.[71] The group's central figures have publicly stated their pro-Palestinian position and animus for Israel. Kersten pointed to an article from 2022, where an EdLib MN figure wrote, "Ethnic Studies explores the colonial roots of the dispossession of Palestinian land and the creation of Zionism."[72]

Observers should note similar language being used in the recent college encampments. One Columbia University professor, whose school was ground zero for the student encampments that shook universities in spring 2024, said, "Perhaps the major achievement of the resistance in the temporary takeover of these settler-colonies is the death blow to any confidence that Israeli colonists had in their military and its ability to protect them."[73]

Usage of the term is more than just wordplay: after rioters disrupted some two-dozen college campuses in the spring of 2024, Jewish community leaders in New York deemed Columbia University unsafe for Jewish students, and universities officials closed the campus to the public around the same time.[74]

The riots destroyed property and violated university rules, a far cry from Forman's call for K–12 students to be given civics instruction that teaches them to "express themselves with candor but not with violence and abuse."[75]

Kersten and the Center for the American Experiment obtained copies of the subject-matter experts who reviewed Minnesota's standards through the Freedom of Information Act, and even those who were sympathetic to ethnic studies recognized the danger in what state officials were proposing to teach in the state's standards.[76] One reviewer described Minnesota's ethnic studies as full of "grievance-mongering," a term that applies just as aptly to the Columbia protests. The reviewer, one who was not opposed to the idea of ethnic studies, said that "calling US foreign policy 'imperialism' shows a lack of international historical, economic, and political understanding. It's a made-up concept, signifying a deep disrespect for Americans who served their country in foreign conflicts and wars."[77]

Writing for *National Review*, Stanley Kurtz points out that Minnesota's ethnic studies concepts do not stand alone as the guide for a single subject but, rather, have been inserted into a litany of subjects, including social studies, geography, and history.[78] Minnesota is not just teaching social studies with an ethnic studies component; state officials have adjusted a host of subjects so that "settler-colonialism" serves as a driving idea behind instruction.

Racism and injustice should be opposed everywhere, but no mention is made of how civil rights laws in the U.S. prohibit discrimination based on race and sex. Minnesota's content can only be described as indoctrination, in stark contrast to *e pluribus unum*. "Minnesota has sleepwalked into an extremist hijacking of our public schools," Kersten writes, emphasizing that Israel "isn't the only nation in the cross hairs of decolonization ideology."[79] The U.S. is the target, too.

Extremists make it appear as though Americans are polarized on civics and America's sense of national identity, but we are not: We want more civics education, not for students to be indoctrinated on how to view themselves as oppressed. We want students taught about character and virtue, not about rioting and violence.

★   ★   ★

In Virginia, it was an immigrant who recently stood up in favor of teaching the moral ideals of our founding documents to K–12 students.

Governor Glenn Youngkin appointed Suparna Dutta to the Virginia Board of Education in 2022, and a Senate committee voted 14-0 in favor of her confirmation in early 2023 (one more meeting and vote by this committee would have been necessary to finalize the nomination).[80]

But after she "dared to speak up for the constitution and against socialism on the Board of Education" at a meeting in February of that year, the Virginia Senate Privileges and Elections committee voted to remove her.[81] One senator accused Dutta—a "minority Hindu woman of color," in Dutta's words—of being aligned with a White-supremacist group.[82]

What exactly did Dutta say that led the senator to accuse her of this?

"I stood up against socialism," Dutta told a local news station.[83] In our conversation, she says that while the board was reviewing updates to Virginia's social studies standards, she objected to a comment from Anne Holton, another board member and wife of Virginia Senator Tim Kaine and former Virginia secretary of education, who described the Constitution and Declaration as documents written "by the privileged and the white," Dutta said.[84]

The social studies standards were several years old, having been drafted under the administration of Governor Terry McAuliffe, a Democrat, and Dutta says the standards "were viewed through a lens of race" and contained "very social-justice-heavy jargon."

Holton said the Declaration of Independence and U.S. Constitution contain ideas that are "fundamental to enshrining slavery" —an inaccurate claim that has been debunked by historians.[85]

★ ★ ★

Dutta's interest in education was personal: she had contacted Youngkin during his campaign because of what was happening at TJ High, the school her son attended.[86] TJ High had long been ranked as one of the highest-achieving public schools in the country, but in 2020, during the summer of protests after the killing of George Floyd, the Fairfax Couty School Board voted to change the school's admissions policies.[87] TJ High is a magnet school, a public school designed to educate the highest-performing students in its enrollment zones. School officials had required prospective students to take an admissions test before being accepted based on their scores, grades, and other merit-based factors.

But some Fairfax board members said the school's policy was racist and that the board needed to "address the under-representation of Black and Hispanic students."[88] The board voted unanimously to remove the testing requirement, which led Dutta to co-found a group called Coalition for TJ to advocate for rigorous academics at the school. The school board created a "holistic" admissions process that considered a student's household income, as well as whether a student attended an "underrepresented middle school," explains the Pacific Legal Foundation, which represented Coalition for TJ in a lawsuit.[89]

The coalition hosted a meeting with Youngkin during his campaign (Dutta says McCauliffe's campaign requested $25,000 to attend a meeting with the coalition, which was declined), and Dutta eventually became a volunteer on Youngkin's campaign team.[90] The coalition sought to preserve the merit-based system that had made TJ High so successful and elevated the work of Virginia's brightest students. Pacific Legal reports that one year after the new admissions standards were used, the share of Asian students at Thomas Jefferson decreased from 73 to 54 percent, evidence of a racially discriminatory impact on these students and grounds for litigation.[91]

★ ★ ★

Dutta's comments defending America's founding documents while she was on the school board struck a nerve. Even though Dutta did not want to remove any content on slavery (an institution she calls "heinous") from the standards, Dutta's comments that socialism and communism are clearly related were "not taken too kindly," Dutta says.[92]

Teachers unions targeted her for removal from the board and started a campaign for her ouster.[93] But that was not all. Representatives from Muslim interest groups, including the head of the Virginia Council of Muslim Organizations, accused Dutta of being an anti-Muslim extremist and contacted then-state Senator Chap Peterson (D-37) with the charges. Writing in RealClearPolitics, Asra Q. Nomani tracked the organizations that opposed Dutta, including teacher unions and these Muslim organizations.[94] None of these groups responded to Nomani's request for evidence that Dutta was an extremist, nor did Chapman provide evidence. Just six days after the Senate committee voted unanimously for her nomination, Democrats in the Senate blocked her final confirmation.[95]

Dutta says local Hindu leaders met with some of the Muslim leaders behind Dutta's ouster. Dutta says, "When they met with these Muslim leaders[, the Muslim leaders said] they wanted to send a message to you guys and to [Indian Prime Minister Narendra] Modi."[96] She continued, "America is definitely becoming a battleground for sectarian politics from all over the world. And as you can see what's happened in Israel, there are so many of these organizations all over the U.S. who are fighting the same Palestinian versus Israel battle in the U.S."[97]

Dutta said she was surprised that she was the only one who spoke out at the meeting to defend the Constitution. "While no nation is perfect," Suparna Dutta says, "the ideals [in the Constitution] are remarkable."

She explained that Americans do not always recognize how fortunate we are. "I was born and brought up in India, which was founded a socialist country. At one point, decades ago, the top personal income tax rate was as high as 97.75 percent," she said.

"But most immigrants don't raise their voices. They are used to being subservient, and the only ones who raise their voices are the ones who are politically connected or the ones who are rich," she says.

"We keep our heads down, work hard, and hope that our kids are getting a good education. But some of us learned otherwise during the summer of 2020," she says, explaining that she had a front-row seat to what she described as her children's indoctrination.

"Growing up in the U.S., people don't realize what you have. You have running water here, 24 hours each day—hot water when you need it," she explains, adding that those living in developing countries cannot always say the same.[98]

★ ★ ★

In a strange twist, and as evidence that racial discrimination still requires our attention, the U.S. Supreme Court declined the Coalition for TJ's request for the high court to consider Thomas Jefferson High School for Science and Technology's new admissions standards.[99] This is odd given the court's earlier decision in *Students for Fair Admissions* that rejected discrimination in college admissions, because both cases deal with the topic of racial preferences (see Chapter 1).

In the Coalition for TJ's case, five of the justices agreed to let stand a Fourth Circuit Court of Appeals decision in favor of Thomas Jefferson's new race-based admissions policy. But Justice Samuel Alito dissented, joined by Justice Clarence Thomas.[100] "What the Fourth Circuit majority held, in essence, is that intentional racial discrimination is constitutional so long as it is not too severe. This reasoning is indefensible, and it cries out for correction," Alito wrote.[101]

Echoing Dutta's comments about immigrants to the U.S. and an appreciation for hard work, freedom, and equality under the law, Alito wrote,

> Asian-American students, many of whom are immigrants or the children of immigrants, have often seen admission to TJ as a ticket

to the American dream. In this respect, their aspirations mirror those of young people from other immigrant groups. Public magnet schools with competitive admissions based on standardized tests have served as engines of social mobility by providing unique opportunities for minorities and the children of immigrants, and these students' subsequent careers have in turn richly contributed to our country's success.[102]

Alito stresses that the Fairfax school board correspondence considered in the case clearly indicated that the members wanted racial rebalancing, irrespective of the hard work or competency of the student body. Prior courts had found "both direct and circumstantial evidence clearly showed that the changes in the admissions process were motivated by racial discrimination," Alito said.[103] It is as though the very essence of *Brown v. Board of Education* had been reversed. Before, schools would not allow Black students to attend because of their skin color, regardless of their skills and efforts. Civil rights advocates of just one or two generations ago wanted everyone to consider character over color, right? Now, the Fairfax board primarily wanted to consider skin color instead of effort.

★　★　★

Dutta's example demonstrates how this issue is affecting statehouses, while Geoghegan and Jackson's story showcases how the topic is affecting homes in neighborhoods across the country. Yet the subject is attracting attention even in the White House. In President Donald Trump's first administration, he created the 1776 Commission, a group of professors and researchers who authored an outline for describing the "history and principles of the founding of the United States."[104] Led by Hillsdale College president Larry Arn and Carol Swain, author and former Vanderbilt professor, the commission drafted a report considering America's founding with relation to slavery, fascism, racism and identity politics, the family, education, and more. Trump reinstituted the commission in his second administration.[105]

In addition to policymakers in the White House, other state officials have worked to clarify the issue. In Florida, Governor Ron DeSantis (R) launched a "model national civic literacy initiative" in 2021.[106] His team set aside more than $100 million to train teachers, and educators could earn $3,000 bonuses for participating.

Tiffany Hoben was a teacher and then social studies curriculum specialist in Manatee County who helped train teachers as part of DeSantis's initiative. She traveled around the state, leading presentations on civics before audiences of hundreds of teachers at a time.

The program was pilloried by the media, which shocked her.

"Everyone [involved in the new program to train teachers to teach civics] was really committed to being super honest about history," Hoben said in our interview.[107] "All the good and the bad and the ugly and the inspiring—all of it."

She met teachers around the state, she says, finding some who were not teaching about slavery because it made them uncomfortable. There were others who were teaching that "America is a bad place to be," she says.

"Our team was unified in [an] intellectually honest endeavor to teach what these things really meant," Hoben says. She explained that her sessions "went way, way deeper than a textbook would go," even covering Cicero and Aristotle and "the philosophical underpinnings of our Republic," she says.

The media remained harshly critical, she says. "We were made out like we were whitewashing history and diminishing the effects of slavery and Jim Crow," Hoben says. "We were really just being as honest as we could and trying to put on display, yes, the flaws and the times when we need to be cognizant of errors and wrong thinking. But how can the Declaration [of Independence] and Constitution have inspired generation after generation to do better?" she asks.[108]

In the model civics course for state educators available on the Florida Department of Education's web site, the issue of slavery is covered early, in the second of five modules in the course.[109] Black Codes, Jim Crow laws, and the civil rights movement are covered in the fourth module.[110]

The New York Times said the Florida program, as well as the new standards in South Dakota discussed earlier in this chapter, "are yet another sign that the nation's schools are on two tracks, with deep divides over what children should learn about their country."[111]

Perhaps. There are competing methods for teaching civics—just as there are techniques in competition for teaching reading—but the divides are not as deep as the *Times* suggests. The survey for this book and other Heritage polling has found consistent results about what parents want taught in schools. And while neither Trump nor DeSantis was elected strictly for their position on K–12 civics, they both share optimistic, patriotic perspectives on the U.S., as demonstrated by their policies.

These positions are popular with Americans. The poll results don't reflect a "deep divide" in the country, despite prominent holdout states such as Minnesota and California, where educators are rejecting parent preferences of lessons about liberty and representative government in favor of activism and identity politics.

★ ★ ★

Forman, the author of *First Lessons in Civics*, the textbook introduced earlier in this section, says, "Surely the development of the ethical nature children should receive formal recognition in a system of education," to which Americans in our surveys agreed.[112]

He designed a "10 Commandments for Students" that include the following:

+ I must not cheat the state.
+ I must not debauch my fellows by bribing them.
+ I must prefer my country to my party.
+ I must tolerate the opinions of others, etc.[113]

Forman laments that in schools—even in his day, when the teaching of Protestant Christian ideas was common—"the formal teaching of morals does not meet with much favor."[114] He continues, "There is but little teaching in our schools that relates to the conduct of life," which he says is a disservice to students and the nation.[115]

Suparna Dutta, Beanie Geoghegan, Melissa Jackson, and others interviewed for this chapter would agree. Yet the experiences of these parents and community leaders were anything but civilized examples of "how the affairs of mankind are managed," to use Forman's terminology.[116] Overbearing school district bureaucracies that were exposed during the pandemic, racial discrimination taught in school curricula and used in admissions processes, opposition to American's core principles—Americans agree that these are not what we want for our children.

Civics instruction is a process of reaching students' "hearts as well as their minds," Forman says, and this is true in every subject today, for better or for worse.[117] Americans want civics to work for the betterment of their children.

★　★　★

"Is this wise? Is it right? Should the moral nature of man be so completely ignored in the scheme of education?"[118] Forman asks. Obviously not, and our survey indicates that parents want educators to instruct students in issues of character and civics—how to live civilly.

At the center of civic life lies marriage and the family.

Nearly one in five state inmates and one in ten federal inmates had lived with a foster family or otherwise spent time in the foster system while growing up.[119] A report from the Chapin Hall Center for Children at the University of Chicago found that half of foster children in their study were involved with the juvenile justice system by age 17.[120] One study of foster children in Pittsburgh found that 90 percent of the children who had been moved to five or more homes had been involved with the justice system.[121]

These statistics are included here not to criticize the foster system nor foster children but to illustrate the outcomes that are common to individuals who are not raised by intact, married parents.

Things do not improve once children leave the system. In a survey that followed individuals who had aged out of the foster care system after turning 18 years old, one in three men and 18 percent of women had been involved in illegal behavior within the last year.[122] Eighty-two percent of men and 59 percent of women in the survey had been arrested at least once between ages 17 and 26.[123]

Even apart from the foster care system, 42 percent of federal inmates reported living primarily with only one parent while growing up, and 47 percent of state inmates reported growing up with only one parent.[124] These figures far outpace the national average—approximately one in four children lives in a single-parent home today, though the rate are much higher for children who are ethnic minorities (more on this later).[125] The negative outcomes for children that stem from nonintact homes and the tragedy of the foster care system are difficult social problems and too much for one survey to solve.

Still, the survey did ask a question about whether Americans want students to be taught the benefits of finishing high school, entering the workforce or college, and getting married before having children.

The survey asked respondents what they think about teaching K–12 students at age appropriate levels to do these three things, which social scientists call the "success sequence."[126] Following this sequence can help reduce the number of single parent families, thereby reducing the number of children who grow up in non-intact homes, and ultimately reducing the share of individuals with a characteristic that frequently coincides with incarceration.

Our survey asked, "According to some researchers, people are much less likely to live in poverty if they follow the Success Sequence: graduating high school, getting a job, and getting married before having children. Should your child's school/assigned public schools teach the Success Sequence?" Fifty percent of our sample from the general population said "yes," while just 18 percent said "no." The remaining third were neutral about teaching the success sequence. The findings were similar for parents: 52 percent were in favor of students learning about the sequence in schools and 21 percent disagreed with teaching this idea, making for clear majorities in favor across the general population and parents.

School board members were even more strongly in favor of teaching the sequence. Seventy-one percent of our subsample of members were in favor and just 13 percent were opposed.

These findings are consistent with prior surveys asking the same question. In a Heritage Foundation survey from 2021, 72 percent of parents were in favor of public school educators teaching the success sequence, and 60 percent of school board members were in favor.[127]

Teaching students that they are more likely to stay out of poverty if they finish high school, then get a job or go to college, and get married before having children is not meant to shame members of non-intact married families. Instructional lessons that teach the benefits from the success sequence are acknowledging what the data demonstrates for individuals who have made these choices and are meant to help young people avoid the choices that derailed the dreams of millions of adults.

Among Millennials (individuals born between 1981 and 1996) who followed the success sequence, nearly all—97 percent—did not live in poverty when they reached their mid-30s.[128] This finding is consistent across racial lines. Yet people do not just want to avoid poverty; they want

Figure 3.3 **Should your child's school teach the success sequence?**

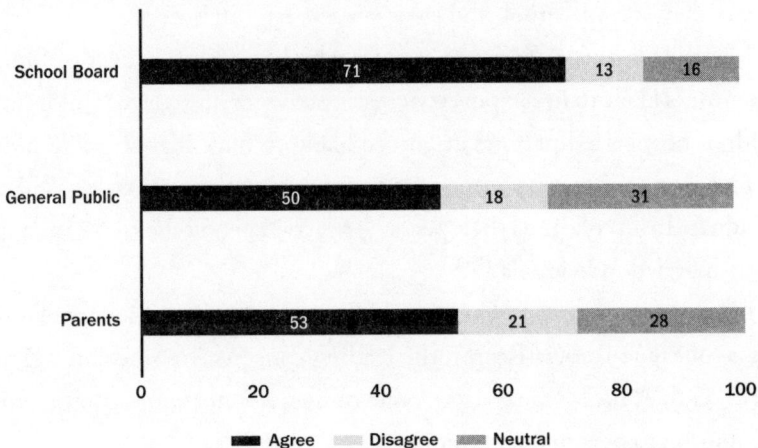

to succeed. And while wealth is not the only indicator of success, wealthier individuals will have better access to health care, successful schools, safer neighborhoods, and more. Sure enough, research on the success sequence finds that 80 percent of Black young adults, 86 percent of Hispanic young adults, and 91 percent of White young adults reached the middle class or higher by their mid-30s.[129]

Between 1975 and 2019, the share of children living with married parents declined from 76 percent to 64 percent.[130] Approximately 25 percent of parents with children ages 0–12 are not married.[131] In the research on families and children and life outcomes—everything from happiness to success in school to income levels later in life—family characteristics (e.g., marital status, parental characteristics such as education) are the variables that are most strongly related to a child's success.[132]

And the findings date back nearly a century. James Coleman's "Equal Education Opportunity" report, released in 1966, shocked educators by finding that a student's family background matters more to a child's later life outcomes than the school they attend.[133] In a summary of Coleman's research and other studies looking at the effects of family characteristics and student outcomes, North Carolina State University associate professor Anna Egalite writes, "In most studies, parental education has been identified as the single strongest correlate of children's success in school, the number of years they attend school, and their success later in life."[134]

Marriage is crucial. Married couples who have children inside of marriage are less likely to live in poverty, creating a better lifestyle for children.[135] Children of married parents are more likely to have higher grade point averages than their peers from non-married parents and are twice as likely to graduate from college as their peers.[136] Married people are twice as happy as non-married individuals.[137b]

In his testimony before Congress in February 2025, my Heritage Foundation colleague Robert Rector, the leading conservative voice on welfare reform, said, "A healthy marriage is one of the two most important factors contributing to personal happiness."[138]

He continued: "Marriage is also a very strong factor in promoting the upward mobility of children. The erosion of marriage has a marked effect on the violent crime rate in communities. Holding race, poverty, and other background variables constant, a 1 percentage point increase in the share of households in the community that are married is associated with a 2 percent decline in violent crime per capita."

One does not have to study the literature for very long before the issue of incarceration comes up again: individuals raised in single-parent homes have an elevated risk of incarceration.[139] Specifically, Black children who are raised in single-parent homes are 1.8 times as likely to spend time incarcerated later in their lives.[140] If we can teach school-age children the value of certain life choices—following the success sequence—that were once common practice among Americans, we could help them avoid making other decisions that could lead to crime and time in prison or jail.

★ ★ ★

Evidence also demonstrates that following the success sequence later in life also leads to positive outcomes.[141] Research from the American Enterprise Institute finds that when mothers who are single at the time they have their baby and later choose to follow any or all of the parts of the success sequence, they are significantly less likely to live in poverty. The poverty rate of mothers who were not married at the time of their child's birth but reached all of the success sequence milestones by the time the child reached age 15 was just 9 percent. AEI's Angela Rachidi explains that 78 percent of the mothers who were not married at childbirth and did not achieve any part of the success sequence later in life were living in poverty when their child reached 15.

Getting these choices right leads to a better life. Of the mothers who attained just one of these milestones by their child's first birthday, the poverty rate was 48 percent. The poverty rate dropped to 25 percent for mothers who attained two of the three success sequence milestones by the time her child reached age one.

Rachidi says that her research answers critics of the success sequence theory who claim that an individual's ability to follow the sequence is "often the result of circumstance" or of "structural factors."[142] She explains that even if parents cannot follow the sequence at younger ages, say, in their later teen years, individuals can still experience the benefits the sequence brings if they attain the key milestones—finishing high school, getting a job or pursuing a terminal degree, and getting married, preferably before having children—later in life.

"It seems plausible that at any point in time, achieving the success sequence milestones could improve prospects for families even when not followed sequentially," Rachidi writes.[143]

★ ★ ★

The next chapter deals with another area in which there is even more widespread agreement: opposition to allowing boys to enter girls' private spaces or play on girls' sports teams. Surveys find that a large share of Americans approve of neither, and the second Trump administration moved quickly and decisively to protect women on this issue.

CHAPTER FOUR

SEX VS. "GENDER"

Truth and freedom are inseparable.

—Calvin Coolidge[1]

Linda T. loves her son.[2] As we talked, she wanted to emphasize that first. But she is fearful of what has happened to him and other children who have been encouraged by educators, doctors, and "gender" activists to try to alter their bodies in an attempt to "transition" to reflect their gender instead of their sex.

"It's kind of like your child is a drug addict, but he is a celebrated one," Linda said. These children who are confused about their sex (confusion that can be diagnosed as "gender dysphoria," defined as a "debilitating sense of "unease" about one's body)[3] are exhibiting behaviors that resemble a dangerous habit. Yet many activists, including too many in the medical community, treat the children as though they are celebrities if they say they were born in the "wrong" body.

For decades, these activists have treated gender as a civil right, even recently trying to redefine sex to mean "sexual orientation and gender identity" (SOGI) in federal law.[4] President Biden's administration circumvented Congress and tried to change a crucial civil rights law by redefining "sex" via the regulatory process, an effort that was quickly challenged by state policymakers and the second Trump administration.[5] State policymakers and advocacy organizations nationwide filed more than a dozen lawsuits to make sure that "sex" means "sex"—your biological makeup, specifically whether you produce sperm or eggs.[6] Yes, there are biological anomalies, but these are rare, and this chapter will address the claim that these anomalies can prove gender is fluid.

★ ★ ★

During his first address to a joint session of Congress, President Trump highlighted his executive order "banning public schools from indoctrinating our children with transgender ideology."[7] He said, "I also signed an order to cut off all taxpayer funding to any institution that engages in the sexual mutilation of youth. And now, I want Congress to pass a bill permanently banning and criminalizing sex changes on children and forever ending the lie that any child is trapped in the wrong body."

He said, "This is a big lie. And our message to every child in America is that you are perfect exactly the way God made you."

President Trump returned to the White House during a period in which surveys had uncovered significant opposition to the "gender" movement, which seeks to affirm young children when those children diagnose themselves as being born in the wrong body.[8] State lawmakers across the country have barred schools from teaching children that there are more so-called genders than male and female.[9] Others have adopted provisions prohibiting the prescription of medicines that block puberty or alter hormones and surgeries on minors to alter their reproductive organs.[10]

Still, the pervasiveness of critical gender theory is remarkable. Hospitals around the country have performed hundreds of procedures on minors, including castration on boys and breast removal on girls.[11] The patient advocacy group Do No Harm, which is "focused on keeping identity politics out of medical education, research, and clinical practice," found that Boston Children's Hospital alone performed 301 such procedures between 2019 and 2023.[12] Hospitals such as Boston Children's also collect billions in federal grants (more than $1 billion in a single calendar year, according to the Washington Examiner) for various activities. That means taxpayers are funding surgical procedures on minors that cause permanent damage in efforts to "change" a child's gender.[13]

Meanwhile, watchdogs report that more than 1,200 school districts in the U.S. governing some 21,300 schools have policies either directing teachers to hide information from parents or not requiring educators to inform parents when a child attends school and says they were born in the wrong body.[14]

★ ★ ★

The term "gender" has become arbitrary in modern parlance. As my colleague Jay Richards, a senior fellow at The Heritage Foundation, explains, the word "gender" used to be synonymous with sex.[15] Etymologically, in English usage, "sex" came to refer to the act of intercourse around the 15th century and "gender" referred to the distinction between males and females.[16]

Today, however, self-described gender advocates are treating gender like an idea, not a biological reality. "Gender ideology does not accommodate the reality of sex—the reproductive strategy of mammals including human beings," Richards writes.[17] Gender is an idea now, an abstraction that people simply choose according to their innate sense of what they feel like. They can even change genders as often as they want.

In biological fact, no one can actually change from a male to a female. The picture on *Glamour* magazine of a pregnant woman who says she is a man only proves that if you keep your reproductive organs intact while claiming you are a different gender, your body still functions according to your biology.[18] Displays such as this are more than enough to confuse young children. And it is troubling that when children tell some adults that they were born in the wrong body, their feelings are rarely questioned, only affirmed—as exhibited by the personnel at the thousands of schools where educators hide a child's sexual confusion from parents. Children suddenly become diagnosticians over a crucial set of medical decisions.

There has been a staggering increase in the number of children confused about their sex in recent years: the number of children who began using puberty blockers or other hormone-altering medicines doubled between 2017 and 2021, according to data analyzed by Reuters.[19] The report's authors note, "These numbers are probably a significant undercount since they don't include children whose [insurance] records did not specify a gender dysphoria diagnosis or whose treatment wasn't covered by insurance." In *Irreversible Damage*, which made *The Economist* magazine's list of "best books of 2020," Abigail Shrier says that the rate of teenage girls in the United Kingdom who tried to change their "gender" increased 4,400 percent between 2008 and 2018.[20] In 2019, data from gender clinics in the U.K. found that nearly three times more females than males were seeking gender medicines or surgeries to alter their reproductive system (624 males and 1,740 females).[21]

Regardless of their sex, these children are being treated like rock stars and guinea pigs at the same time. According to reports from around the U.S., children expressing confusion about their sex are being encouraged to experiment with medicines meant for other specific medical treatments (called "off-label" uses).[22] Doctors are giving Lupron, for example, to confused children to suppress puberty.[23] The drug was designed to treat prostate cancer, however, and puberty suppression is just a known side effect.[24] Spironolactone was designed to treat high blood pressure, but because it suppresses testosterone, doctors are also providing this to males who think they are women.[25]

Notably, the U.S. Food and Drug Administration has not approved puberty blockers and other "sex hormones" for "gender care."[26] "No clinical trials have established their safety for such off-label use," said the Reuters report.[27]

Some school districts, however, are making "'gender-affirming' hormone treatment" available on school grounds.[28] Neighborcare Health, a nonprofit health care provider that operates clinics in schools and other locations around Seattle and Olympia, Washington, offers "comprehensive, evidence-based, gender-affirming care services to our students and families who need them," according to an email obtained by Parents Defending Education (now called Defending Education).[29] In the emails, Neighborcare said it had already been offering student counseling that promoted "social identity," which means they had already been affirming students' confusion about their sex. The health care organization said that parent consent would be required for hormone-altering medicines, but neither Seattle Public Schools nor the

Olympia School District requires educators to notify parents if their child wants to be addressed by a name and pronouns that do not correspond to the child's birth certificate.[30]

Research on "Gender" and Medicine

For privacy reasons, Linda T. asked that I not use her real name.[31] But she has been speaking out more often in recent years after meeting parents like her—parents of children struggling with their hormones and who tried to change their bodies, doing irreparable damage in some cases. She has met hundreds of parents who feel isolated and have "been through the war," as Linda calls it, of watching loved ones take medicines for off-label uses to delay puberty or change hormone activity.

In 2024, England's National Health Service released what is known as "The Cass Report," which reviewed research evidence on so-called transgender interventions.[32] The paper is significant: *The Times* of London called it "the world's biggest review into the contested field of transgender healthcare," with *The Wall Street Journal* dubbing it a "landmark review."[33] Dr. Hilary Cass, a pediatrician and former president of the Royal College of Pediatrics and Child Health, led the investigative team, who returned damning findings for doctors conducting these experiments on young people. The Cass Report could not find any "good evidence on the long-term outcomes of interventions to manage gender-related distress."[34]

Among the specific results in the Cass report, the authors found:

+ Children can be confused about their sex, but, in general, we should not be surprised if a young person's "sense of identity is not always fixed and may evolve over time."[35] In, fact, other research has found that, in 80–95 percent of cases of children confused about their sex, this confusion resolves naturally, without interventions, as the children complete puberty and enter adulthood.[36]

- Children may feel "an urgency to transition," but "young adults looking back at their younger selves would often advise slowing down."[37]
- The evidence on how to treat someone who is confused about their sex is "weak," and "clinicians [say] they are unable to determine with any certainty which children and young people will go on to have an enduring trans identity."[38]
- We do not know what "gender" medicine is going to do to young people. "Our current understanding of the long-term health impacts of hormone interventions is limited and needs to be better understood," the Cass authors wrote.[39]

The Reuters article mentioned earlier also said that sex hormone drugs' "long-term effects on fertility and sexual function remain unclear."[40] The report also said that no research has been conducted to see how adults are functioning after attempting to "transition" as children—we do not know how satisfied they are or how many have detransitioned. After the release of her report, Cass said she could not use public transportation any longer out of fear for her safety.[41] She said she received "'vile' abusive emails" and had "been given security advice to help keep her safe." All this over a report that found doctors need to know more about medical interventions on "gender-related distress" before continuing to conduct procedures on or prescribe medicines to young people.

Since the Cass report, still more research has found that medical practitioners do not have reliable evidence on the effects of puberty-blocking and hormone-related drugs.[42] The effect of administering puberty blockers to individuals to treat depression found mixed results. Researchers, however, found that 92 percent of individuals who used puberty blocking interventions "progressed to receiving gender affirming hormone therapy," which means puberty blockers may not address any significant medical issues but are likely to be the first step on the path to more significant medical treatments. Another study released in early 2025 found inconclusive results from the use of certain hormone treatments, again demonstrating that medical professionals do not know enough about the effects of these treatments to confidently prescribe them.[43]

The research is still coming. In 2025, *The Journal of Sexual Medicine* published by Oxford University released a study that found, "Gender-affirming surgery, while beneficial in affirming gender identity, is associated with increased risk of mental health issues, underscoring the need for ongoing, gender-sensitive mental health support for transgender individuals' post-surgery."[44] Translation: patients should not expect surgery that alters their reproductive organs to resolve depression or anxiety, and once they undergo the procedure, they will need more counseling to affirm their decision.

Across Europe, lawmakers have adopted policies that stop "gender" interventions for minors. Officials in Sweden, Finland, England, Wales, Scotland, Denmark, and Norway have stopped these practices.[45] Policymakers in still other nations such as Australia, Italy, and France are considering such prohibitions.

★ ★ ★

In my conversation with Linda, she said, "If the doctors would just say 'no'" to children who feel confused about their sex and want to manipulate their bodies, "that would resolve a ton of this."[46] Today, while we do not allow minor-age children to diagnose themselves with strep throat or pneumonia—or as autistic or clinically depressed—some adults allow children to decide they were born in the wrong body and be treated accordingly.[47] Too often adults unquestioningly allow children to pursue medical treatments that alter their hormones or even physical bodies according to the child's "feeling."[48] Authors such as Shrier, Ryan Anderson, Kathleen Stock, and Mary Margaret Olohan have chronicled many examples.[49]

Linda says that all of her advocacy now is meant to help parents with sexually confused children and detransitioners. Her position is one formed by "love and concern, not to shame and 'other' and despise some group of people."[50]

She has told her son that she knows he is doing everything he can to "blend in," but "there are too many in your community that... are trying to shove this down our throats," which calls to mind the threats to Cass's safety. J. K. Rowling has received death threats for saying men who insist that they are women should not be allowed in women's intimate spaces such as bathrooms and changing rooms.[51]

"That is a problem," Linda says.

As the survey for this book and several other surveys demonstrate, Linda is speaking for many. A 2023 Gallup survey found that 55 percent of Americans think it is "morally wrong" to change your gender, an increase of 4 percentage points from 2021.[52]

Another survey, this one by the Public Religion Research Institute (PRRI), a nonpartisan research center that counts *The Atlantic* and left-of-center Brookings Institution among its partners, found in 2023 that the share of Americans who say there are only two "genders" (a term they are using interchangeably with sex) was increasing.[53] Fifty-nine percent of all Americans in their survey (respondents were also disaggregated by political affiliation, religion, age, and more) said there are only two genders in 2021, a figure that increased to 65 percent in 2023. The share of Republicans increased from 87 to 90 percent over this period, while Democrats went from 38 percent to 44 percent.[54]

As explained previously, "gender" and "sex" were once interchangeable, but radical critical theorists have helped make the term a mutable concept. This redefinition, along with the medical concerns about individuals attempting to change their physical makeup, leaves many questions about the movement unanswered. "Gender identity," explains Stock, author of *Material Girls* and critic of gender theory, is an "inner state," detached from a physical body. As a concept, "gender" can even be defined as "a matter of culture" and cultural notions about what constitutes "masculine" and "feminine"—or something else.[55]

By gender advocates' own admission, "gender" refers to a feeling. The radical gender theorist Gale Rubin says "sex" means both gender and gender identity, reducing biological reality to a malleable idea.[56] Judith Butler, queer theorist and professor, says "gender is in no way a stable identity…it is an identity…instituted through a *stylized repetition of acts*" (emphasis in the original).[57] This means your gender identity can be in your head, even if this thought does not match your biology.

Richards, my Heritage colleague, says gender theorists want their idea to be considered "as a simple deliverance of science and sweet reason, rather than a dogma."[58] The ambiguity in the definition of "gender" serves their purposes.

In truth, we are born as one sex or another—specifically with the ability to produce sperm or eggs. As Richards and other researchers have explained, there are sexual anomalies in a very few number of cases, perhaps as rare as 0.018 percent of the human population.[59] Yet even in these instances, the anomalies do not make a person two sexes or a third sex. Richards and Ethics and Public Policy Center President Ryan Anderson both document that these individuals are still one sex who would produce sperm or eggs if not for the anomalies that prevent them from doing so.[60] Just because an individual's sex is hard to determine does not make them any less of a specific sex. They are just not physically able to reproduce like the majority of the population.

★ ★ ★

Americans agree that they do not want teachers to provide classroom instruction on sexual orientation and "gender identity" to most school-age children. In our survey, among parents and the general population, strong majorities said they do not want these ideas taught to children in kindergarten, elementary, or middle school. School board members opposed teaching these ideas to students before middle school.

My results are similar to a New York Times/Siena poll from 2022 where 70 percent of respondents were "somewhat" or "strongly" opposed teaching about sexual orientation and gender identity to elementary school students.[61] Opposition decreased when respondents were asked about older children,

Figure 4.1 Should public school teachers provide classroom instruction on sexual orientation and "gender identity" to children in kindergarten through 3rd grade?

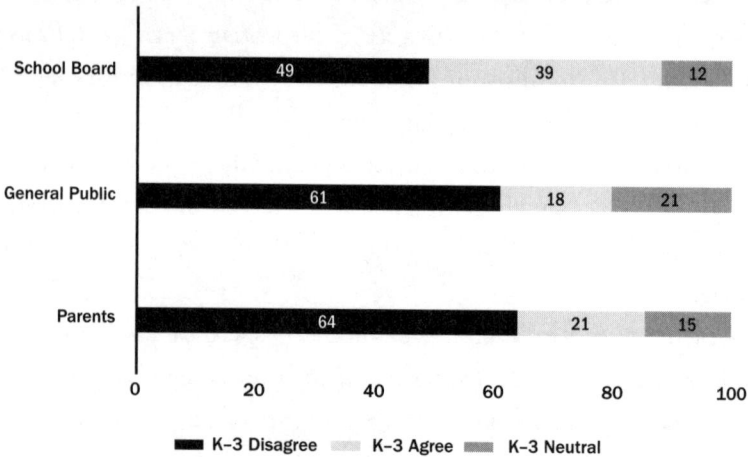

	K-3 Disagree	K-3 Agree	K-3 Neutral
School Board	49	39	12
General Public	61	18	21
Parents	64	21	15

Figure 4.2 Should public school teachers provide classroom instruction on sexual orientation and "gender identity" to children in elementary school?

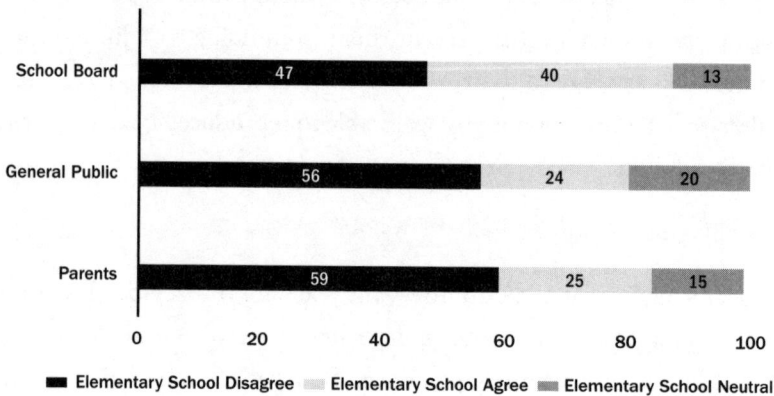

	Elementary School Disagree	Elementary School Agree	Elementary School Neutral
School Board	47	40	13
General Public	56	24	20
Parents	59	25	15

but 54 percent still said they opposed teaching middle school students about gender and 42 percent reported being "strongly" or "somewhat" opposed to teaching high school students.

Still, in the survey for this book and the New York Times/Siena poll, there are high levels of agreement that "gender" should not be taught to elementary and middle-school-age children.

Figure 4.3 Should public school teachers provide classroom instruction on sexual orientation and "gender identity" to children in middle school?

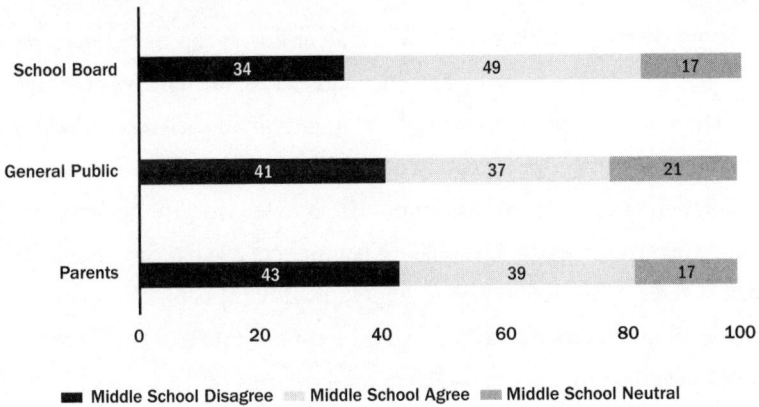

	Middle School Disagree	Middle School Agree	Middle School Neutral
School Board	34	49	17
General Public	41	37	21
Parents	43	39	17

Figure 4.4 Should public school teachers provide classroom instruction on sexual orientation and "gender identity" to children in high school?

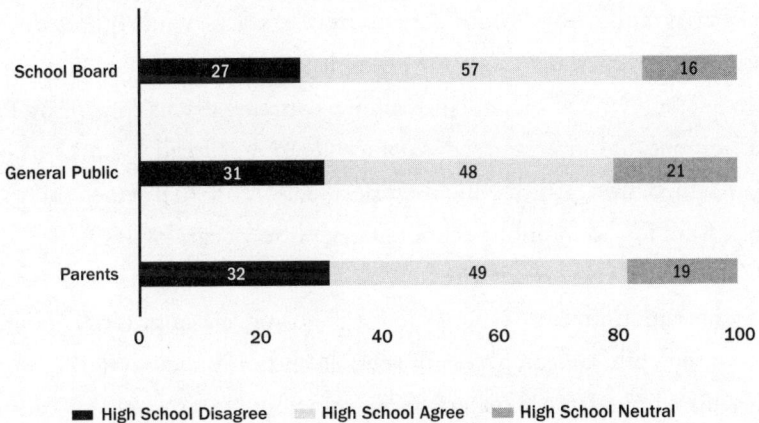

	High School Disagree	High School Agree	High School Neutral
School Board	27	57	16
General Public	31	48	21
Parents	32	49	19

Some lawmakers are already designing policies that seem to reflect these findings. Florida went first, adopting provisions in 2022 that prohibited the teaching of "gender" to children in grades K–3.[62] The state board of education expanded the provisions to include all students in K–12.[63] Lawmakers in other states, including Alabama and Arkansas, have adopted similar proposals, with still more considering the provisions.[64]

Sexually Explicit Materials and Minors

Classroom instruction is not the only way children can be exposed to the idea of gender and the sexually graphic material that often accompanies the topic. The books available in school libraries and on classroom shelves are the subjects of much debate today over who should decide on the content that is age-appropriate for students. The left-leaning PEN America, an advocacy group for writers, says state lawmakers are banning books from library shelves.[65] But when researchers looked for specific titles that PEN claimed policymakers or educators had banned, most of the books were readily available. One report found that 74 percent of the books that PEN claimed had been removed from school libraries were still available when researchers looked through the school computer catalogues—with some copies currently checked out at the time of the article's publication.[66]

And the books in question are not titles by Dr. Seuss. Some of these books are graphic novels with depictions of sex acts, while others discuss erotic encounters. *Lawn Boy*, for example, a fictional account of a young Hispanic boy who works in landscaping, contains discussions of oral sex and homosexual intercourse.[67] *Gender Queer* has lurid pictures of oral sex, masturbation, girls having their period, homosexual acts—and these books were found in public school district library catalogues.[68]

The issue at hand is not whether some books should be "banned." Rather, it is whether adults are responsible for choosing age-appropriate content that young children can access in schools and only including the books, magazines, and reference materials that contribute to a school's educational program. Public school libraries do not need to carry every book available in print. When school board members and teachers take time to determine the age-appropriate nature of a book and choose not to make it available in a school library, this does not mean they are banning the book. Rather, these educators are deciding what is appropriate for school-age children. The materials are still available on Amazon, at Barnes & Noble, or often at a local public library.

The process of choosing what books should be made available to students is an important one. The survey I conducted asked respondents who they believed should decide which books are available in school libraries. Among parents and the general public, 47 percent of respondents said that parents and school personnel should have the most influence—as opposed to school personnel making these decisions apart from parents. The school board survey was more evenly divided, but even here, one-third of respondents said parents and school personnel should have the most influence.

Figure 4.5 **Who do you believe should decide which books are available in public school libraries?**

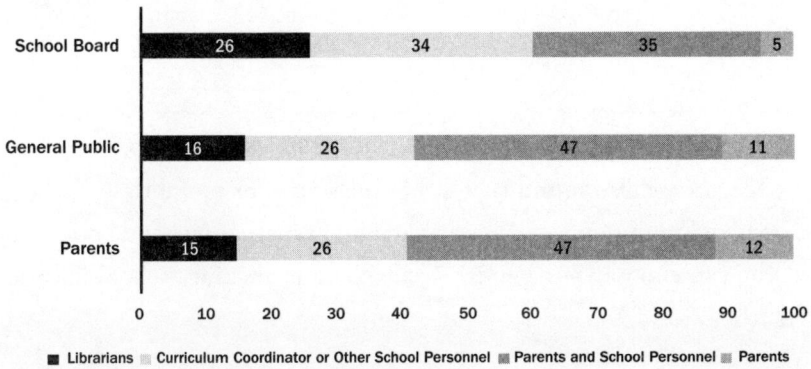

■ Librarians ▨ Curriculum Coordinator or Other School Personnel ▨ Parents and School Personnel ▨ Parents

Figure 4.6 **Should elementary age children have access in public school libraries to books that say you can choose your "gender" and you are not born with a biological sex?**

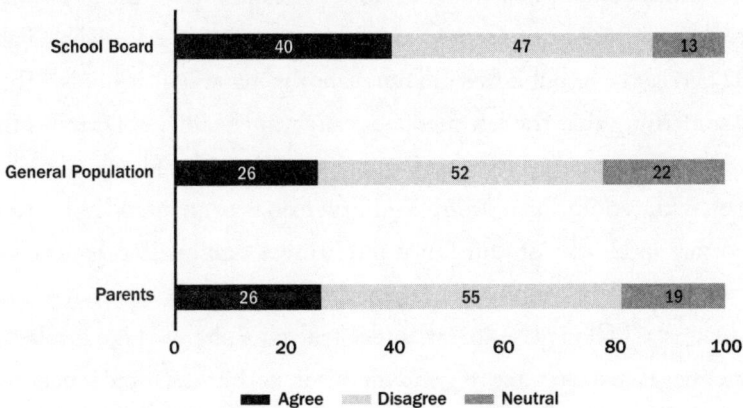

■ Agree ▨ Disagree ▨ Neutral

Figure 4.7 **Do you believe that elementary and secondary students should have access to books with graphic depictions of sex acts?**

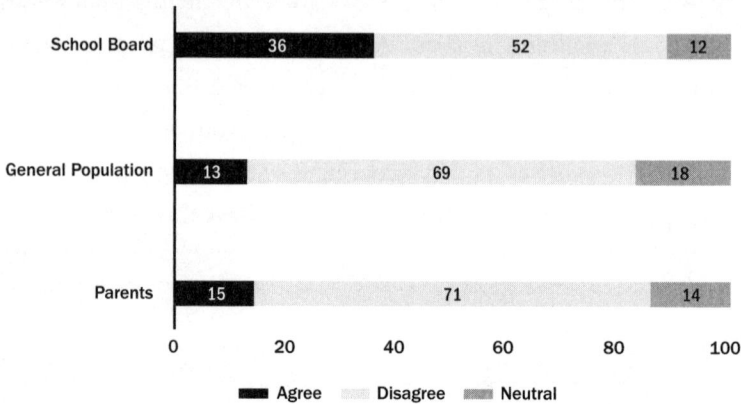

The survey also found that either majorities or pluralities in all our respondent groups opposed making graphic sexual content and books that say you can choose your "gender" available in elementary school libraries (Figures 4.6 and 4.7).

★   ★   ★

The survey results found agreement across party lines against including graphic sexual content in school libraries. For example, for the question in Figure 4.7, 58 percent of Democrats did not want this material available and 82 percent of Republicans did not want the material in schools. "That's really something that the left media doesn't want really publicized—that many Democrats are against what is going on with our children and what is going on in the educational realm," said Erin Friday in an interview.[69] Friday, an attorney and leader of Our Duty and Protect California, organizations trying to help families who are concerned about sexualized content in schools, says she was a "lifelong Democrat" and a "true blue liberal." Like Linda, she does not have a partisan axe to grind on this issue, but the topic is personal.

When Friday's daughter began to exhibit gender dysphoric symptoms, Friday became concerned, politics aside. She opposed the gender ideology being taught in her daughter's school, but she found few in her home state of California who were willing to listen.

"We are ignored or recast as Republicans or right-wing bigots," Friday says.

"I was absolutely gob smacked by what I heard in the classroom," Friday says after visiting her daughter's school, where Friday was first exposed to the notion of "gender ideology." She says that her child's school hired consultants to introduce a new sex education curriculum. She attended an information session explaining how the material was going to be included in her daughter's classroom and felt that the message was "If you are not GI Joe, the ultimate epitome of a man, or Barbie, the ultimate epitome of a woman, you are somewhere on the spectrum" of LGTBQ+.[70]

"Even if you were trying to follow their reasoning, it was impossible," Friday says. She describes a handout from the presentation with "nonsense terms" on it. They had to create an entire vocabulary to explain the convoluted concept of gender. "I'm looking around absolutely confused that no one is raising their hand to ask what these two young men [presenting the gender-infused curriculum] are espousing. What they are saying is nonsensical," she says.

Like Beanie Geoghegan and Melissa Jackson, the concerned moms who founded Freedom in Education to improve civics instruction in schools, Friday was surprised at what was not happening the classroom, too. Erin said she noticed that the expectations began to fall in her daughter's class and "homework was disappearing."

But the lack of rigor was a small concern compared to what was happening to her daughter.

★ ★ ★

These gender consultants at Friday's school were not the only ones using the ambiguous definition of "gender," essentially rewriting the dictionary. The American Medical Association (AMA), the nation's largest association of medical professionals, has released its own glossary of terms to conform to the radical gender orthodoxy.[71] The new handbook says, "In all cases, pursuing equity requires disavowing words that are rooted in systems of power that reinforce discrimination and exclusion," a remarkable statement in several respects.[72] First, why is an association of doctors pursuing "equity" instead of accuracy? Second, why is the AMA using Marxist concepts such as "systems of power" to guide their organization?

The AMA has made race and gender its priorities instead of health. The AMA has banned the words "vulnerable," "high-risk," "target," "tackle," "combat," "hard-to-reach," "disadvantaged" and "at-risk." Medical professionals must say "equity" instead of "equality," and cannot call people who do not have health care "people who do not seek health care."[73] A research report cannot be called a "white paper," and the list goes on.[74] Language must be policed because, as the organization says, "Patriarchal narratives enforce rigidly defined traditional norms, and reinforce inequities based on gender."[75] The AMA's guidebook calls critical race theory and gender studies part of a "rich tradition" that provides a "foundation for an alternative narrative."[76]

The AMA's redefinitions are important because gender dysphoria and a child's confusion about his or her sex are medical issues. If the nation's largest association representing doctors is prepared to change the definition of words to depart from "traditional norms," that has wide-reaching implications for families and schools.

★ ★ ★

Things went from bad to worse for Friday after she learned more about the new curriculum at her daughter's school. Her daughter and her daughter's friends came home suddenly sexualized: "Why were these girls who were between 11 and 12 using language that was not appropriate for their age?" Friday asked.[77] "Girls coming over to my house with long blond hair down to their waist wanting to be called 'Evan,'" she says.

"My daughter started going down a very dark hole," Friday explains. Her daughter was "a pleasant, kind child," but, over the course of two years, she began turning her schoolwork in late and had new friends who were giving themselves tattoos. She created anonymous social media accounts and started talking about suicide.

She cut her hair and drew "sexualized pictures," Friday says. Her daughter sank into depression during the COVID-19 pandemic. "She would say awful, vicious things," Friday says, when her family tried to set boundaries and help her with her depression.[78]

Friday's example demonstrates why school officials should not withhold information from parents when children say they are confused about their sex. Those who favor such secrecy argue that not informing parents about their child's confusion over sex is appropriate because parents would rather have a "live son than a dead daughter"—implying that a child will commit suicide if their "gender" choice is not affirmed.[79]

Yet research does not support the claim that policies in favor of secrecy—such as in California and New Jersey, where school officials do not have to inform parents when a child wants to live as a gender that does not match their sex—result in lower suicide rates.[80] Rather, suicide rates appear to be higher among young people in states with lax laws regarding access to puberty blockers and cross-sex hormones.[81]

The survey for this book found that Americans are not polarized on this issue: we do not want educators to keep secrets from parents about their children. In the survey, we asked respondents if they believe school officials should notify parents if their child "identifies as transgender or has questions related to his or her gender identity." Here, strong majorities from all of our respondent groups were in favor of school policies that inform parents when their child expresses confusion about their sex while at school. Seventy-four percent of school board members agreed, with Democrats registering higher levels of approval (81 percent) than Republicans (73 percent).

Parents wanted to be "in the know" about what their children are going through at school. Among parents in our survey, 61 percent favored policies that would inform them if a child expressed confusion about their sex at school, with Democrats and Republicans registering their agreement in almost equal measure (64 percent and 66 percent respectively).

"This is not a right–left issue. Most of the parents I know who are caught up in this would consider themselves to be hard-core liberal Democrats, but now they are horrified and politically homeless," Linda said.[82] She explains that her experience with her son involved a school official who provided counsel in favor of "transitioning," and the official put her son in contact with others who encouraged him to "transition." Furthering an individual's sexual confusion in this way is often referred to as "social affirmation," but as Linda and hundreds of other parents know, it is hardly affirming.

"Many Democrats are against what is going on with our children and what is going on in the educational realm [advocating for gender-based instruction]," says Friday.[83]

Like Linda, Friday has gotten to know other parents through social media. Many of these parents, she says, are also trying to help their young children who are receiving "affirmative" messages about their sex from social media, and the internet in general, as well as school curricula and other activities.

She wanted to know how she could take action. "I hopped from group to group to find out who was *doing*," Friday said, which led to her involvement with Our Duty.[84]

Figure 4.8 Some public school districts have policies preventing school staff from disclosing to parents any information related to their child's gender identity (for example, a boy stating that he now identifies as a girl). Should your child's school inform parents that their child identifies as transgender or has questions related to his or her gender identity?

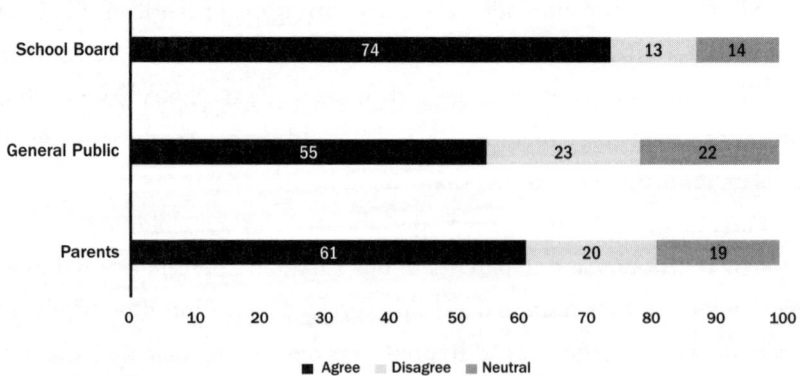

Friday would endure the "hardest year and a half of my life" after she took all of her daughter's devices—phone, tablets, etc.—and kept her off social media. In an interview with *The Daily Signal*, Friday says she does not know what the "recipe" is for helping a child grow out of sexual confusion, but Friday says she "threw everything at it."[85] Therapy, changing schools, setting boundaries, holding to those boundaries, being consistent. Even when her daughter said terrible things to her, Friday said, "Parents have forgotten that we are not supposed to be liked all the time."[86]

After about 18 months, her daughter began to emerge from depression and stopped rejecting her physical body. It was a lot of work, Friday says, but having her daughter back was worth the battle.

"Once my daughter was stable, I decided I was going to be vocal," she said.

★ ★ ★

Our survey respondents were also in favor of educators addressing students by names and pronouns that corresponded with the child's birth certificate unless school officials received consent from parents to do otherwise. Among school board members, 70 percent were in favor of this policy, with 73 percent of Democrats in favor and 75 percent of Republicans agreeing.

Figure 4.9 **Should school employees address by the name [and pronouns] listed on/consistent with your child's birth certificate unless the staff receive express permission from you/parents?**

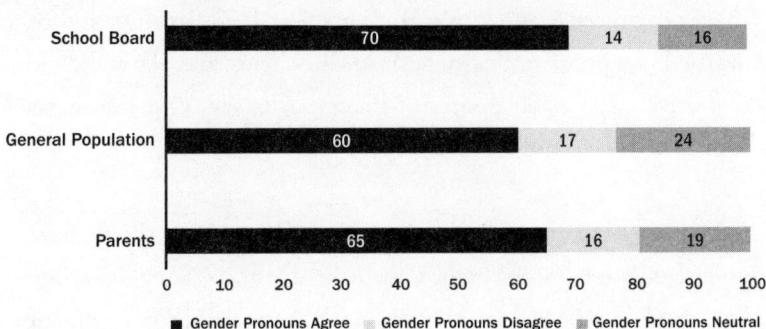

	Agree	Disagree	Neutral
School Board	70	14	16
General Population	60	17	24
Parents	65	16	19

■ Gender Pronouns Agree   Gender Pronouns Disagree   Gender Pronouns Neutral

This book's final chapter will discuss the "Given Name Act" and how it can protect children and families from social affirmation. The "rock star" scenario described earlier, in which adults simply affirm a child's self-diagnosis of being born in the wrong body, is a form of this affirmation. This process of affirmation can be the starting point for a child who then proceeds to find more affirmation from school-sponsored counselors, which can lead to medical interventions and dangerous off-label uses of medicines and surgeries. By requiring that school personnel alert parents when a child shows signs of gender dysphoria, families can intervene and prevent minor-age children from making dangerous health decisions.

★ ★ ★

In 2024, a woman who called herself "Kay" told an audience in Oklahoma that she was raped and beaten by a man who said he was a woman.[87] Kay described herself as a feminist who was in favor of pro-gender policies until the assault. According to the *Daily Mail*, Kay said, "Up until that point I was like everybody else, live and let live." She added, "One time it took to change my mind. To open my eyes and see how our rights and protections are being eroded away."

A 15-year-old girl, also from Oklahoma, was "severely beaten" by a "transgender" student in the bathroom at her school in 2022.[88] That same year, two incidents occurred in Broward County, Florida, public schools involving sexual assault or "groping" by boys who said they were girls in school bathrooms.[89]

These are precisely the kinds of events that J. K. Rowling and others have warned can occur under state or local policies that allow individuals to access private spaces for people of the opposite sex.[90] So, the survey for this book asked the sample,

In 2015, the Department of Justice argued that students should have "unfettered access" to the bathroom, locker room, or changing facility that matches their gender identity. Should the federal government require your local school to provide students with "unfettered access" to the bathrooms, locker rooms, and changing facilities aligned with their professed gender identity?

A plurality of the sample from the general population was opposed (42 percent), with nearly 68 percent of Republicans opposing and just under half (45 percent) of Democrats opposing or saying they were neutral on the question. Responses were nearly identical when asked if schools should give students this access. And responses were also nearly identical to those from the general population across our sample of parents.

Advocates for "gender transitioning" dismiss fears about men who access female spaces by saying they are women. Some advocates say the idea of a trans "predator" is a myth, even a "red herring," according to *Time* magazine.[91] The left-leaning site Vox says there is "hysteria" among those who oppose allowing individuals to use facilities of the opposite sex if they claim to be of a different "gender."[92]

Such claims are hard to support today:

+ In Virginia, a boy dressed as a girl assaulted girls on two different occasions at different schools.[93] One of the victims and her

---

Figure 4.10 **Should the federal government require your local school to provide students with "unfettered access" to bathrooms, locker rooms, and changing facilities aligned with their professed gender identity (agree or disagree)?**

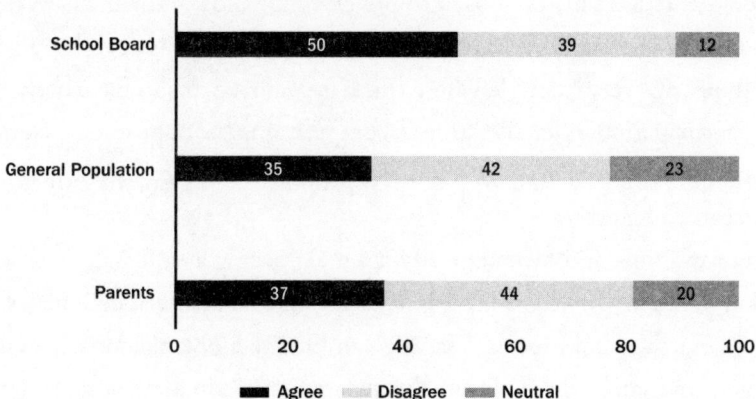

	Agree	Disagree	Neutral
School Board	50	39	12
General Population	35	42	23
Parents	37	44	20

family sought $30 million from Loudoun County public schools in a lawsuit. The Loudoun County public school board fired superintendent Scott Ziegler after a state grand jury report on the district's response to the assaults.[94]

+ In New Mexico, a 12-year-old girl was assaulted by a boy in a school bathroom and was fearful of even reporting the incident to her parents.[95] The girl became suicidal, and after she did report the assault, two other students said they had been assaulted by the same male student posing as a female.

+ In Wisconsin, an 18-year-old male who said he was a woman exposed himself to 14-year-old girls in a locker room after swimming during gym class.[96]

+ A California teen said she was "terrified" when she saw a man's genitalia in the locker room at a YMCA.[97] She said children change in those locker rooms after childcare programs during the summer and could be exposed to naked men who say they are "trans."

+ In South Carolina, a man saying he was a woman tried to admit himself to a women's shelter but was evicted after stabbing a staff member.[98]

★ ★ ★

Respondents were also opposed to policies that allow individuals to participate in single-sex athletic competitions with individuals of the opposite sex. In nearly every example where this has occurred, males have been the ones participating in female athletic competitions (as opposed to women competing against men)—giving males an overwhelming, and sometimes dangerous, advantage.

For example, in November 2023, a male posing as a female in a field hockey game hit another player in the face and caused serious injuries to the victim's face and mouth.[99] In 2022 in Guam, a boy playing on a girls' rugby team injured three players during a match.[100] In 2018, a male damaged a woman's eye socket in a mixed martial arts fight.[101] Swimmer Riley Gaines has appropriately raised awareness about unfair competition between males and females (Gaines, a female, competed against Lia Thomas, a male, in college swimming) and has since continued to press the issue, stressing the harm that can come to females competing against males.[102] Gaines has drawn national attention in recent years, especially after her federal testimony in which she told Rep. Summer Lee (D-Pa.) that if her testimony was "transphobic" then Rep. Lee's remarks were "misogynistic."[103]

Similar to the other questions regarding radical "gender" policy, a larger share of school board members were in favor of allowing "gender"-based athletics than respondents from the general population or parents. Overall, 40 percent of school board members were in favor, with 42 percent opposed.

Gallup has found results similar to those from the parent and general public respondents in the survey for this book. The Gallup results mentioned earlier on Americans' opinions on the morality of gender changes also found approval for only allowing individuals to compete on sports teams that match their biological sex.[104] Sixty-nine percent of Americans were in favor of policies on athletic participation according to biological sex, a 7 percentage point increase from 2021.

Figure 4.11 Should K–12 students who "identify" as a "gender" that is contrary to their biological sex participate on single-sex sports teams?

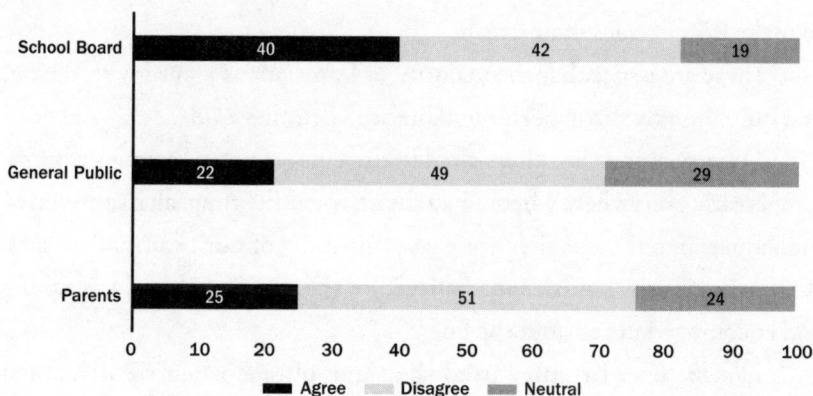

	Agree	Disagree	Neutral
School Board	40	42	19
General Public	22	49	29
Parents	25	51	24

The growing list of examples in which men dominated and even injured women while playing in girls' and women's sports leagues cannot be restated enough—until it stops happening. In February 2024, five men who had "assumed" a female gender identity "hijacked" a women's college volleyball game.[105] At least both teams were fielding "trans" players, three on one side and two on another. Yet these players played the entire game, according to reports, which raises the question: what were the spectators watching, a women's volleyball game or something else? The game should have been called a coed match.

★ ★ ★

The Biden administration released a revised rule in favor of using "sexual orientation and gender identity" in federal law in April 2024, and the rule was immediately met by eight lawsuits representing public officials in twenty-six states.[106]

Louisiana State Superintendent Cade Brumley, who helped revise the state's social studies standards described in Chapter 3, was vocal in his opposition to the Biden administration's proposed change. In 2024, Brumley wrote a letter to all educators in his state saying they should not change their policies and redefine "sex" to mean "gender."[107]

He knew that he was not alone in his opposition to the Biden administration's policy. In an interview, Brumley told me, "The White House tried to make fringe issues mainstream."[108]

"These are issues that the majority of Louisianans agreed with me on, and quite frankly the majority of America," Brumley said.

Our survey and the others cited in these pages prove Brumley is right.

"Nearly everywhere where I had the opportunity to speak to a crowd of individuals in our state, they were very affirming of our position," he says. "Overwhelmingly, Louisianans believed in the position that I was taking and encouraged me to hold the line."[109]

Hold the line. Brumley used the same phrase when we discussed his decision to revise the state's social studies standards and include a positive perspective of American history. The standards still dealt with slavery and the failures of prior generations of Americans to live up to our founding ideals, but, on net, the instruction gives students a set of positive, aspirational examples from our nation's history. Brumley says that many, if not most, in his state held this perspective, and he just needed to stay the course and not be intimidated by radical ideologies.

"Even when I would talk to individuals in purple or blue states about the position I was taking in Louisiana, more often than not they agreed with me that it was the right position to take," he said.

"These far-left extreme views really put the Democratic Party in jeopardy and made them seem like a fringe party on the issues," Brumley said. In rejecting the Biden administration's policies, "I think in many ways people were voting for common sense," he said.[110]

★ ★ ★

In an attempt to preserve a relationship with her son, Linda says she has tried to keep her advocacy anonymous, though as mentioned above, she has been actively talking with parents around the country about their experiences. She continues to be active with the families she has met.

"There is no accountability for [medical gender interventions]," she says. "No one stays a minor. At 18 the wheels come off," she says.[111]

"We have no idea what the long term effects are going to be," Linda says.

Friday joined Our Duty, an advocacy organization that initially formed in the United Kingdom and has branches in New Zealand, Australia, Canada, and Germany, as well as Friday's group in California. She explains that they are a group of nonpartisan parents who "hold the line."[112] She says, "We are parents who don't believe that gender ideology just hurts kids; it hurts the adult population also."

In turn, Our Duty supports Friday's other project, called Protect Kids California.[113] A group of advocates formed Protect Kids CA in an effort to put a measure on the state ballot that would prohibit all gender interventions on minors, including puberty blockers and cross-sex surgeries.[114] The measure would also prohibit males from competing in girls' athletics or using intimate facilities such as locker rooms and bathrooms. And the measure would also prevent educators from hiding information about children and sexual confusion from their parents.

Friday feels like she had to act because as she looked around, so few were doing so. "I kept waiting for the white knight to come in, but there wasn't any."[115]

In 2024, Linda offered anonymous testimony in Arizona in favor of a bill that would require insurance providers who cover "gender transition" procedures to also cover "gender detransition procedures."[116] State Senator Janae Shamp, the bill sponsor, read Linda's testimony.

"I worry about his long-term health and well-being," Linda wrote in her testimony about her son. As she has met more and more parents going through similar situations with their children, she has learned of "both trans-identified and detransitioned adults suffering health consequences."[117]

Policymakers need not criminalize "gender," but neither should policies put others in danger just because someone says they should use a bathroom that does not match their sex. Considering the results from surveys on these issues, Americans are not polarized when it comes to sex.

★ ★ ★

So who favors these policies—who wants young children taught about "gender" or for sexualized books to be made available in public school libraries? The most outspoken, and well-funded, group in education that supports radical "trans" policies is the same group that supports critical race theory, DEI, and cueing as reading instruction: teachers unions. In fact, the central offices of the two largest teachers unions—the National Education Association (NEA) and American Federation of Teachers (AFT)—advocate for many of the causes that my survey found Americans oppose.

The AFT advocates for gender to be taught to young children and wants students to become revolutionaries in favor of these causes: "We support the independent mass actions of youth to defend their existence, dignity, and rights of the LGBTQIA+ community," while opposing legislative proposals that prohibit the teaching of gender theory to elementary and middle school students.[118]

Conservatives and parents who are fearful of the effects of gender-based medical interventions are not opposing the "existence" of people confused about their gender, only seeking research-based boundaries on introducing these ideas to young people and preventing minor children from making decisions about their bodies without parental input. As discussed earlier, the intersection of gender and medicine is an issue of safety and health.

Adults who choose to live by a gender identity that does not correspond with their biology are free to do so, but they should not be allowed to coerce other people—children in particular—to share changing spaces with them according to their gender instead of their biology or compete against them in sports according to their gender.

Notably, though, the AFT is in favor of boys competing on girls' sports teams, which overlaps with males accessing females' private spaces for changing clothes. AFT President Randi Weingarten issued a statement in favor of such policies in April 2023.[119] The NEA offers teaching materials for educators on LGTBQ+ topics and supports the gender-based sports policies.[120]

The NEA also recommends that teachers read books that promote DEI and gender theory, including *White Fragility*, a guidebook for implementing DEI and critical race theory, and *Gender Queer*.[121] The AFT promotes similar resources on its website.[122]

Given all of these examples and more, teachers union influence is significant enough to warrant its own chapter.

CHAPTER FIVE

OUR OUT OF TOUCH
TEACHERS UNIONS

*But better education doesn't mean a bigger Department of Education. In
fact, that Department should be abolished. Instead, we must do a better
job teaching the basics, insisting on discipline and results, encouraging competition and, above all, remembering that education does not begin with
Washington officials or even State and local officials. It begins in the home,
where it is the right and responsibility of every American.*
—Ronald Reagan, "Radio Address to the Nation on Education,"
March 12, 1983[1]

Every year, the National Education Association (NEA), the nation's
largest teacher union, holds an annual meeting and adopts a series
of resolutions, many of which have little if anything to do with what goes
on in the classroom.[2] Recently adopted resolutions include provisions in
favor of the United Nations' Charter and international disarmament agree-
ments, support for the International Court of Justice, a freeze on nuclear
weapons, ending world hunger, "respect for individual names and pronouns,"
reparations for the institution of slavery in America's history, and an end
to supposed "white supremacy culture."[3] That last resolution reads in part:

...the Association believes that the norms, standards, and organizational structures manifested in white supremacy culture perpetually
exploit and oppress people of color and serve as detriments to racial
justice. Further, the invisible racial benefits of white privilege, *which
are automatically conferred irrespective of wealth, gender, and other factors,* severely limit opportunities for people of color and impede full
achievement of racial and social justice. The Association believes that,
to aid in the efforts to eradicate hate caused by prejudice, stereotypes,

and biases, school districts must provide training in cultural competence, implicit bias, restorative practices and techniques, and racial
justice [emphasis added].[4]

This resolution echoes the DEI content described in Chapter 1 and
the ethnic studies standards from California and Minnesota outlined in
Chapter 3. This special interest group is seizing on the areas in which the
media and left-of-center policymakers want Americans to think we are
polarized—when in fact, racial preferences are unpopular (Chapter 1), parents want virtues taught in school (Chapter 3), and Americans do not want
men to access women's private spaces (Chapter 4). Voters must recognize
that the unions are not in the business of education reform nor seeking to
improve outcomes for teachers and students. Instead, as this chapter will
explain, teacher unions are political machines that advocate for distinctly
progressive causes and fund, with few exceptions, left-wing candidates and
left-of-center interest groups.

The ideological slant cannot be overstated. For example, in the Heritage Foundation survey from 2021, respondents were asked about "White
Supremacy Culture." The survey included a question using text consistent
with the NEA resolutions on slavery and "white supremacy" and asked
parents and school board members if students should be taught that slavery
is the "center of our national narrative."[5] A full 50 percent of all parents and
70 percent of school board members disagreed with the union position and
responded that they did *not* want schools to use instructional materials
based on this premise.[6]

In Chapter 1 the survey questions on DEI and CRT found that Americans are split on these terms even if they oppose their application, which
means the union resolutions in favor of these issues still represent extreme
positions. Furthermore, over the last three years, there has been a widespread
withdrawal from DEI initiatives, from companies abandoning DEI hiring
to colleges closing DEI offices to state lawmakers prohibiting taxpayer
spending on DEI programs.[7] Note, as well, President Trump's executive

order prohibiting DEI in the federal government, an order issued on his first day in office in 2025.[8] Here again, unions are out of step with many large corporations, universities, state policymakers, and the White House, as well as the voters who elected the state and federal officials who oppose DEI.

There are several other teacher union resolutions that demonstrate similar disconnects between voters and unions.

For example, while Americans oppose racial preferences, the NEA has attempted to tie segregation to modern-day school choice programs in attempt to brand school choice as racist. A recent resolution reads:

> The Association also opposes any governmental attempts to resegregate public schools through any means, including vouchers, charters, and other school-choice initiatives.[9]

Yet research has demonstrated that school choice options in K–12 education leads to *integration* rather than segregation.[10] Economist Philip Magness has pointed to examples from Virginia in which segregationists opposed early vestiges of school choice in the state for fear that such programs would lead to integration.[11] Other researchers have found that 9 out of the 10 studies investigating a causal relationship between school choice and segregation have found that parent choice in education does not cause segregation.[12]

Meanwhile, parents overwhelmingly support school choice. According to a 2022 Harvard/Education Next survey, 52 percent of parents support school choice with only 27 percent opposed.[13] Fifty-seven percent support school vouchers for all students, 51 percent support education savings accounts, and a full two-thirds (66 percent) of parents support tax credit scholarships.[14] Support among Black families for these school choice options was the highest of any group, with a whopping 72 percent supporting vouchers for all students, 57 percent supporting education savings accounts, and 72 percent of Black respondents supporting tax credit scholarships.[15] High levels of support among Black families make it hard for the NEA to support their claims that school choice leads to "segregation."

The disconnect doesn't stop there. Another recent resolution from the NEA reads:

> The Association acknowledges that students and educators experience discrimination from the effects of mispronunciations, misgendering, misrepresentations, incorrect documentations in systems of record, or the usage of deadnames.[16]

Laws like the Given Name Act, which prohibits schools from calling a child by a different name or pronoun without a parent's permission, have spread widely in recent years. Lawmakers in eight states have adopted a version of the law since 2022.[17] Lawmakers in still other states are considering such proposals.[18]

Other resolutions undermine safe school environments, something parents also care deeply about. In the survey results provided in Chapter 2, when parents were asked to name the most important factor for them in choosing a school for their child, one in five respondents said "school safety" was most important.

The survey also asked respondents how they think school administrators should design student discipline policies. Some of the tragic events in recent years involving school violence, such as the school shootings in Parkland, Florida, and Nashville, involved non-students committing acts of violence (though they were former students at the respective schools).[19] Americans certainly agree on protecting students from outsiders with bad intentions, but managing the behavior of students in the classroom is also the topic of much research and debate.[20]

Again, since school safety is among parents' primary concerns when they can choose a school instead of sending their child to the local assigned public school, the union's resolution on "restorative justice" calls into question whether their views align with parents' perspectives (and as discussed below, effective policy). A recent NEA resolution reads:

The Association believes that all staff must be trained in conflict resolution strategies, trauma informed practices, and restorative practices to help students in the promotion of safe schools.[21]

As the survey for this book will demonstrate, if you are not familiar with "restorative justice" or have yet to form an opinion, you are in good company. Restorative justice is an approach to dealing with student infractions where, "rather than punishing the perpetrator," teachers view "any delinquency or victimization" as "harm done to a web of relationships."[22] The technique is a consequence-free, punishment-free approach to dealing with misbehavior.

And on this issue, there is significant debate among researchers and policymakers. In 2014, President Barack Obama's administration issued a directive (called a "Dear Colleague Letter") to schools nationwide stating that if educators suspended or expelled Black and Hispanic students more than White students, schools could be subject to a federal investigation.[23] Many schools complied, even adopting policies that kept track of student discipline according to race, even though the policies violate federal court rulings.[24] As a replacement, the Obama administration advocated for restorative justice practices by highlighting the school districts using such techniques.[25] The first Trump administration rescinded this guidance, but the Biden administration reinstated much of this practice.[26]

My survey found respondents from the general public and parent sample were almost evenly divided between those in favor, opposed, and neutral on this issue. Respondents were asked:

Advocates of "Restorative Justice," which uses meetings between victims and offenders instead of punishments, argue that this is important for reducing disparities in discipline outcomes. Opponents fear that Restorative Justice's lack of consequences leads to increased disruption and violence, threatening school safety. Should the federal government require your child's school/assigned public schools to adopt Restorative Justice practices?

Figure 5.1 **Federal Government Should Require Restorative Justice**

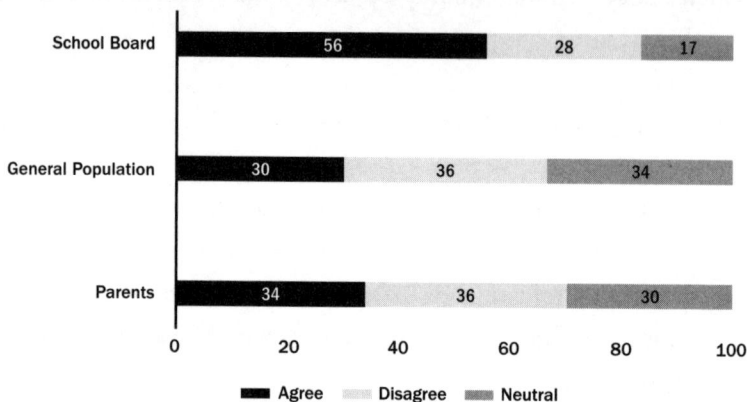

	Agree	Disagree	Neutral
School Board	56	28	17
General Population	30	36	34
Parents	34	36	30

Figure 5.2 **Should your child's school adopt restorative justice practices?**

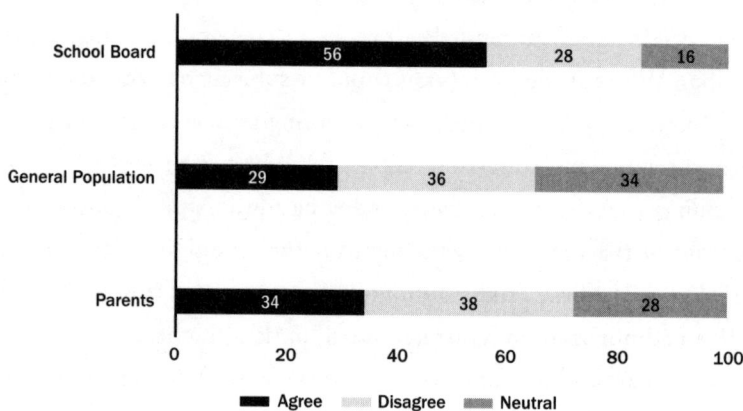

	Agree	Disagree	Neutral
School Board	56	28	16
General Population	29	36	34
Parents	34	38	28

On the question of federal policy, 34 percent of parents were in favor, 30 percent were neutral, and 36 percent disagreed. Slightly more parents were opposed when asked if their local school should adopt these practices: 34 percent in favor, 28 percent neutral, and 38 percent opposed. The results were similar across our sample from the general population, with approximately equal thirds of respondents registering in favor, neutral, and opposed.

As I leaned against the divided results from the survey questions on phonics and critical race theory and called for strong advocacy for the former based on research and opposition to the latter based on civil rights law, so, too, should policymakers and educators lean against the divides on school discipline. Note, too, that the union's support for restorative justice does not rest on broad-based support among the general public or parents according to the survey for this book.

The topic is crucial because evidence finds that the technique is frequently used in K–12 schools nationwide even as incidents of student misbehavior are increasing.[27] In July 2022, a survey of public school officials around the country found that 87 percent reported that "the COVID-19 pandemic has negatively impacted student socio-emotional development during the 2021–22 school year."[28] The specifics are particularly discouraging:

> Respondents attributed increased incidents of classroom disruptions from student misconduct (56 percent), rowdiness outside of the classroom (48 percent), acts of disrespect towards teachers and staff (48 percent), and prohibited use of electronic devices (42 percent) to the COVID-19 pandemic and its lingering effects.[29]

Another survey of teachers and school administrators conducted by *Education Week* in 2023 found that most respondents—70 percent—say that students are misbehaving more now than before the pandemic in 2019.[30] In another poll from *Education Week*, 80 percent of respondents said that students are less motivated than before the COVID-19 school years.[31]

So regardless of what the sample for this book's survey thinks about restorative justice, student behavior is worsening, and this makes teachers' jobs more difficult.

Restorative Justice and Research

The origins of restorative justice as it is practiced in schools today trace back to attempts to reform the criminal justice system in the 1970s. Some researchers contend that the technique of allowing the accused to make "restitution" with their victims originated in Canada in 1974, where the officials allowed two vandals to meet with those who owned the damaged property.[32] An essay by a Canadian professor written for the Administrative Office of the U.S. Courts notes that the concept can be found in a paper written in 1971 by two graduate students at the University of Minnesota who wanted to improve their state's criminal justice system.[33] The students outlined how restorative justice could be used in the corrections system. Minnesota Department of Corrections commissioner Dr. David Fogel allowed for a small experiment to be conducted on incarcerated individuals that would "bring victims and offenders together to negotiate a reparations agreement covering the form of restitution to be made, the amount of damages to be repaid, the expected schedule of repayments, and the ongoing contact to be maintained between victims and their offenders."[34] The original idea was to create a process by which guilty individuals would repair the damage done by their crimes, with in-person meetings with the victims a part of the process. "Restitution" was a key component of restorative justice in its early iterations.[35]

Restorative justice, as practiced in K–12 schools today, though, has changed significantly from its first iterations in corrections settings.

The NEA says that restorative justice practices are intended to lower the rate at which students are suspended from school and reduce student interaction with the criminal justice system (dubbed the "school-to-prison pipeline")—a notable shift from the restorative justice's origins as a way to improve what happens within the justice system.[36] Nevertheless, restorative justice is used as a substitute for out-of-school suspensions and expulsions. Educators are encouraged to use "classroom circles" where students discuss their feelings and create a "community built on kindness, not consequences."[37] The practice "emphasizes dialogue and mutual agreement" and "turns to mediation" instead of "punishment."[38]

While this sounds nice, the increasing levels of misbehavior in schools and the sad truth that school shootings continue to occur—albeit, and mercifully, rarely—mean that consequences must be a larger part of student discipline systems. In fact, research finds that restorative interventions that keep disruptive students in the classroom result in negative outcomes for the students sitting around them in class.

A study of discipline policies in Philadelphia schools, where school officials banned exclusionary discipline (out-of-school suspensions and expulsions), found that officials within the system had problems implementing the new policy—including negative outcomes for the peers of disruptive students.[39] Researchers found that "most schools did not comply with the ban" on suspensions, while another survey of teachers in Philadelphia found that 85 percent of those surveyed said suspensions are "useful for removing disruptive students so that others can learn," 89 percent said suspensions are "useful for sending messages to parents about the seriousness of infractions," and 84 percent said these student removals help "ensure a safe school environment."[40]

On the other side of Pennsylvania in Pittsburgh, RAND researchers found that reducing suspensions and expulsions did not improve student achievement and did not reduce the number of violent incidents or arrests.[41] These researchers note that over a short period—two years—there was a decrease in the most violent forms of behavior in the Pittsburgh-area schools studied, but the academic achievement of middle school students declined as well, making the results decidedly mixed if not negative, on net. The researchers also said that "[r]estorative practices did not...reduce suspensions for middle school students or suspensions for violent offenses." Researchers said their findings show that suspension rates decreased on average as educators carried out policies calling for such reductions, but educators' objectives should not be to simply reduce exclusionary discipline—the goal should be to create safer schools.[42]

A study of schools in Chicago found that when educators shortened the length of student suspensions, easing back on the consequences students face for misbehavior, the school climate worsened and the test scores of suspended students did not improve.[43]

Even before the pandemic, parents said that school discipline was too lax. In a 2019 poll by *Phi Delta Kappan* magazine, 51 percent of parents of public school students and 64 percent of public school teachers said school discipline was not strict enough.[44] The poll quoted a teacher in Delaware public schools who said, "School discipline is too lenient because of the political correctness that has now invaded the schools, along with government intrusion into the public schools. The teacher has very little control regarding classroom discipline."[45]

Following the Parkland tragedy of 2018, when a very disturbed teen entered his former high school and took the lives of 19 individuals, researchers and the media began to ask more about restorative justice and its effects. In the 2019 *Education Next* survey, nearly 50 percent of the general public opposed the idea that Washington should tell schools not to suspend or expel students based on a child's race or ethnicity.[46] While the Parkland murders were committed by a White individual, the school discipline policies in place at Marjory Stoneman Douglas High School, located in Broward County, Florida, were specifically designed to limit student interaction with law enforcement, not to protect innocent students from disruptive, even violent, peers.[47]

Former Broward County Superintendent Robert Runcie, who resigned and was charged with perjury after the tragedy, had worked with then-President Barrack Obama's education secretary, Arne Duncan, in Chicago before coming to Broward (as of 2025, Runcie's perjury case was still moving through the court system).[48] President Obama and Secretary Duncan touted Broward as a model for the country on limiting student suspensions based on a child's race.[49]

Like many of the topics in this book, K–12 student discipline is worthy of its own book-length treatment (and has, in fact, received such attention[50]). For the purposes of this book, though, parents should recognize that research exists demonstrating restorative justice's negative impacts on students. Furthermore, the way restorative justice is used in schools today leaves out the "restorative" part that was essential in the technique's original design for correctional settings. Taken together, this means unions are pushing a policy on schools while research points in a different direction and surveys find either opposition to the practice (the 2021 Heritage survey) or inconclusive results (the survey for this book).

★ ★ ★

There are still more NEA resolutions that have little if any relevance to K–12 education. The NEA has decided they are well-positioned, as a group representing teachers, to approve a resolution on "covert operations and counterintelligence activities," which reads: "The Association also believes that all such activities should be conducted under the jurisdiction of all three branches of the federal government and that individuals/agencies must be held accountable when they work outside of the specific directives issued for a given operation."[51] Why is a teacher union considering such language and what does the resolution have to do with schools?

The NEA also takes a position on nuclear weapons: "The Association also believes the United States and all other nations should adopt a verifiable freeze on the testing, development, production, upgrading, emplacement, sale, distribution, and deployment of nuclear weapons, materials, and all systems designed to deliver nuclear weapons."[52]

Although it's easy to chuckle at a union with, presumably, near zero expertise on nuclear warfare opining on national security issues, this resolution demonstrates that this interest group is devoting time and energy to topics that have no bearing on students and classrooms.

Considering the overtly political positioning from NEA resolutions and that these resolutions have nothing to do with either teacher working conditions or student welfare, I lean against the mixed opinions of teachers' unions from my survey. The survey asked respondents what they thought about teacher unions and found considerable ambiguity. More than half of the sample from the general population and parents said teacher unions were somewhere in between helpful and harmful (the question asked respondents to rate teacher unions on a scale of 1 to 10, and most rated unions between 4 and 7). More school board members had a favorable opinion of unions.

Figure 5.3 **Rate Teacher Unions**

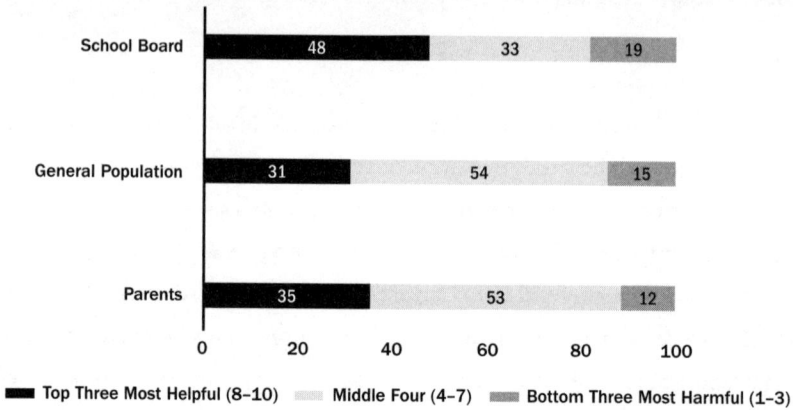

	Top Three Most Helpful (8–10)	Middle Four (4–7)	Bottom Three Most Harmful (1–3)
School Board	48	33	19
General Population	31	54	15
Parents	35	53	12

Notably, unions reliably support Democrats, giving 94 percent of their political contributions to candidates and officials to the left side of the aisle.[53] This is particularly problematic as teachers unions are public sector unions, generating their revenue from public school teachers and staff, the salaries of whom are paid by taxpayers. Their wildly lopsided giving is out of step with the percentage of Americans who self-identify as Democrats. According to *Gallup* in 2024, the party ID split was as follows:

+ Republican – 28%
+ Democrat – 28%
+ Independent – 43%[54]

It is the case, however, that the political preferences of the nation's 3.8 million teachers[55] are to the left of the average American, but they aren't overwhelmingly so. Approximately 43 percent of K–12 teachers describe themselves as moderate, 29 percent as liberal or "very liberal," and 27 percent as conservative or "very conservative," according to a 2017 survey by *Education Week*.[56] Teachers unions reliably represent one side of the political aisle—the left side.

These education interest groups are membership organizations that were originally created to represent teachers and improve their working conditions, but they spend more on politics than the welfare of their members. A review of union expenses in 2022–2023 found that the NEA "spent $10 million more on politics and lobbying" than on representing its member educators.[57]

The NEA's audacity is matched by the actions of Randi Weingarten, president of the American Federation of Teachers (AFT).[58] In a move that baffled many, Weingarten made a trip to war-torn Ukraine in 2022, stating in a post on social media that she was "Heading to the border now to assess the situation."[59] What about the situation with low reading scores, or dismal civics achievement, or women being threatened in private spaces? Weingarten's Ukraine visit did not improve the working conditions of her members, but it may have increased her clout with lawmakers as her union and the NEA use their considerable resources and influence to advance progressive political aims.

Teachers have needed help in recent years, not distractions. COVID-19 brought with it a great deal of uncertainty, along with declining test scores and increases in student misbehavior, and instead of helping teachers with materials to clean surfaces or provide protection, unions lobbied to keep schools closed.[60] The dramatic declines in student achievement following the pandemic demonstrate that the prolonged closures had negative impacts on students, which would impact teachers' working conditions once schools reopened.

★ ★ ★

Unions also dominate school board elections. These elections are typically held off-cycle, which means the elections take place on years when there is not a congressional or presidential election.[61] The off-cycle nature of school board elections depresses voter turnout and concentrates turnout among well-organized special interest groups.[62] As University of California, Berkeley, professor Sarah Anzia explains, holding elections off-cycle "is a way to put a limit on the number of people who will participate and to affect the kinds of people who participate."[63] Special interest groups like the teachers unions, Anzia notes, "work behind the scenes to reinforce the structures that encourage low-turnout elections," increasing the likelihood that the voters who do turnout to vote have a vested interest in maintaining the status quo.[64]

As a result, many voters learn about school board candidates after picking up materials from the teachers' unions table right before stepping into the voting booth. According to John Chubb, former distinguished visiting fellow at the Hoover Institution, turnout in school board elections "is the lowest of any general election, averaging perhaps 10 percent of local voters."[65] But it's not just manipulation of who turns out to vote in school board elections that is driven by the unions; their endorsement of particular candidates continues to have a significant impact on school board election outcomes. Union endorsements increase voters' support of a given candidate by an average of 6 percentage points, with support for a candidate increasing by between 10 to 20 percentage points among Democrats as a result of a union endorsement.[66] As Michael Hartney writes in a report for the Manhattan Institute, "the union seal of approval buoys candidates' electoral prospects because voters believe union-favored candidates hold shared interests on important education issues."[67]

Hartney goes on to explain that

> voters are largely mistaken about what union endorsements convey and what drives endorsement decisions. For example, union support for incumbents is unrelated to academic achievement gains. Instead, the only consistent predictor of union support for incumbents is whether the district raised salaries for senior teachers prior to an election.[68]

These elections matter, especially when voters and families need public officials to respond effectively to a crisis. Even at a time (fall 2020) when most parents wanted schools to return to in-person instruction, teachers unions resisted. In school districts with a stronger union presence, schools were statistically less likely to reopen: Hartney and Leslie K. Finger found little correlation between school reopening and COVID severity/prevalence, while "mass partisanship and teacher union strength best explain how school boards approached reopening."[69] Indeed, in places like Chicago[70] and Philadelphia,[71] the teachers unions dragged their feet on returning to in-person instruction, largely in an attempt to extract political concessions in exchange for school reopening. National unions like the American Federation of Teachers encouraged their local affiliates to strike if they didn't want to go back to work in person.[72]

Parents understandably worried that their children would learn less while at home during the pandemic than they would if schools remained open. Unfortunately, results from the Nation's Report Card provided in these pages bear out their concerns.

In addition to dominating local school board elections, teachers' unions have historically had an outsized impact on spending on state and federal elections. A 2010 report found that the NEA had a $355 million budget and outspent ExxonMobil, Microsoft, Walmart, and the AFL-CIO combined during the 2007–2008 election cycle.[73] In addition to the millions in campaign contributions, the NEA provides hundreds of thousands of dollars in member dues to left-leaning groups such as Americans United for Change and the Democratic Congressional Campaign Committee.[74]

Unions and the Origin of the U.S. Department of Education

One of the most headline-grabbing executive orders from the second Trump administration was the president's directive to U.S. Department of Education Secretary Linda McMahon to close the very agency she led.[75] The NEA and AFT opposed the agency's closure, even filing lawsuits to stop the efforts.[76] On this issue, the unions are not just reliably siding against a policy proposed by the political party they oppose (as indicated by their campaign contributions). The union is trying to protect the very education bureaucracy they helped create. From the time of America's founding, education has been a local issue.[77] In the early Puritan era, parents and local communities were responsible for educating children. The Colonial Acts of 1642 and 1647 codified the notion early on, calling on parents to teach their children to read in English, understand religious tenets, and know the capital laws of the Commonwealth of Massachusetts.[78] The Colonial Act of 1647, also known as the Old Deluder Satan law, mandated that every town with more than 50 households hire a teacher, and once a town had more than 100 families, a grammar school would have to be established.[79] As the population of New England began to swell, the schools that grew out of the Colonial Act of 1647 also began to increase in number.[80] "Academies" appeared during the late 18th century and spread throughout New England in the years following the American Revolution. During this time in the colonial era, parents were viewed as their children's primary teachers, and their voices were essential parts of the education structure of the community.[81]

Changes to the nature of work from agrarian to industrial during the mid-19th century combined with westward expansion encouraged a fragmented system of academies to give way to widespread public schooling. These "common schools," championed by Massachusetts State Board of Education head Horace Mann (cited in Chapter 2 for his opposition to phonics-based instruction), led to significant formalization of public education.[82] In his *Twelfth Annual Report* (1848), Mann lauded the promise of the common school to become "the most effective and benignant of all the forces of civilization."[83] The common school era eventually gave way to the Progressive era in the early 20th century and what would be recognized today as a system of public schools.[84]

Throughout this time period—from the colonial era through the mid-20th century—the federal government played virtually no role in K–12 education. Lawmakers created a federal education office in 1867, but the agency only lasted one year.[85] Some initiatives and programs popped up from time to time, such as the provisions that would create the National School Lunch program, which first appeared in 1943.[86] But education remained a local and state issue.

Federal policies and appropriations for education began to change after the Soviets launched the Sputnik satellite in 1957.[87] Dwight D. Eisenhower had already established the office of Health, Education, and Welfare (HEW) in 1953, but the Sputnik satellite added urgency to federal efforts attempting to help U.S. students catch up to their Soviet peers.[88] When the Soviets launched a second satellite (Sputnik II) just one month after the first, "the success of academically talented students became the foremost preoccupation of the nation's schools."[89] President Eisenhower argued that the United States needed to best the Soviet Union "on the Communists' own terms—outmatching them in military power, general technological advance, and specialized education and research."[90] In response, Congress passed, and Eisenhower signed into law, the National Defense Education Act (NDEA) on September 2, 1958, providing hundreds of millions in federal funding to improve science education and international competitiveness during the Cold War.[91]

The NDEA's central concern was national defense, providing justification for increased federal intervention in education under the auspices of national security, which the federal government has a responsibility and mandate to provide. Federal involvement in education would be supersized in 1965 when President Lyndon Johnson shifted the focus on education spending from Washington and fighting a Cold War with the Soviets to fighting a domestic "War on Poverty."[92]

In his speech describing his plan for fighting this new war, Johnson said, "A third place to build the Great Society is in the classrooms of America. There our children's lives will be shaped."[93] The various Great Society programs—from Head Start (a preschool program), to increased federal spending on elementary and secondary education, to more spending on college loans and grants—sought to cure the many perceived societal ills of the day.[94]

Hardly. The Great Society failed to improve student achievement or help individuals escape poverty, but the initiatives did manage to grow federal programs and spend taxpayer money.[95] Since the time Johnson launched the Great Society education programs, inflation-adjusted per-pupil spending has tripled, but academic outcomes have remained flat.[96] A long-term study of Head Start found the program to be ineffective.[97] And of considerable concern is data demonstrating that the gap between the top (90th percentile) and bottom (10th percentile) of K–12 students according to family income remains the same as it was when the War on Poverty began—a difference that is the equivalent of four grade levels' worth of learning.[98]

Instead of improving academic outcomes for poor children, massive federal spending and programs introduced as part of the War on Poverty have led to an ongoing staffing surge. As Kennesaw State professor Ben Scafidi has documented, from 1950 to 2019, while the number of students increased 100 percent, the number of teachers increased 243 percent and the number of administrators and all other staff increased 709 percent.[99] As of 2022, teachers made up just 47.5 percent of school staff.[100]

With this surge in hiring, no interest group would want a cabinet-level U.S. Department of Education more than the teachers unions.

In September 1976, the NEA made its first presidential candidate endorsement.[101] Speaking at the special interest group's annual meeting, vice presidential candidate Walter Mondale promised the group that if they supported him and his running mate Jimmy Carter, the administration would establish a stand-alone, cabinet-level agency for education.[102] Mondale's brother was an NEA official, so his selection as Jimmy Carter's running mate was key to the union's first-ever endorsement of a presidential candidate.[103] More consequential was Carter's commitment to establish a cabinet-level agency. Carter told the NEA that he was "in favor of creating a separate cabinet-level Department of Education," in order to consolidate grant programs and provide "a stronger voice for education at the federal level."[104] As a result, the union endorsed Carter (the NEA had an estimated 1.8 million members by this point), with the union representing Carter's largest bloc of delegates at the nominating convention in July of 1976.[105]

It would take until the end of Carter's presidency before he was able to make good on his promise to the teachers unions. In 1979, stretching from the winter months to the spring and summer, a bill to create the U.S. Department of Education finally passed the Senate by a vote of 72 to 21, followed by narrow passage in the House (210 to 206).[106] President Carter signed into law the Department of Education Organization Act on October 17 of that year, and the agency opened its doors on May 4, 1980.[107]

The purpose of including this history here is to explain why the teachers unions wanted a federal Department of Education, a department that would oversee an area of American life for which the federal government has no enumerated power in the U.S. Constitution. As Carter stated outright, such an agency would be "a stronger voice" for education in Washington, even though education is a state priority. Organized special interest groups would be best situated to lobby Congress and engage with federal agencies and regulators—not parents or teachers, who do not have the political capital of interest groups with billion-dollar coffers.

Decades later, after mediocre student results and whopping budget increases, federal officials investigated the agency to determine what, exactly, the office was doing.[108] In 1998, after an exhaustive series of state hearings and testimony on the effects of the increased federal involvement in education, a congressional subcommittee published *Education at a Crossroads*, documenting just how ineffective the department had become.

Led by then Congressman and Chairman of the Commission William Goodling along with Congressman Pete Hoekstra, the commission found that federal involvement in K–12 education had led to a program-for-every-problem mentality. The agency fostered "shadow" state-level departments of education, with three times as many federally funded employees in state agencies as the number of staff in the federal Department of Education, all tasked with carrying out federal requirements.[109] The *Crossroads* report documented how federal programs and spending had created a "cottage industry in selling information on program descriptions, application deadlines and filing instructions for each of the myriad federal education programs."[110] The report explained that millions of manhours were required every year to complete the federal paperwork burden created by the Education Department.[111] More manpower was needed for all of this, which meant more dues-paying members for the unions.

Ultimately, then, the *Crossroads* report is crucial evidence demonstrating how unions benefit from the growth of this federal office. More will be said about the Trump administration's efforts to close the agency in the concluding chapter.

Unions are an issue that deserves more than ambivalence from Americans. Voters only have the time and interest for a select number of topics, but the interest groups' influence over politics and advocacy for radical causes that have far-reaching implications make them a formidable presence opposing cultural and political issues on which surveys find Americans are in agreement.

★ ★ ★

Finally, to get beyond the myth of polarization in American life, individuals, families, and policymakers need solutions for the issues that matter most to Americans—the limited role that government should play in our lives, the importance of policies being rooted in merit, the teaching of character and virtue to the next generation, and more. Policymakers should be confident in efforts to devolve decisions from Washington, putting them closer to the local communities those decisions affect. We are, after all, a nation rooted in a robust civil society—those "little platoons" first noted by Edmund Burke—and the spirit of association identified by Alexis de Tocqueville.[112]

The findings from the survey in this book should give Americans confidence that they agree on vital cultural issues while experts insist we are polarized on these topics. For these subjects involving sex and race and the other topics on which we found agreement, citizens should speak up before school boards and with their state and federal representatives. We can confidently say there are others with us.

The concluding chapter will offer examples of policies that are supported by the polling and research provided in this book to make children safer, uphold civil rights laws, and protect individual liberty. What follows is a guide for parents, community leaders, and policymakers, as civil society realigns policies to reflect the agreement we share as Americans.

CONCLUSION

The real problem is not lack of money but failure of vision.
—William J. Bennett, "Our Greedy Colleges"

The purpose of this book is to help Americans connect the prevailing public opinions during the years of the Biden administration (2021–2025) to the politics and policies of the second Trump White House. Public opinion during the Biden years should be viewed against the backdrop of the policies this administration adopted (which are easy to identify) as well as the cultural changes also taking place during the period (which are observable but harder to identify). Admittedly, the survey conducted for this book offers a snapshot in time, describing a particular moment. I make no claim that public opinion is etched in stone.

Still, some of the results from the survey represent significant shifts from the policies of prior administrations, and the federal and state laws that officials are adopting now that are consistent with such polling could be changes that last for many years. Multiple surveys conducted around the same time, combined with research evidence supporting certain laws and policies, help to substantiate the positions Americans take on topics in the headlines and in their daily lives. Together, surveys and research help describe the culture and society and political climate in which we live. In this respect, I repeat my agreement with the Brookings scholars quoted in this book's introduction, that studying "what citizens think about politics and policy is a genuine contribution to democracy."[1]

The survey results demonstrate that Americans are more closely aligned on key issues than the "experts" described in the introduction would have us believe.

Education lies at the center of many of these issues. From race to sex to the value of marriage and getting a job, we cannot investigate any of these topics for long without arriving at schools and instruction.

It may seem counterintuitive, but the Trump administration's most consequential effort at fostering student success and social cohesion around education policy and cultural questions is the administration's attempt to close the federal education agency. Chapter 5 traced the origins of the U.S. Department of Education to teacher union lobbying efforts while also listing the myriad radical policy positions of unions. This origin story offers reason enough to question the necessity of the agency's existence.

Additionally, for 45 years, taxpayers and policymakers have witnessed the agency's budget steadily increase and staff ranks swell while student results remain, at best, uninspiring or, at worst, mediocre. The agency has become so bloated that few realize just how much money is being distributed to schools and for what purposes.

To wit, in February 2025, the Trump administration cancelled $600 million in federal grants to K–12 schools that promoted racial preferences through DEI programs—grants that likely violate civil rights statutes by promoting racial discrimination through DEI.[2] The administration also canceled hundreds of millions in federal taxpayer spending for Columbia University and other colleges, monies that taxpayers surely did not know were going to these purposes or at least in such staggering amounts.[3]

Closing the Education Department is not a dereliction of federal education responsibilities. Rather, it is an essential effort at promoting fiscal transparency and giving parents and local educators more authority over education institutions because they will have the ability to run their local schools and provide students with more learning options without federal interference.

★ ★ ★

On March 11, 2025, the Trump administration initiated a reduction in force at the Department of Education, cutting in half the number of employees from 4,133 to 2,183.[4] Less than two weeks later, on March 20, President Trump signed an executive order—*Improving Education Outcomes by Empowering Parents, States, and Communities*—directing Education Secretary Linda McMahon to "take all necessary steps to facilitate the closure of the Department of Education" to the "maximum extent permitted by law."[5] On March 22, Trump announced college student loans and programs for K–12 students with special needs (the Individuals with Disabilities Education Act, or IDEA), two of the largest programs run by the Education Department, would be "coming out of the Department of Education immediately," with loans moving to the Small Business Administration and programs for students with special needs moving to the U.S. Department of Health and Human Services.[6]

These steps, reducing staff and moving two programs out of the agency, are major developments in the generations-long goal to eliminate the Education Department. As discussed in Chapter 5, closing the agency has been a longstanding goal for conservatives. Arguing that "federal aid became federal interference," President Ronald Reagan attempted from the beginning of his administration to abolish what he called Carter's "new bureaucratic boondoggle."[7]

"It's time to face the truth," Reagan said in a March 13, 1983, weekly radio address. "Advocates of more and more government interference in education have had ample time to make their case and they've failed."[8] Later in the address he said, "Better education doesn't mean a bigger Department of Education. In fact, that department should be eliminated."

Notably, the list of those who supported the agency's closure is long and distinguished. Nobel laureate Milton Friedman supported abolishing the Department of Education.[9] Former senate majority leader and presidential hopeful Bob Dole voted against the creation of the Department of Education in 1979[10] and vowed to eliminate the agency when he was running for president in 1996.[11] Former education secretaries Bill Bennett and Lamar Alexander (also a former member of Congress) support abolishing the department,[12] as does Betsy DeVos, education secretary during President Trump's first term. Liberal MSNBC commentator and erstwhile Republican Joe Scarborough introduced a bill to eliminate the Department of Education during his tenure in the 104th Congress.[13] The bill, which Scarborough introduced in June 1995, received an impressive 120 cosponsors in the House of Representatives.[14] Members of Congress ranging from Lindsey Graham, Rand Paul, Thomas Massie, and Bill Cassidy to former Speaker John Boehner and the late Senator John McCain have supported eliminating the agency.[15]

More recently, state leaders have become increasingly vocal that the federal Department of Education is redundant at best and counterproductive at worst. Governors Kim Reynolds (Iowa), Ron DeSantis (Florida), Bill Lee (Tennessee), Mike DeWine (Ohio), Greg Abbott (Texas), Jeff Landry (Louisiana), Brad Little (Idaho), Jim Pillen (Nebraska), and Mike Braun (Indiana) attended the March 20 executive order signing at the White House to wind down the department.[16] Other state leaders like Alaska Commissioner of Education Deena Bishop and Wyoming Superintendent of Public Instruction Megan Degenfelder were also in attendance.[17] State education chiefs have also vocally supported the administration's moves to eliminate the agency, including Oklahoma Superintendent of Public Instruction Ryan Walters,[18] former Florida Commissioner of Education Manny Diaz,[19] and Louisiana Superintendent of Public Instruction Cade Brumley (whose comments on social studies and protecting women and girls from "gender" ideology were included in Chapters 2 and 4),[20] among others. These state officials have said they are ready to be handed the education baton from Washington.

The Department of Education Has Reached Its Expiration Date

Increases in federal spending on K–12 schools are not correlated with improved student achievement.[21] Likewise, federal spending has had negative effects on postsecondary education. In education research, the "Bennett Hypothesis" is the theory that as the federal government increases the amount of money that it makes available to students in the form of loans for college tuition, so, too, will college tuition increase. Former Education Secretary William J. Bennett originated the idea in 1987 in commentary for *The New York Times* entitled "Our Greedy Colleges," which succinctly describes his argument.[22] Obviously these tuition increases create challenges for families and students trying to pay for college on their own, without federal loans.

Bennett decried college administrators who had chosen to increase tuition in the mid-1980s at a rate higher than inflation.[23] He also tied the tuition increases to ever-growing federal loan subsidies that "would help cushion the increase" for students.[24] Time—and research—have proved him correct. Since 1970, inflation-adjusted tuition rates have quintupled at both public and private colleges.[25] Research from the Federal Reserve Bank of New York found that every $1 increase in federal subsidized loans creates a 60-cent increase in college tuition.[26]

Not all of the spending appears to be going to classrooms. Mirroring the hiring spree in K–12 education, the number of non-teaching employees and administrators in America's colleges and universities increased 50 percent faster than teaching faculty from 2001 to 2011.[27] Non-instructional staff at universities across the country now accounts for more than half of university payroll costs.[28] Just 40 percent of full-time employees at non-doctoral colleges are instructional staff, a figure that drops to 28 percent at doctoral-granting universities.[29]

Preston Cooper, a researcher at the American Enterprise Institute, found that "since 2003, only one-third of the increase in colleges' and universities' core expenditures has gone to spending on instruction. Almost all the rest has fed the growth of the vast administrative apparatus of these institutions."[30]

The increasing federal subsidies have insulated colleges from making tough choices over the years, from cutting ineffective or low-enrollment academic departments to keeping staffing levels in check. And ever-increasing college costs have muddied colleges' value proposition. The six-year completion rate for students pursuing a bachelor's degree stood at just 64 percent in 2020, meaning slightly more than 6 in 10 students complete a four-year bachelor's degree in six years.[31] This can be explained in part by the fact that the typical *full-time* college student spends only 2.76 hours per day on all education-related activities, including attending class and completing homework and assignments.[32]

When students do finish college, they too often find themselves ill-prepared for the workforce. One-third of college graduates are under-employed, working in jobs that do not require a bachelor's degree.[33] For example, 75 percent of engineering majors are in jobs that require a bachelor's degree, but that figure drops to just 40 percent for communications majors.[34] At the same time, business leaders report that college courses do not prepare graduates for the workforce or provide them with the practical or technical skills needed to be successful in their careers.[35] A 2018 survey conducted by the National Association of Colleges and Employers found that although almost 80 percent of students believed they were proficient in oral and written communication, just 42 percent of employers agreed.[36] Those findings reinforced earlier survey data from the Association of American Colleges and Universities, which found that while 62 percent of students felt they were competent in oral and written communication, just 28 percent of employers agreed.

Federal subsidies, on their own, do not underprepare college students for the workforce, but the increasing number and size of federal loans do usher more students to campus for experiences they do not necessarily need (or that do not effectively prepare students) to be successful in the job market.

★ ★ ★

The *Education at a Crossroads* report introduced in Chapter 5 arrived at conclusions on federal education spending and programs that are still true now:

> It is time for America to take a careful look at what billions of federal education dollars have purchased, and to make hard decisions about whether to continue expanding the federal role, or to return control to parents and teachers.... It is time for the burden of proof to shift to

the federal government. If it cannot be demonstrated that a particular federal program is more effectively spending funds than state and local communities would otherwise spend them, Congress should return the money to the states and the people, without any burdensome strings attached.[37]

Fortunately, state lawmakers have adopted a host of innovative policies focused on parent choice in education over the last 30 years, demonstrating that the future of learning depends on the laboratories of democracy that are U.S. states, not Washington, D.C.[38] State officials are offering families and students more options than the public school to which a child is assigned based on his or her ZIP code. What started as a trickle of small private education options for students that met certain eligibility criteria has turned into a virtual flood of learning opportunities that, in some states, are available to all students.

Wisconsin lawmakers adopted the first modern-day private school choice program in 1990, the Milwaukee Parental Choice Program (MPCP).[39] The MPCP allows K–12 students from low-income families to attend a private school of their choice.[40] The adoption of this voucher proposal was followed in 1996 by Ohio's Cleveland Scholarship Program, another private school scholarship option for children in low-income families (and, at the outset, only children in grades K–3).[41] Lawmakers in different states continued to adopt isolated choice programs, generally for students that met limited eligibility criteria (for example, Florida adopted a scholarship program for children with special needs in 1999, and federal lawmakers approved a voucher program for children from low-income families in Washington, D.C., in 2004).[42]

By 2010, eight years after a crucial U.S. Supreme Court opinion ruled that vouchers do not violate the U.S. Constitution, lawmakers in 13 states had adopted private learning options for students.[43] Lawmakers in Arizona expanded the concept of a private school voucher in 2011 and allowed students to use scholarships to pay for more than just private school tuition.[44]

With these new education savings accounts, parents could pay for personal tutors, hire education therapists, and buy textbooks and more with their child's account. These accounts were introduced as part of the education reforms adopted by Mississippi lawmakers. Lawmakers in Florida and Tennessee had adopted similar accounts by 2017.[45]

Following the COVID-19 pandemic, as millions of parents like Melissa and Beanie were frustrated with public school closures and other responses to the pandemic, school choice exploded across states. In 2021, West Virginia lawmakers adopted a scholarship program open to every child in the state.[46] As of this writing, lawmakers in 17 states have adopted education savings accounts similar to those in Arizona and West Virginia, open to every child in their respective states.[47]

Education is emerging out of an era in which students attend a public school based on where they live, with state and even local education policies broadly overseen by a cabinet-level agency in Washington, to a catalogue of options from which parents can choose, not unlike on-demand TV and music services. Increasingly, parents can choose how and where their children learn.

Researchers have measured the effects of such programs on students and schools and found strong returns for both participants and students in the public schools that scholarship students left to attend private schools.

To date, researchers have conducted 17 randomized controlled trial (RCT) evaluations of the effect of school choice on students' academic outcomes.[48] RCTs are the "gold standard" of scientific research because, as a result of randomization, researchers can draw causal conclusions to a high degree of certainty about the impact of a given program or policy.[49] Of the 17 RCTs conducted on the academic effects of school choice to date, 11 find positive effects for some or all students, four find neutral effects, and two find negative effects.[50] It is worth noting, however, that those two negative evaluations were unique to a scholarship program in Louisiana where lawmakers placed stringent regulations on participating private schools.[51] The bulk of scientifically rigorous evaluations are unambiguous about the positive academic effects school choice has on student success.

In addition to improving academic achievement outcomes, access to school choice significantly increases students' likelihood of graduating high school and enrolling in college.[52] Of the seven experimental evaluations conducted to date on the effect of school choice on academic attainment (e.g., outcome variables such as graduating high school, enrolling in college, earning a college degree), five find statistically significant positive effects for some or all students, and two find no effects. No rigorous studies find a negative effect on academic attainment.[53]

Researchers have also evaluated the competitive effects of education choice (that is, the effect on public school students when their peers use a scholarship to leave and attend a school of their choice).[54] Of the 29 empirical evaluations to date, 26 find positive benefits for all students, one finds no effect, and two found a negative effect.[55]

Additionally, researchers have also found other, non-academic positive outcomes from policies that offer parents and students choices in education. Education choice has positive effects on students' civic engagement[56] (researchers measured "political tolerance, voluntarism, political knowledge, political participation, social capital, civic skills, and patriotism"), reduces crime rates among high-school seniors who participated in school choice programs,[57] increases levels of parent and student perceptions of school safety among participating families,[58] and more.[59]

Policy Recommendations

The closure of the U.S. Department of Education and the adoption of "universal" education choice in the states—learning options available to students regardless of income or area of residence—are remarkable policy changes that will reshape the daily lives of parents and students nationwide.

Based on the polling and research results provided in these pages, there are still other policies that lawmakers should consider:

Empowering parents with curriculum transparency

In furtherance of each of the prior items, and addressing the concerns raised by Latasha, Melissa, Beanie, Suparna, and others in our earlier chapters, K–12 school administrators and teachers should make classroom content available to the public. Educators should post the titles of textbooks and reading assignments online, along with worksheets from the internet and course syllabi.

During COVID-19 all schools that moved to online learning had to make assignments available on the internet, so there are no logistical reasons schools cannot do so now. Schools do not have to post full textbooks online, but parents should at least know the source of the classroom instruction being delivered to students. There are many online platforms that schools use today to communicate with parents, including FACTS, Blackboard (now called "Anthology"), Daily Connect, ParentSquare, and more.[66] Educators already have tools at their disposal to exchange messages with families. Taxpayers and policymakers should not have to wait until an enterprising parent or reporter finds an alarming school assignment and exposes the material for the public to be aware of what is happening in classrooms.

Adopting traditional school discipline policies over "restorative justice" practices

Teachers and principals should be allowed to maintain order in their classrooms without state or federal directives to keep quotas according to race about the children they suspend or expel.[67] No one wants a child to be expelled from school, but if a student is found to be so threatening and violent that the other children in his or her class or even an entire school is at risk, then educators have a responsibility to protect their school communities.

Policies that trade "restorative circles," where perpetrators discuss infractions with their peers, for consequences administered due to misbehavior are policies that endanger victims. Because each school and every student has unique characteristics, there is no single policy that guarantees school safety and adequate student discipline. However, documents such as the Federal Commission on School Safety Report from 2018 offer examples from schools around the country on how to enforce discipline on a case by case basis and adopt security measures that protect educators and students.[68]

Weakening the power of teachers unions through teacher certification reform, removing colleges of education as gatekeepers to the classroom, and decentralizing education decision-making from Washington to the states and local governments.

The teaching profession is constrained by policies that mandate that aspiring teachers obtain paper credentials (certificates, additional degrees, etc.), often at a substantial cost.[69] Requiring several years of certification work can be a significant deterrent for people who would otherwise become teachers, such as mid-career professionals.

Yet research has shown little if any connection between teacher certification and a teacher's impact on student academic achievement.[70] As researchers Thomas J. Kane, Jonah E. Rockoff, and Douglas O. Staiger said, "To put it simply, teachers vary considerably in the extent to which they promote student learning, but whether a teacher is certified or not is largely irrelevant to predicting his or her effectiveness."[71]

States and school districts should remove unnecessary barriers to entering the classroom—namely, requirements for certification—while simultaneously demanding excellent performance from teachers in the classroom.

Teaching the success sequence

State and local boards of education have the authority to adopt curricular materials and instructional strategies. Administrators should work with teachers and parents to include the research and lessons from the "success sequence" in K–12 schools.[72] Lawmakers in states such as Alabama and Tennessee have already adopted provisions to include the success sequence in K–12 curriculum.[73]

Since the material concerns romantic relationships, sex, and careers, parents and educators should introduce these ideas at age-appropriate levels. Students deserve to know that finishing high school, entering the workforce or enrolling in a terminal degree, and getting married before having children not only decreases the odds that they will live in poverty as young adults but also increases in the likelihood they will reach the middle class or better, regardless of race or other socioeconomic characteristics.

Parent bill of rights

Lawmakers in half of all states (twenty-five as of this writing) have adopted provisions that are considered a parent bill of rights.[74] State officials should use these laws as models of how to protect families and children and keep parents informed about health-related issues affecting their child. The provisions should state that parents are a child's primary caregiver and have the right to direct their child's moral, religious, and educational upbringing. Public officials may not interfere with a parent's role unless they can demonstrate a compelling interest and the intervention is exercised with the least restrictive means necessary.

Officials can combine these provisions with the prohibition on compelled speech provided above, as well as the academic transparency and Given Name Act proposals, to create a comprehensive suite of provisions empowering and protecting children and families.

★ ★ ★

Much of this book covers the results of public opinion surveys. But can public opinion be trusted? The Brookings research provided in the introduction thinks so. Again, however, lawmakers should not base public policies on polling alone. In the first scene of Shakespeare's *Julius Caesar*, Murellus, a conspirator against Caesar, criticizes "commoners" for so quickly changing their allegiance from Pompey to Caesar after Caesar's victory:

> You blocks, you stones, you worse than senseless things!
> O you hard hearts, you cruel men of Rome, Knew you not Pompey?
>   Many a time and oft
> Have you climb'd up to walls and battlements…
> To see great Pompey pass the streets of Rome…
> And do you now strew flowers in his way,
> That comes in triumph over Pompey's blood?

Critics may say that the survey in this book merely represents a populace following the lead of the White House, just agreeing with pronouncements from the second Trump administration. Had the survey been issued at a different time, the responses would have been different, they may argue. Yet the poll was conducted well before the 2024 election. The survey measured public opinion in the midst of President Joe Biden's administration, an administration that was moving in the opposite direction from where conservatives believed the nation should go.

Others may argue that some of the results, such as the questions on DEI and unions, do not align with conservatives' preferred answers—thus conflicting with the thesis that America is not polarized on the issues. But the answers do not show united support for unions or for DEI, among the other questions on which there were not conclusive results, but rather divided opinions that could be the result of ambiguity or simply indecision. Respondents were often split on the answers, with a nontrivial amount of neutrality. For example, half of our respondents did not know what to make of union influence on schools and rated them in the middle of the spectrum between "most helpful" to K–12 schools and "most harmful."

As explained in the introduction, Americans do not have the time or even the interest to be experts on every subject. Likewise, not every respondent may connect one policy (racial preferences in college admissions) to its underlying philosophy (critical race theory and DEI). The opposition to teaching radical gender theories to young children and allowing boys who say they are girls to have access to girls' private spaces actually means there is more opposition to teacher unions—or at least the policies that teacher unions support—than many realize, because unions support such practices.

As for whether public opinion is too fickle to rely on, the survey results are supported by findings from other polling, even if public opinion is never final. The same public that turned from Pompey to Caesar went on to split again, but the trends in current opinion, when paired with research findings, build support for policies that align with prevailing opinions. This information is especially helpful when politicians and the media want us to think that certain positions are isolated and that Americans are polarized, when in fact Americans agree on important issues. We can hope that the opinions binding Americans on cultural and even moral questions point not to a pending civil war but rather to the prospect that our nation has more holding us together than driving us apart.

APPENDIX A

TITLE: Heritage Foundation Survey of Public Opinion

SURVEY FUNDER: The Heritage Foundation

SURVEY DATA COLLECTION AND QUALITY CONTROL: Braun Research, Inc.

INTERVIEW DATES:
- Gen Pop. 7/10/23–8/3/23
- Parents. 7/10/23–7/30/23
- Members. 7/10/23–9/27/23

SAMPLE FRAMES: Gen Pop 18+, Parents in the U.S. (K–12 Students) and School Board Members (K–12 Schools)

SAMPLING METHODS: Non-probability panel via Pure Spectrum (https://www.purespectrum.com/) for Parents and Gen Pop; email for School Board Members based on Heritage-provided sample (email invitation attached)

LANGUAGE: English only per each group (School Board, Gen Pop, Parents)

INTERVIEW METHODS: Online only

AVERAGE INTERVIEW LENGTH: 12 minutes per each group (School Board, Gen Pop, Parents)

SAMPLE SIZES AND MARGINS OF ERROR
- Gen Pop 18+ = n2022, ± 1.52 percent (17.5% response rate, 95% confidence level)
- Parents of children 18+ (K–12) = n1581, ± 2.018 percent (21.3% response rate, 95% confidence level)

- School Board Members = n519, ± 1.9 percent (5.44% response rate, 95% confidence level)

Significance testing was performed on both 90% and 95% confidence levels.

SCHOOL BOARD MEMBER SAMPLE

Our school board member sample was smaller than our general population and parent samples. Like these samples, there was a small number of respondents who overlapped.

A breakdown of the geographic region of our school board sample is provided here:

TOTAL ANSWERING	519
Northeast	109
	21.00%
Midwest	109
	21.00%
South	188
	36.22%
West	113
	21.77%

Some of our school board member sample came from our sample of parents and the general population. The table below provides the share of overlapping responses:

TOTAL ANSWERING	519
General Population	216
	41.62%
Parents	148
	28.52%
School Board Members	155
	29.87%

School Board Member Email

K–12 School-Board Member Survey

Subject Line: Survey with School-board Members of Public Schools (K–12)

Greetings!

We would like to invite school-board members of public schools (K–12) to contribute to a market research survey pertaining to education. The questions will ask your opinions about issues you feel are most important to you and will help inform curriculum offerings to students.

All answers will be kept strictly confidential and aggregated, so individuals cannot be identified by their responses.

The survey is being fielded by Braun Research, an independent, international market research company, based in Princeton, New Jersey, in the United States.

Would you please provide your valuable input by taking about ten minutes to answer our survey questions?

To begin the survey, please use this link:

[Survey link]

We greatly appreciate your taking the time to share your thoughts with us!

If you have any questions about this research, please contact [Braun Contact].

Thank you again!

Sincerely,

[Braun Contact]

NOTES

INTRODUCTION

1 Arthur Schlesinger Jr., *The Disuniting of America: Reflections on a Multicultural Society* (New York, N.Y.: W.W. Norton & Co., 1998), p. 11.

2 Phone interview with Latasha Fields, March 3, 2025.

3 *Poverty in America: Economic Realities of Struggling Families: Hearing Before the U.S. House Budget Committee*, 116th Cong. (2019–2020), June 19, 2019, (testimony of Pastor Latasha Harrison Fields), https://www.congress.gov/116/meeting/house/109649/witnesses/HHRG-116-BU00-Wstate-FieldsP-20190619.pdf.

4 Ibid.

5 1776 Unites, "Activists: About Latasha Harrison Fields," available at https://1776unites.org/essays/author/latashaharrisonfields/.

6 Phone interview with Latasha Fields, March 3, 2025.

7 Charles Bethea, "The Americans Prepping for a Second Civil War," *The New Yorker*, November 4, 2024, https://www.newyorker.com/magazine/2024/11/11/among-the-civil-war-preppers.

8 Geoffrey Skelley and Holly Fuong, "3 in 10 Americans Named Political Polarization as a Top Issue Facing the Country," *FiveThirtyEight*, June 14, 2022, https://fivethirtyeight.com/features/3-in-10-americans-named-political-polarization-as-a-top-issue-facing-the-country/.

9 Federal Elections Commission, "Federal Elections: 2012," July 2013, https://www.fec.gov/resources/cms-content/documents/federalelections2012.pdf.

10 Federal Elections Commission, "Federal Elections: 2016," December 2017, https://www.fec.gov/resources/cms-content/documents/federalelections2016.pdf.

11 Federal Elections Commission, "Federal Elections: 2020," October 2022, https://www.fec.gov/resources/cms-content/documents/federalelections2020.pdf.

12 Federal Elections Commission, "Official 2024 Presidential General Election Results," January 16, 2025, https://www.fec.gov/resources/cms-content/documents/2024presgeresults.pdf.

13 Rachel Kleinfeld, "Polarization, Democracy, and Political Violence in the United States: What the Research Says," Carnegie Endowment for International Peace, September 5, 2023, https://carnegieendowment.org/2023/09/05/polarization-democracy-and-political-violence-in-united-states-what-research-says-pub-90457#:~:text=American%20politicians%20are%20highly%20ideologically,steady%2C%20unpunctuated%20manner%20for%20decades.

14 Mark Murray and Alexandra Marquez, "Here's What's Driving American's Increasing Political Polarization," *Meet the Press Blog*, June 15, 2023, https://www.nbcnews.com/meet-the-press/meetthepressblog/s-s-driving-americas-increasing-political-polarization-rcna89559.

15 Yascha Mounk, "The Doom Spiral of Pernicious Polarization," *The Atlantic*, May 21, 2022, https://www.theatlantic.com/ideas/archive/2022/05/us-democrat-republican-partisan-polarization/629925/.

16 Elizabeth Kolbert, "How Politics Got So Polarized, *The New Yorker*, December 27, 2021, https://www.newyorker.com/magazine/2022/01/03/how-politics-got-so-polarized.

17 David Sims, "A Civil-War Movie with No One Cheering," *The Atlantic*, March 15, 2024, https://www.theatlantic.com/culture/archive/2024/03/civil-war-movie-review/677759/.

18 See Lewis M. Andrews, "The Subtle Tyranny of the 'Expert' Class," *The American Conservative*, May 11, 2020, https://www.theamericanconservative.com/the-subtle-tyranny-of-the-expert-class/.

19 Rotten Tomatoes, *The Boondock Saints*, https://www.rottentomatoes.com/m/boondock_saints.

20 Tom Disalvo and Diego Pineda Pacheco, 15 Notable Divides Between Audience and Critic Scores on Rotten Tomatoes, April 15, 2024, at https://collider.com/notable-divides-between-audience-critic-scores-on-rotten-tomatoes/; Rotten Tomatoes, *The Last Jedi*, https://www.rottentomatoes.com/m/star_wars_the_last_jedi.

21 Ibid.

22 Zeynep Tufekci, "We Were Badly Misled About the Event That Changed Our Lives," *The New York Times*, March 16, 2025, at https://www.nytimes.com/2025/03/16/opinion/covid-pandemic-lab-leak.html#.

23 See, for example, Mark Mazzetti et al., "Trump Officials Are Said to Press Spies to Link Virus and Wuhan Labs," *The New York Times*, January 5, 2021, https://www.nytimes.com/2020/04/30/us/politics/trump-administration-intelligence-coronavirus-china.html and Mark Harrington, "New York Times Changes Its Tune on Lab-Leak Theory," *UnHerd*, March 17, 2025, https://unherd.com/newsroom/new-york-times-changes-its-tune-on-lab-leak-theory/.

24 Tufekci, "We Were Badly Misled About the Event That Changed Our Lives."

25 John Ehrenreich, "School Closures Were Not a Crisis," *Slate*, December 18, 2023, at https://slate.com/technology/2023/12/school-closures-covid-pandemic-learning-loss.html.

26 Nancy Lee, COVID-19, School and Resilient Kids, Biscayne Times, November 2, 2020, at https://www.biscaynetimes.com/viewpoint/covid-19-school-and-resilient-kids/.

27 Liv Finne, "WEA Union President Says We Shouldn't Worry About How Closed Schools Are Harming Children, Because They Are All Falling Behind Together," Washington Policy Center, September 9, 202, at https://www.washingtonpolicy.org/publications/detail/wea-union-president-says-we-shouldnt-worry-about-how-closed-schools-are-harming-children-because-they-are-all-falling-behind-together.

28 National Center for Education Statistics, "Table 203.10 Enrollment in public elementary and secondary schools, by level and grade: Selected years, fall 1980 through fall 2031," 2023 *Digest of Education Statistics*, https://nces.ed.gov/programs/digest/d23/tables/dt23_203.10.asp.

29 Eric A. Hanushek and Bradley Strauss, "A Global Perspective on US Learning Losses," Hoover Education Success Initiative, February 2024, https://www.hoover.org/sites/default/files/research/docs/Hanushek-Strauss_WebreadyPDF_240229.pdf.

30 Chloe Shoemaker and Jonathan Butcher, "Youth Mental Health Crisis Gives More Urgency to School Choice Movement," *The Daily Signal*, March 30, 2022, https://www.dailysignal.com/2022/03/30/youth-mental-health-crisis-gives-more-urgency-to-school-choice-movement/.

31 Deni Mazrekaj and Kristof De Witte, The Impact of School Closures on Learning and Mental Health of Children: Lessons from the COVID-19 Pandemic, *Perspectives on Psychological Science*, Vol. 19, Issue 4, July 10, 2023, at https://journals.sagepub.com/doi/full/10.1177/17456916231181108.

32 Dana Goldstein and Sarah Mervosh, What We've Learned About School Closures for the Next Pandemic, *The New York Times*, March 13, 2025, at https://www.nytimes.com/2025/03/13/us/school-closures-future-pandemic.html.

33 Skelley and Fuong, "3 in 10 Americans Named Political Polarization as a Top Issue."

34 "Congress and the Public," Gallup, January 2, 2022, https://news.gallup.com/poll/1600/congress-public.aspx.

35 "Heading into Trump's Second Term, Americans Are Deeply Divided," Ipsos, January 18, 2025, https://www.ipsos.com/en-us/heading-trumps-second-term-americans-are-deeply-divided.

36 E. J. Dionne Jr. and Thomas E. Mann, "Polling & Public Opinion: The Good, the Bad, and the Ugly," Brookings, June 1, 2003, https://www.brookings.edu/articles/polling-public-opinion-the-good-the-bad-and-the-ugly/.

37 Ibid.

38 Ibid.

39 Ibid.

40 Ibid.

41 Different sources count the orders and other presidential actions differently, but reliable sources put the figure above 40. See "Presidential Actions," The White House, https://www.whitehouse.gov/presidential-actions/ and Sarah Fortinsky, "Trump Executive Orders and Actions: By the Numbers," *The Hill*, January 21, 2025, https://thehill.com/homenews/administration/5098445-trump-executive-orders-first-day/.

42 "2021 Joseph R. Biden, Jr. Executive Orders," *Federal Register*, https://www.federalregister.gov/presidential-documents/executive-orders/joe-biden/2021.

43 The White House, "Defending Women from Gender Ideology Extremism and Restoring Biological Truth to the Federal Government," Presidential Actions, January 20, 2025, https://www.whitehouse.gov/presidential-actions/2025/01/defending-women-from-gender-ideology-extremism-and-restoring-biological-truth-to-the-federal-government/.

44 The White House, "Protecting Children from Chemical and Surgical Mutilation," Presidential Actions, January 28, 2025, https://www.whitehouse.gov/presidential-actions/2025/01/protecting-children-from-chemical-and-surgical-mutilation/.

45 The White House, "Ending Illegal Discrimination and Restoring Merit-Based Opportunity," January 21, 2025, *https://www.whitehouse.gov/presidential-actions/2025/01/ending-illegal-discrimination-and-restoring-merit-based-opportunity/* and The White House, "Ending Radical and Wasteful Government DEI Programs and Preferencing," January 20, 2025, https://www.whitehouse.gov/presidential-actions/2025/01/ending-radical-and-wasteful-government-dei-programs-and-preferencing/.

46 The White House, "Ending Radical Indoctrination in K-12 Schooling," Presidential Actions, January 29, 2025, https://www.whitehouse.gov/presidential-actions/2025/01/ending-radical-indoctrination-in-k-12-schooling/.

47 The White House, "Reinstating Common Sense School Discipline Policies," Presidential Actions, April 23, 2025, https://www.whitehouse.gov/presidential-actions/2025/04/reinstating-common-sense-school-discipline-policies/.

48 White House, "Improving Education Outcomes by Empowering Parents, States, and Communities," Presidential Actions, March 20, 2025, https://www.whitehouse.gov/presidential-actions/2025/03/improving-education-outcomes-by-empowering-parents-states-and-communities/.

49 "Congress and the Public," Gallup.

50 *Students for Fair Admissions, Inc. v. President and Fellows of Harvard College,* 600 U.S. 181 (2023), 15.

51 Craig Trainor, "Dear Colleague" letter, February 14, 2025," U.S. Department of Education, https://www.ed.gov/media/document/dear-colleague-letter-sffa-v-harvard-109506.pdf.

52 Lindsey M. Burke et al., "Created Equal: A Road Map for an America Free of the Discrimination of Racial Preferences," Special Report No. 274, The Heritage Foundation, June 29, 2023, https://www.heritage.org/sites/default/files/2023-07/SR274.pdf; *Students for Fair Admissions v. Harvard.*

53 Trainor, "Dear Colleague" letter.

54 Megan Brenan, "American's Confidence in Higher Education Down Sharply," Gallup, July 11, 2023, https://news.gallup.com/poll/508352/americans-confidence-higher-education-down-sharply.aspx.

55 Jon Marcus, "A Looming 'Demographic Cliff': Fewer College Students and Ultimately Fewer Graduates," NPR, January 8, 2025, https://www.npr.org/2025/01/08/nx-s1-5246200/demographic-cliff-fewer-college-students-mean-fewer-graduates.

56 U.S. Department of Education, "U.S. Department of Education to Begin Federal Student Loan Collections, Other Actions to Help Borrowers Get Back into Repayment," Press Release, April 21, 2025, https://www.ed.gov/about/news/press-release/us-department-of-education-begin-federal-student-loan-collections-other-actions-help-borrowers-get-back-repayment.

57 Prableen Bajpai, "An Overview of the Trillion-Dollar Economies in the World," Nasdaq, April 29, 2022, https://www.nasdaq.com/articles/an-overview-of-the-trillion-dollar-economies-in-the-world; "Postsecondary Institution Revenues," National Center for

Education Studies, August 2023, https://nces.ed.gov/programs/coe/indicator/cud/postsecondary-institution-revenue; U.S. Department of Education, "U.S. Department of Education to Begin Federal Student Loan Collections, Other Actions to Help Borrowers Get Back into Repayment," Press Release, April 21, 2025, https://www.ed.gov/about/news/press-release/us-department-of-education-begin-federal-student-loan-collections-other-actions-help-borrowers-get-back-repayment.

58 For a review of the research demonstrating these findings, including research from the Brookings Institution and the American Enterprise Institute, as well as research journals, see the Heritage Foundation, "Teaching the Success Sequence to Help Every Child Succeed in School and in Life: Model State/District School Board Policy," Model Legislation, November 16, 2023, https://www.heritage.org/model-legislation/teaching-the-success-sequence-help-every-child-succeed-school-and-life-model-statedistrict. See also Brian Goesling, Hande Inanc, and Angela Rachidi, "Success Sequence: A Synthesis of the Literature," Administration for Children and Families, OPRE Report No. 2020-41, December 2020, p. 15, https://www.acf.hhs.gov/sites/default/files/documents/opre/Success_sequence_review_2020_508_0.pdf.

59 Brad Wilcox and Wendy Wang, "The Power of the Success Sequence," American Enterprise Institute, May 26, 2022, https://www.aei.org/research-products/report/the-power-of-the-success-sequence/.

60 The Nation's Report Card, "Fourth Graders' Mathematics Scores Improve Following Historic Drops, Eighth Graders Show No Change," Press Release, January 30, 2025, https://www.nationsreportcard.gov/reports/mathematics/2024/g4_8/supporting-files/2024rm-press-release.docx and The Nation's Report Card, "National Assessment of Educational Progress: Reading, 8th Grade," 2024 Results, available at https://www.nationsreportcard.gov/reports/reading/2024/g4_8/?grade=8.

61 Johnny Dodd and Lizzie Hyman, "After Revealing He Couldn't Read, Former Convict Is Inspiring Others on TikTok: Here's How (Exclusive)," *People*, December 2, 2023, https://people.com/after-revealing-he-couldnt-read-former-convict-inspiring-others-tiktok-exclusive-8408297; "Ryan Hudgins, "Oliver James, 34, Is Learning to Read and Posting About It on TikTok," *Today*, March 4, 2023, https://www.today.com/popculture/books/oliver-james-tiktok-illiteracy-reading-journey-rcna73255.

62 Governor's Early Literacy Foundation, "Early Literacy Connection to Incarceration," https://governorsfoundation.org/gelf-articles/early-literacy-connection-to-incarceration/; Elizabeth Greenberg et al., "Literacy Behind Bars: Results from the 2003 National Assessment of Adult Literacy Prison Survey," U.S. Department of Education, May 2007, https://nces.ed.gov/pubs2007/2007473.pdf; Herrick, E. "Prison Literacy Connection," *Corrections Compendium*, Volume: 16 Issue: 12 (December 1991) Pages: 1, 5-9, https://www.ojp.gov/ncjrs/virtual-library/abstracts/prison-literacy-connection#:~:text=The%20relationship%20between%20illiteracy%20and,is%20estimated%20at%2075%20percent.

63 "Know Your Rights: A Guide for Transgender and Gender Nonconforming Students," ACLU and GLSEN, July 26, 2017, https://assets.aclu.org/live/uploads/document/07-26-17TGNCStudentBrochure.pdf.

64 Marni Rose McFall, "Maps Shows States Which Passed Anti-Trans Legislation in 2024," *Newsweek*, November 29, 2024, https://www.newsweek.com/map-shows-states-which-passed-anti-trans-legislation-2024-1992353.

65 Jonathan Butcher, *Splintered: Critical Race Theory and the Progressive War on Truth* (Bombardier Books, 2022).

66 "A Look at the National Education Association's Spending, 2022–2023," Americans for Fair Treatment, https://americansforfairtreatment.org/resources-and-data/nea-where-do-your-union-dues-go/.

67 2022-2023 NEA Resolutions, I-54. White Supremacy Culture, at https://www.nea.org/sites/default/files/2022-08/nea-resolutions_2022-2023.pdf; Diana Lambert, John Fensterwald, and Zaidee Stavely, "Bill to Mandate 'Science of Reading' in California Schools Faces Teacher Union Opposition," *EdSource*, April 5, 2024, https://edsource.org/2024/bill-to-mandate-science-of-reading-in-california-schools-faces-teachers-union-opposition/709193.

68 Maxford Nelson, "Does the Montana Teachers Union Support Racist Organizations?" Freedom Foundation, April 7, 2025, https://www.freedomfoundation.com/labor/does-the-montana-teachers-union-support-racist-organizations/; Maxford Nelson, "Free Ride: How Idaho Tax Dollars Support Teachers Unions," Freedom Foundation, January 31, 2024, https://www.freedomfoundation.com/labor/free-ride-how-idaho-tax-dollars-support-teachers-unions/.

69 Jon Levine, "Powerful Teachers Union Influenced CDC on School Reopenings, Emails Show," *New York Post*, May 1, 2021, https://nypost.com/2021/05/01/teachers-union-collaborated-with-cdc-on-school-reopening-emails/.

70 See, for example, Matteo Cina, "San Francisco Mandates Teaching Gender Identity in Elementary School: 'Parental Involvement Not Required,'" Fox News, December 13, 2022, https://www.foxnews.com/us/san-francisco-mandates-teaching-gender-identity-elementary-school-parental-involvement. Despite the obvious evidence, it bears repeating today: "there are two—and only two—sexes: male and female, which refer to the two body structures (phenotypes) that, in normal development, correspond to one or the other gamete—sperm for males and ova for females." Source: Heritage Foundatoin, "Defining Sex Act," available at https://www.heritage.org/model-legislation/defining-sex-act.

71 Jonathan Butcher and Lindsey M. Burke, Ph.D., "The Education Lesson from COVID-19: School Choice Is Imperative for Every Child," The Heritage Foundation Backgrounder No. 3582, February 1, 2021, https://www.heritage.org/sites/default/files/2021-02/BG3582.pdf; see also Miranda Cyr, "New Mexico Education Officials: 12,000 Students Enrolled in the Spring Now Unaccounted for," Las Cruces Sun News, November 16, 2020, https://www.lcsun-news.com/story/news/education/2020/11/16/12-000-new-mexico-students-unaccounted-for-accordin gnmped/6320036002/?utm_content=bufferf96f9&utm_medium=social&utm_source=twitter.com&utm_campaign=buffer; Lily Altavena, "50,000 Students Are Gone From Arizona Public Schools. Where Did They Go?" *USA Today*, October 29, 2020, https://www.usatoday.com/story/news/local/arizona-education/2020/10/29/arizona-public-school-enrollment-down-50-k-where-did-students-go/6056383002/; Stephen Sawchuck and Christina A. Samuels, "Where Are They? Students Go Missing in Shift to Remote Classes," *Education Week*, April 10, 2020, https://www.edweek.org/leadership/where-are-they-students-go-missing-in-shift-to-remote-classes/2020/04; Michael Burke, "Thousands of Los Angeles High School Students Are Not Accessing Online Learning During School Closures," *EdSource*, March 30,

2020, https://edsource.org/2020/thousands-of-los-angeles-high-school-students-are-not-accessing-online-learning-during-school-closures/627448.

72 Return2Learn Tracker, "Enrollment Tracker: 2020-2022," https://www.returntole-arntracker.net/2020-22-enrollment-changes/.

73 Centers for Disease Control, "Emergency Department Visits for Suspected Suicide Attempts Among Persons Aged 12-25 Years Before and During the COVID-19 Pandemic—United States, January 2019-May 2021," June 18, 2021, https://www.cdc.gov/mmwr/volumes/70/wr/mm7024e1.htm.

CHAPTER ONE

1 *Students for Fair Admissions v. President and Fellows of Harvard College*, 600 U.S. 181 (2023).

2 Jonathan Butcher phone interview with Chad Ellis, February 26, 2024. See also Jonathan Butcher, "DEI, Sold as a Way to Promote Racial Harmony, Does Just the Opposite," The Heritage Foundation, March 11, 2024, https://www.heritage.org/civil-rights/commentary/dei-sold-way-promote-racial-harmony-does-just-the-opposite. The case documents for Ellis's lawsuit are available at Oklahoma Supreme Court, Case Number CV-2023-34, Pltiff's Brief in Chief, https://www.oscn.net/dockets/GetCaseInformation.aspx?db=osage&number=CV-2023-00034&cmid=2111069.

3 Ibid., Case No. CV-2023-34, Exhibit A, Letter from Susan E. Brandon to Chad Ellis, October 3, 2023.

4 Ibid., Case No. CV-2023-34, Proposition I, p. 15.

5 Ibid.

6 Case No. CV-2023-34, pp. 7, 9 .

7 Ibid., Exhibit A.

8 Ibid.

9 Ibid.

10 Ibid.

11 Frank Dobbin and Alexandra Kalev, "Why Doesn't Diversity Training Work? The Challenge for Industry and Academia," *Anthropology Now* 10 (2018): 48–55, https://scholar.harvard.edu/sites/scholar.harvard.edu/files/dobbin/files/an2018.pdf.

12 Jonathan Butcher, "Restoring Equality in Employment: Sinking the DEI Ship," Backgrounder No. 3875, The Heritage Foundation, November 27, 2024, https://www.heritage.org/sites/default/files/2024-11/BG3875.pdf.

13 Office of Florida Attorney General Ashley Moody, "Attorney General Moody Calls for Investigation into Starbucks Race-Based Quota Hiring Program," press release, May 22, 2024, https://www.myfloridalegal.com/newsrelease/attorney-general-moody-calls-investigation-starbucks-race-based-quota-hiring-program.

14 "Attorneys General of 13 States Issue Warning to Fortune 100 Companies Regarding Their Diversity and Inclusion Programs in Wake of Supreme Court's Decision Overturning Affirmative Action in Higher Education," Gibson Dunn, July 18, 2023, https://www.gibsondunn.com/attorneys-general-of-13-states-warning-to-fortune-100-companies-regarding-their-diversity-and-inclusion-programs-in-wake-of-supreme-court-decision/.

15 The White House, "Ending Racial and Wasteful Government DEI Programs and Preferencing," Presidential Actions, January 20, 2025, https://www.whitehouse.gov/presidential-actions/2025/01/ending-radical-and-wasteful-government-dei-programs-and-preferencing/; The White House, "Ending Illegal Discrimination and Restoring Merit-Based Opportunity," Presidential Actions, January 20, 2025, https://www.whitehouse.gov/presidential-actions/2025/01/ending-illegal-discrimination-and-restoring-merit-based-opportunity/.

16 Butcher, "Restoring Equality in Employment"; Jessica Guynn, "Inside Robby Starbuck's anti-DEI War on Tractor Supply, John Deere, and Harley-Davidson," USA Today, August 27, 2024, https://www.usatoday.com/story/money/2024/08/02/robby-starbuck-harley-davidson-john-deere-dei/74608637007/; Christopher F. Rufo, "Trump's DEI Move Is One to Celebrate," City Journal, January 21, 2025, https://www.city-journal.org/article/donald-trump-dei-executive-order.

17 Vincent Lloyd, "A Black Professor Trapped in Anti-Racist Hell," Compact, February 10, 2023, https://compactmag.com/article/a-black-professor-trapped-in-anti-racist-hell.

18 "What Is DEI?" McKinsey & Company, August 17, 2022, https://www.mckinsey.com/featured-insights/mckinsey-explainers/what-is-diversity-equity-and-inclusion.

19 Rohini Anand and Mary-Francis Winters, "A Retrospective View of Corporate Diversity Training from 1964 to the Present," Academy of Management Learning & Education, 7, no. 3, (September 2008): 356–72, https://ideas.wharton.upenn.edu/wp-content/uploads/2018/07/Anand-Winters-2008.pdf.

20 "DEI Study Group Report and Recommendations," Iowa Board of Regents, November 15–16, 2023, 2, https://www.iowaregents.edu/media/cms/1123_ITEM_11__DEI_Study_Group_Repor_CBA91840D4213.pdf.

21 "DEI Required: 67 Percent of Universities Mandate 'Diversity' Indoctrination," Speech First, April 15, 2024, https://speechfirst.org/news/dei-required-67-of-universities-mandate-diversity-indoctrination/.

22 Lloyd, "A Black Professor Trapped in Anti-Racist Hell."

23 Ibram X. Kendi, How to Be an Antiracist (New York: One World, 2019), 19; Rachel Poser, "Ibram X. Kendi Faces a Reckoning of His Own," New York Times Magazine, June 4, 2024, https://www.nytimes.com/2024/06/04/magazine/ibram-kendi-center-for-antiracist-research.html.

24 Kendi, How to Be an Antiracist, 180.

25 Ibram X. Kendi, "The Civil Rights Act Was a Victory Against Racism. But Racists Also Won," The Washington Post, July 2, 2017, https://www.washingtonpost.com/news/made-by-history/wp/2017/07/02/the-civil-rights-act-was-a-victory-against-racism-but-racists-also-won/; Richard Delgado, "The Shadows and the Fire: Three Puzzles for Civil Rights Scholars: An Essay in Honor of Derrick Bell," Alabama Civil Rights and & Civil Liberties Law Review 6 (2014): 21–44, https://scholarship.law.ua.edu/fac_essays/64.

26 Ibid., pp. 26–27.

27 Tabia Lee, "A Black DEI Director Cancelled by DEI," Compact, March 31, 2023, https://compactmag.com/article/a-black-dei-director-canceled-by-dei.

28 Doug Most, "As BU Launches Inquiry into Center for Antiracist Research, Interim President Freeman Explains Goal and Reasoning," *BU Today*, September 21, 2023, https://www.bu.edu/articles/2023/bu-launches-inquiry-into-center-for-antiracist-research/; Poser, "Ibram X. Kendi Faces a Reckoning."

29 Dobbin and Kalev, "Why Doesn't Diversity Training Work?"; Elizabeth Levy Paluck and Donald P. Green, "Prejudice Reduction: What Works? A Review and Assessment of Research and Practice," *Annual Review of Psychology* 60 (January 10, 2009): 339–67, https://www.annualreviews.org/doi/full/10.1146/annurev.psych.60.110707.163607; Patrick S. Forscher et al., "A Meta-Analysis of Procedures to Change Implicit Measures," *Journal of Personality and Social Psychology* 117 (August 9, 2019): 522–59, https://psyarxiv.com/dv8tu/; Carol T. Kulik and Loriann Roberson, "Common Goals and Golden Opportunities: Evaluations of Diversity Education in Academic and Organizational Settings," *Academy of Management Learning & Education* 7, no. 3 (2008), https://journals.aom.org/doi/abs/10.5465/amle.2008.34251670; C. K. Lai et al., "Reducing Implicit Racial Preferences: II. Intervention Effectiveness Across Time," *Journal of Experimental Psychology: General* 145, no. 8 (2016), 1001–16, https://doi.org/10.1037/xge0000179.

30 Akita Jagdeep et al., "Instructing Animosity: How DEI Pedagogy Produces the Hostile Attribution Bias," Network Contagion Research Institute and Rutgers University Social Perception Lab, November 2024, https://networkcontagion.us/wp-content/uploads/Instructing-Animosity_11.13.24.pdf.

31 Steph Solis, "BU Closes Antiracist Research Center as Founding Director Leaves," *Axios*, January 31, 2025, https://www.axios.com/local/boston/2025/01/31/bu-closes-antiracist-research-center-ibram-x-kendi-leaves.

32 Nikki Graph, "Most Americans Say Colleges Should Not Consider Race or Ethnicity in Admissions," Pew Research Center, February 25, 2019, https://www.pewresearch.org/short-reads/2019/02/25/most-americans-say-colleges-should-not-consider-race-or-ethnicity-in-admissions/.

33 Vianney Gómez, "As Courts Weigh Affirmative Action, Grades and Test Scores Seen as Top Factors in College Admissions," Pew Research Center, April 26, 2022, https://www.pewresearch.org/short-reads/2022/04/26/u-s-public-continues-to-view-grades-test-scores-as-top-factors-in-college-admissions/.

34 "Asian Americans Hold Mixed Views Around Affirmative Action," Pew Research Center, June 8, 2023, https://www.pewresearch.org/race-and-ethnicity/2023/06/08/asian-americans-hold-mixed-views-around-affirmative-action/.

35 See the essays in "Toward a Critical Cultural Pluralism: Progressive Alternatives to Mainstream Civil Rights Ideology," in Kimberlé Crenshaw et al., eds., *Critical Race Theory: The Key Writings That Formed the Movement* (The New Press: New York, 1995), 124–200.

36 See, for example, Allison Davis-White Eyes, "Statement from the VP of DEI: The U.S. Supreme Court's Affirmative Action Ruling," Fielding Graduate University, June 29, 2023, https://www.fielding.edu/statement-from-the-vp-of-dei-on-the-us-supreme-courts-affirmative-action-ruling/.

37 Please note, again, that my sample of school board members is not nationally representative.

38 Civil Rights Act of 1964, 42 U.S.C., § 2000d, https://www.govinfo.gov/content/pkg/USCODE-2008-title42/html/USCODE-2008-title42-chap21-subchapV.htm.

39 Phone interview with Wayne Lewis, conducted by Jonathan Butcher, March 15, 2024.

40 Ibid.

41 Ibid.

42 Ibid.

43 Over the last decade, many parents have soured on the use of tests to evaluate their children, arguing that schools "overtest" pupils. While the 5–7 percentage point difference between the share of parents who favored the use of student GPA and the shares of school board members and the general public who said GPA was more important than standardized test is not a large difference, parental dissatisfaction with testing in recent years may help explain that difference. See, for example, Amanda Paulson, "Standardized Test Backlash: More Parents Pull Kids from Exams as Protest," *Christian Science Monitor*, April 30, 2015, https://www.csmonitor.com/USA/Education/2015/0430/Standardized-test-backlash-More-parents-pull-kids-from-exams-as-protest.

44 Andrew D. Martin, "Our Commitment to Diversity," Letter to the Washington University of St. Louis Community, June 29, 2023, https://andrewdmartin.washu.edu/our-commitment-to-diversity/.

45 *Students for Fair Admissions, Inc. v. President and Fellows of Harvard College*, 600 U.S. 181 (2023), 230–31.

46 Martin, "Our Commitment to Diversity," Letter to the Washington University of St. Louis Community.

47 Doug Hicks, "Supreme Court College Admissions Decision," Davidson College Press Release, July 3, 2023, https://newsofdavidson.org/2023/07/03/61505/supreme-court-college-admissions-decision/.

48 Oberlin Office of the President, "The Supreme Court Decision on Affirmative Action," Oberlin College & Conservatory, June 29, 2023, https://www.oberlin.edu/president/supreme-court-decision-affirmative-action; University of Michigan Office of the President, "Statement on the Supreme Court's Affirmative Action Ruling," University of Michigan, June 29, 2023, https://president.umich.edu/news-communications/messages-to-the-community/statement-on-supreme-courts-affirmative-action-ruling/; BU Today Staff, "Disappointed and Determined, BU Community Reacts to SCOTUS Affirmative Action Ruling," *BU Today*, June 29, 2023, https://www.bu.edu/articles/2023/bu-community-reacts-to-scotus-affirmative-action-ruling/#:~:text=While%20we%20are%20disappointed%20with,talents%20will%20contribute%20to%20the.

49 Phone interview with Wayne Lewis, conducted by Jonathan Butcher, March 15, 2024.

50 Ibid.

51 Civil Rights Act, §2000d.

52 Iowa Board of Regents DEI Study Group Report and Recommendations, provided to the governor and General Assembly on November 27, 2023, pp. 11–12, https://www.legis.iowa.gov/docs/publications/DF/1387350.pdf.

53 Ibid., p. 12.

54 Ibid., p. 13.

55 Senate Bill 17, 88th Regular Session (2023), Texas Education Code § 51.3525, https://capitol.texas.gov/tlodocs/88R/billtext/html/SB00017F.htm.

56 Senate Bill 266, 2023 Regular Session, Florida Statutes § 1004.06, https://www.flsenate.gov/Session/Bill/2023/266/BillText/er/PDF.

57 See Heritage Foundation Data Visualizations, "DEI: A State Legislation Tracker," available at https://datavisualizations.heritage.org/education/dei-a-state-legislation-tracker/.

58 Robby Soave, "Berkeley Weeded Out Job Applicants Who Didn't Propose Specific Plans to Advance Diversity," *Reason*, February 3, 2020, https://reason.com/2020/02/03/university-of-california-diversity-initiative-berkeley/.

59 "The New Loyalty Oaths," Goldwater Institute, January 17, 2023, https://www.goldwaterinstitute.org/policy-report/the-new-loyalty-oaths/.

60 Steve McGuire (@sfmcguire79), "UPDATE: a new factsheet released by Arizona State University addresses the use of DEI statements in hiring," July 15, 2023, Twitter, https://twitter.com/sfmcguire79/status/1680235793808252928?s=61&t=EP8g_wipfg-ejvL4tqi1rg.

61 Matt Beienburg, "Billions for DEI in Higher Ed: The Cost of Indoctrination," Goldwater Institute, January 15, 2025, https://www.goldwaterinstitute.org/policy-report/billions-for-dei-in-higher-ed-the-cost-of-indoctrination/; U.S. Department of Education, "U.S. Department of Education Cuts Over $600 Million in Divisive Teacher Training Grants," press release, February 17, 2025, https://www.ed.gov/about/news/press-release/us-department-of-education-cuts-over-600-million-divisive-teacher-training-grants.

62 "About," Harvard Office for Equity, Diversity, Inclusion & Belonging, https://edib.harvard.edu/about.

63 Knight Foundation, "College Student Views on Free Expression and Campus Speech 2024," July 2024, https://knightfoundation.org/wp-content/uploads/2024/07/Knight-Fdn_Free-Expression_2024_072424_FINAL-1.pdf.

64 "UChicago/AP-NORC Free Expression Poll," The University of Chicago and Associated Press-NORC, https://apnorc.org/wp-content/uploads/2023/09/UChicago_AP-NORC-Free-Expression-Poll-Topline-Final.pdf. The survey interviews were conducted September 7–11, 2023.

65 Zach Kessel, "Jewish Students Hid in NYC College Library as Pro-Palestinian Protestors Banged on Doors, Called for 'Intifada,'" *National Review*, October 26, 2023, https://www.nationalreview.com/news/jewish-students-hid-in-nyc-college-library-as-pro-palestinian-protesters-banged-on-doors-called-for-intifada/.

66 Salvador Hernandez, "Pro-Palestinian Protestors Shut Down Event Organized by Jewish Student Groups at UC Berkeley," *Los Angeles Times*, February 27, 2024, https://www.latimes.com/california/story/2024-02-27/pro-palestinian-protesters-shut-down-event-organized-by-jewish-students-at-uc-berkeley.

67 "Fairfax County Schools Defending $20K Presentation from Anti-Racism Scholar," Fox 5 Washington DC, September 25, 2020, https://www.fox5dc.com/news/fairfax-county-schools-defending-20k-presentation-from-anti-racism-scholar.

68 Rik Kirkland and Iris Bonnet, "Focusing on What Works for Workplace Diversity," McKinsey & Company, April 7, 2017, https://www.mckinsey.com/featured-insights/gender-equality/focusing-on-what-works-forworkplace-diversity#; Butcher, *Splintered: Critical Race Theory and the Progressive War on Truth*, p. 107.

69 "GrantED: Exposing $1 Billion in Department of Education Grant Funding that Has Entrenched Far-Left Ideologies in Education," Parents Defending Education, December 12, 2024, https://defendinged.org/investigations/granted/.

70 Beienburg, "Billions for DEI."

71 Emily Peck, "Americans Are Fine with Corporate DEI," *Axios*, January 17, 2025, https://www.axios.com/2025/01/17/diversity-initiatives-workers-trump.

72 See, for example, Carol T. Kulik and Loriann Roberson, "Common Goals and Golden Opportunities: Evaluations of Diversity Education in Academic and Organizational Settings," Academy of Management Learning & Education, Vol. 7, No. 3 (2008), https://journals.aom.org/doi/abs/10.5465/amle.2008.34251670; Patrick S. Forscher et al., "A Meta-Analysis of Procedures to Change Implicit Measures," PsyArXiv, August 9, 2019, https://psyarxiv.com/dv8tu/; Elizabeth Levy Paluck and Donald P. Green, "Prejudice Reduction: What Works? A Review and Assessment of Research and Practice," *Annual Review of Psychology*, Vol. 60 (January 10, 2009), pp. 339–367, https://www.annualreviews.org/doi/full/10.1146/annurev.psych.60.110707.163607; and C. K. Lai et al., "Reducing Implicit Racial Preferences: II. Intervention Effectiveness Across Time," *Journal of Experimental Psychology: General*, Vol. 145, No. 8 (2016), pp. 1001–1016, https://doi.org/10.1037/xge0000179.

73 Richard Delgado and Jean Stefancic, *Critical Race Theory: An Introduction* (New York: New York University Press, 2001), 3.

74 Jamelle Bouie, "What Americans Really Think About 'Critical Race Theory,'" *The New York Times*, February 26, 2022, https://www.nytimes.com/2022/02/26/opinion/critical-race-theory-survey.html.

75 Peter Ramjug, "Seven Out of 10 People Don't Know What Critical Race Theory Is, US Poll Finds," December 23, 2021, https://news.northeastern.edu/2021/12/23/critical-race-theory-survey/.

76 Crenshaw et al., eds., *Critical Race Theory*, xvii–xviii.

77 Ibid., xviii.

78 Ibid., xv.

79 Richard Delgado, "The Shadows and the Fire: Three Puzzles for Civil Rights Scholars: An Essay in Honor of Derrick Bell," University of Alabama Law School, April 2017, p. 44, https://www.law.ua.edu/acrcl/files/2017/04/The_Shadows_And_The_Fire.pdf.

80 Kendi, "The Civil Rights Act."

81 Parents Defending Education, "POLL: Americans Overwhelmingly Reject 'Woke' Race and Gender Policies in K–12 Education," press release, May 10, 2021, https://defendinged.org/press-releases/poll-americans-overwhelmingly-reject-woke-race-and-gender-policies-in-k-12-education/.

82 Zoe Kalen Hill, "Majority of Americans Hold Negative View of Critical Race Theory amid Controversy," *Newsweek*, June 16, 2021, https://www.newsweek.com/majority-americans-hold-negative-view-critical-race-theory-amid-controversy-1601337.

83 Lindsey Burke et al., "The Culture of American K–12 Education: A National Survey of Parents and School Board Members," Special Report No. 241, The Heritage Foundation, January 11, 2021, https://www.heritage.org/sites/default/files/2021-01/SR241.pdf.

84 Joshua Dunn, "Critical Race Theory Goes to Court," in *The Critical Classroom: How Critical Theory Undermines Academic Excellence and Individual Agency in Education*, Lindsey Burke, Jonathan Butcher, and Jay Greene, eds. (Washington, D.C.: The Heritage Foundation, 2022), p. 55.

85 "Affinity Groups," Parents Defending Education, https://defendinged.org/resources/affinity-groups/#:~:text=Affinity%20groups%20are%20school%2Dsponsored,%E2%80%9D%20and%20%E2%80%9Chealing%20spaces.%E2%80%9D.

86 Ibid.; James Sidanius et al., "Ethnic Enclaves and the Dynamics of Social Identity on the College Campus: The Good, the Bad, and the Ugly," *Journal of Personality and Social Psychology* 87, no. 1 (2004): 96–110, https://dash.harvard.edu/bitstream/handle/1/3205411/Sidanius_EthnicEnclaves.pdf?sequence=1.

87 "Affinity Groups."

88 Jonathan Butcher phone interview with Wayne Lewis, March 15, 2024.

CHAPTER TWO

1 Aristotle, *Nicomachean Ethics*, trans. D. P. Chase (London: Henry Hammans, 1861), p. 317.

2 Melissa Jackson and Beanie Geoghegan, interview with Jonathan Butcher, October 27, 2023.

3 Black Lives Matter, "Act Now to Defund the Police and Invest in Communities," https://blacklivesmatter.com/actions/act-now-to-defund-the-police-and-invest-in-communities/; Black Lives Matter at School Week of Action, "Guiding Principles," https://www.blacklivesmatteratschool.com/guiding-principles.html.

4 Mike Gonzalez, *BLM: The Making of a New Marxist Revolution* (New York: Encounter, 2021), Kindle edition, location 1315.

5 Michelle Watson, "Black Lives Matter Executive Accused of 'Syphoning' $10M from BLM Donors, Suit Says," CNN, September 5, 2022, https://www.cnn.com/2022/09/04/us/black-lives-matter-executive-lawsuit/index.html.

6 Juliana Menasce Horowitz et al., "Support for the Black Lives Matter Movement Has Dropped Considerably from Its Peak in 2020," Pew Research, June 14, 2023, https://www.pewresearch.org/social-trends/2023/06/14/support-for-the-black-lives-matter-movement-has-dropped-considerably-from-its-peak-in-2020/.

7 Jackson, interview.

8 Melissa Jackson and Beanie Geoghegan, interview with Jonathan Butcher, October 27, 2023.

9 Megan Brenan, "Americans' View of K–12 Education Improves from 2023 Low," Gallup, August 28, 2024, https://news.gallup.com/poll/649385/americans-view-education-improves-2023-low.aspx.

10 Lydia Saad, "Americans' State of the Nation Ratings Remain at Record Low," Gallup,

February 5, 2025, https://news.gallup.com/poll/656114/americans-state-nation-ratings-remain-record-low.aspx.

11 Michael B. Henderson et al., "Pandemic Parent Survey Finds Perverse Pattern: Students Are More Likely to Be Attending School in Person Where Covid Is Spreading More Rapidly," *Education Next* 21, no. 2 (spring 2021), https://www.educationnext.org/pandemic-parent-survey-finds-perverse-pattern-students-more-likely-to-be-attending-school-in-person-where-covid-is-spreading-more-rapidly/.

12 "Survey of Public Opinion: Trends Through 2022," *Education Next*, https://www.educationnext.org/ednext-poll-interactive-trends-through-2022-public-opinion/.

13 Megan Brenan, "K-12 Education Satisfaction in U.S. Ties Record Low," Gallup, August 31, 2023, https://news.gallup.com/poll/510401/education-satisfaction-ties-record-low.aspx.

14 "Public School Enrollment," National Center for Education Statistics, May 2023, https://nces.ed.gov/programs/coe/indicator/cga/public-school-enrollment.

15 "Public Charter School Enrollment," National Center for Education Statistics, May 2023, https://nces.ed.gov/programs/coe/indicator/cgb/public-charter-enrollment; Peter Jamison et al., "Home Schooling's Rise from Fringe to Fastest-Growing form of Education," *The Washington Post*, October 31, 2023, https://www.washingtonpost.com/education/interactive/2023/homeschooling-growth-data-by-district/.

16 Melissa Jackson and Beanie Geoghegan, interview with Jonathan Butcher, October 27, 2023.

17 Claudine Geoghegan, "Testimony to the U.S. House of Representatives Committee on the Judiciary Subcommittee on the Constitution and Limited Government," April 16, 2024, p. 1, https://www.iwf.org/wp-content/uploads/2024/04/Beanie-Geoghegan-written-testimony-House-Judiciary-4.16.2024.pdf.

18 Ibid., p. 2.

19 Sarah Mervosh and Francesca Paris, "Why School Absences Have 'Exploded' Almost Everywhere," *The New York Times*, March 29, 2024, https://www.nytimes.com/interactive/2024/03/29/us/chronic-absences.html. The *Times* report is citing American Enterprise Institute data from C2i, Return2Learn Tracker, which is available at https://www.returntolearntracker.net/.

20 Danyela Souza Egorov, "Chronic Absenteeism Is Hampering School Improvement Efforts in New York City: What Can Be Done About It, Table 1," Manhattan Institute Issue Brief, March 6, 2025, https://manhattan.institute/article/chronic-absenteeism-hampering-school-improvement-efforts-new-york-city?.

21 Institute for Education Sciences, National Center for Education Statistics, *Digest of Education Statistics*, Table 215.30 Enrollment, poverty, and federal funds for the 120 largest school districts, by enrollment size in 2021: School year 2019-20 and fiscal year 2022, https://nces.ed.gov/programs/digest/d22/tables/dt22_215.30.asp?current=yes.

22 Mervosh and Paris, "Why School Absences Have 'Exploded' Almost Everywhere," *The New York Times*.

23 Institute for Education Sciences, National Center for Education Statistics, "2024 Mathematics and Reading at Grades 4 and 8," press release, January 29, 2025; Insti-

tute for Education Sciences, National Center for Education Statistics, "Program for International Student Assessment (PISA) 2022 U.S. Results," https://nces.ed.gov/surveys/pisa/pisa2022/index.asp#/.

24 Institute for Education Sciences, National Center for Education Statistics, "Program for International Student Assessment (PISA) 2022 U.S. Results."

25 The Nation's Report Card, "NAEP Report Card: Reading, National Trends and Student Skills, 4th Grade," https://www.nationsreportcard.gov/reports/reading/2024/g4_8/national-trends/?grade=4.

26 The Nation's Report Card, "Civics," https://www.nationsreportcard.gov/civics/; The Nation's Report Card, "History," https://www.nationsreportcard.gov/ushistory/; The Nation's Report Card, "Geography," https://www.nationsreportcard.gov/highlights/geography/2018/.

27 Lindsey M. Burke, Ph.D., Jonathan Butcher, Emilie Kao, and Mike Gonzalez, "The Culture of American K-12 Education: A National Survey of Parents and School Board Members," Heritage Foundation Special Report No. 241, January 11, 2021, https://www.heritage.org/sites/default/files/2021-01/SR241.pdf. This report found that school board members believe civics should be taught more in schools. See also Jack Miller Center, "New Poll Shows Parents Overwhelmingly Agree: Stop Politicizing Civic Education, Prioritize Founding Documents and Ideas," Press Release, December 8, 2022, https://www.jackmillercenter.org/press-release/nationwide-parents-poll-on-civic-education. This poll found, "Among those surveyed, 89% agree that a civic education about our nation's founding principles is 'very important.' Over 92% of parents believe that the achievements of key historical figures should be taught even if their views do not align with modern values."

28 Ibid.

29 See APM Reports, "Reading," available at https://features.apmreports.org/reading/; Eliza Billingham and Emily Hanford, "'This Is My Kid, This Is Our Story,' Messages from Listeners," *Sold a Story*, May 11, 2023, https://www.apmreports.org/story/2023/05/11/sold-a-story-messages-from-listeners.

30 See Emily Hanford, *Sold a Story*, Podcast and Reporting, AMP Reports, available at https://features.apmreports.org/sold-a-story/.

31 Billingham and Hanford, "'This Is My Kid, This Is Our Story,' Messages from Listeners."

32 Emily Hanford, *Sold a Story*, https://features.apmreports.org/sold-a-story/; Emily Hanford, "Experts Say Widely Used Reading Curriculum Is Failing Kids," *The Educate Podcast*, January 27, 2020, https://www.apmreports.org/episode/2020/01/27/lucy-calkins-reading-materials-review. For more research on phonics, see Anderson, Richard C. et al., *Becoming a Nation of Readers* (Urbana: Illinois University, 1985), available at https://files.eric.ed.gov/fulltext/ED253865.pdf.

33 Anderson et al., *Becoming a Nation of Readers*, and this is the main topic of Hanford's research cited in this book. See also James S. Kim, "Research and the Reading Wars" in *When Research Matters*, Frederick Hess and Lorraine M. McDonnel, eds. (Cambridge: Harvard Education Press, 2008), https://scholar.harvard.edu/sites/scholar.harvard.edu/files/jameskim/files/bookch2.pdf and Jeanne S. Chall, *Learning to Read: The Great Debate* (New York: McGraw Hill, 1967).

34 Andrew J. Coulson, *Market Education: The Unknown History* (New Brunswick: Transaction Publishers, 1999), p. 16.

35 Ibid., See also Anderson et al., p. 46, 50.

36 Teacher interview via e-mail with Jonathan Butcher, April 4, 2024 (teacher requested name be withheld).

37 Susan Wise Bauer and Jessie Wise, *The Well-Trained Mind* (New York: W. W. Norton & Company, 2009), p. 33; Anderson et al., pp. 22–23, 33. "Phonics is the student of speech equivalents of printed symbols and their use in pronouncing printed and written words," see Chall, p. 14.

38 Emily Hanford, "Sold a Story, Episode 1: The Problem," Podcast, October 20, 2022, transcript available at https://www.apmreports.org/episode/2022/10/20/sold-a-story-e1-the-problem#transcript; see also Wise Bauer and Wise, pp. 221-225.

39 Anderson et al., pp. 22–23, 33.

40 University of Chicago, "Phonics v. Whole Word: The Science of Reading, with Adrian Johns," University of Chicago News, https://news.uchicago.edu/phonics-vs-whole-word-science-reading; see also Wise Bauer and Wise, p. 222.

41 Wise Bauer and Wise, pp. 221–225; Coulson, pp. 161–168.

42 Emily Hanford, "Influential Literacy Expert Lucy Calkins Is Changing Her Views," APM Reports, October 16, 2020, https://www.apmreports.org/story/2020/10/16/influential-literacy-expert-lucy-calkins-is-changing-her-views.

43 Emily Hanford, "Sold a Story E3: The Battle," October 22, 2022, https://www.apmreports.org/episode/2022/10/27/sold-a-story-e3-the-battle; see also Coulson, pp. 161-168.

44 Hanford, "Influential Literacy Expert Lucy Calkins Is Changing Her Views."

45 See Anderson et al. *Becoming a Nation of Readers*; Kim, "Research and the Reading Wars", p. 93.

46 Coulson, p. 161–168; Wise Bauer and Wise, pp. 221–225.

47 Ibid.

48 Christopher Peak, "New Reading Laws Sweep the Nation Following Sold a Story," APM Reports, November 18, 2024, https://www.apmreports.org/story/2024/11/18/legislators-reading-laws-sold-a-story.

49 A recent study that found these results is Student Achievement Partners, "Comparing Reading Research to Program Design," January 2020, https://achievethecore.org/content/upload/Comparing%20Reading%20Research%20to%20Program%20Design_An%20Examination%20of%20Teachers%20College%20Units%20of%20Study%20FINAL.pdf. See also Kim, "Research and the Reading Wars" in *When Research Matters*, p. 93.

50 Ibid.

51 The Nation's Report Card, "Fourth Graders' Mathematics Scores Improve Following Historic Drops, Eighth Graders Show No Change," press release, January 30, 2025, https://www.nationsreportcard.gov/media.aspx.

52 Ibid.

53 E. D. Hirsch, Jr., "Curriculum and Competence," in *A Primer on America's Schools*, Terry Moe, ed., (Stanford: Hoover Institution Press, 2001), p. 197.

54 See Core Knowledge Foundation, "Knowledge-Based Schooling," available at https://www.coreknowledge.org/knowledge-based-schooling/.

55 See Rachel Alexander Cambre, Ph.D., "Classical Schools in America: A Movement of Hope," Heritage Foundation First Principles No. 100, August 2024, https://www.heritage.org/sites/default/files/2024-08/FP100_0.pdf. Cambre's report provides the characteristics that classical schools tend to share in common, such as instruction in Latin and Greek, requirements that students memorize large sections of text, dividing students within the school into different "houses" for competitions, and more.

56 Governor's Early Literacy Foundation, "Early Literacy Connection to Incarceration," https://governorsfoundation.org/gelf-articles/early-literacy-connection-to-incarceration/; Elizabeth Greenberg et al., "Literacy Behind Bars: Results from the 2003 National Assessment of Adult Literacy Prison Survey," U.S. Department of Education, May 2007, https://nces.ed.gov/pubs2007/2007473.pdf.

57 Hirsch, Jr., "Curriculum and Competence," p. 199.

58 Governor's Early Literacy Foundation, "Early Literacy Connection to Incarceration."

59 Herrick, E. "Prison Literacy Connection," *Corrections Compendium*, Volume: 16 Issue: 12 (December 1991) Pages: 1, 5–9, https://www.ojp.gov/ncjrs/virtual-library/abstracts/prison-literacy-connection#:~:text=The%20relationship%20between%20illiteracy%20and,is%20estimated%20at%2075%20percent.

60 U.S. Department of Justice, "Special Report: Profile of Prison Inmates, 2016," Office of Justice Programs, December 2021, p. 6, https://bjs.ojp.gov/content/pub/pdf/ppi16.pdf.

61 Bobby D. Rampey et al., "Highlights from the U.S. PIAAC Survey of Incarcerated Adults: Their Skills, Work Experience, Education, and Training," Program for the International Assessment of Adult Competencies: 2014, November 2016, p. 6, https://nces.ed.gov/pubs2016/2016040.pdf.

62 Governor's Early Literacy Foundation, "Early Literacy Connection to Incarceration."

63 Rampey et al., "Highlights from the U.S. PIAAC Survey of Incarcerated Adults: Their Skills, Work Experience, Education, and Training," p. 9.

64 "In 2010, the institutionalization rate for this group [Black men aged 20 to 24] dropped to 26%, but, as was the case in 2000, they were more likely to be institutionalized than they were to be employed (19% employment rate in 2010)." See George Gao, "Chart of the Week: The Black-White Gap in Incarceration Rates," Pew Research Center, July 18, 2014, https://www.pewresearch.org/short-reads/2014/07/18/chart-of-the-week-the-black-white-gap-in-incarceration-rates/.

65 Institute for Education Sciences, National Center for Education Statistics, "2024 Reading Trial Urban District Snapshot Report, Chicago, Grade 4," https://nces.ed.gov/nationsreportcard/subject/publications/dst2024/pdf/2024220XC4.pdf.

66 Chicago Public Schools, FY 2025 Budget, March 5, 2025, https://www.cps.edu/about/finance/budget/budget-2025/; Samantha Smylie, "While the State Faces a Tighter Budget, Illinois' Schools Chief Asks for a Boost in Education Funding," *Chalkbeat Chicago*, January 15, 2025, https://www.chalkbeat.org/chicago/2025/01/15/illinois-education-officials-approve-2026-budget-proposal/; Illinois' Governor's Office of Management and Budget, "FY 2025 Illinois Economic and Fiscal Policy Report," p. 15, https://budget.illinois.gov/content/dam/soi/en/web/budget/documents/

economic-and-fiscal-policy-reports/Economic_and_Fiscal_Policy_Report_FY25_
FINAL_11.1.24.pdf.

67 Kim, "Research and the Reading Wars", p. 102,

68 *The New England Primer*, available at https://dn790002.ca.archive.org/0/items/
newenglandprimer00fordiala/newenglandprimer00fordiala.pdf and Robert Emans,
"History of Phonics," Elementary English 45 (May 1968), pp. 602–608, https://
www.jstor.org/stable/41386374.

69 Emans, pp. 602–608.

70 Emans, pp. 602–608.

71 Kim, p. 89.

72 Horace Mann, "Lecture on the mode of preparing and using spelling books, delivered
before the American Institute of Instruction, etc." United States: n.p., 1841, available
at https://babel.hathitrust.org/cgi/pt?id=hvd.32044028949212&seq=18.

73 Ibid., p. 16.

74 Coulson, p. 164.

75 Ibid.

76 Kim, p. 90.

77 Kim, p. 92.

78 Coulson, *Market Education: The Unknown History*, p. 163.

79 Emans, p. 602.

80 Wise and Wise Bauer, p. 222.

81 Anderson et al., *Becoming a Nation of Readers*.

82 Kim, "Research and the Reading Wars," p. 95.

83 Anderson et al., *Becoming a Nation of Readers*, p. vi.

84 Ibid, p. 37. See footnote 50 on that page for a list of resources documenting the
effectiveness of phonics, including J.S. Chall, Learning to Read: The Great Debate
(2nd ed.), (New York: McGraw-Hill, 1983).

85 Emily Hanford, "At a Loss for Words," APM Reports, August 22, 2019, https://www.
apmreports.org/episode/2019/08/22/whats-wrong-how-schools-teach-reading.

86 Ibid. and Hanford cites Keith E. Stanovich, "Romance and Reality," *The Reading
Teacher*, December 1993, Vol. 47, No. 4, pp. 280–291, available at http://www.
keithstanovich.com/Site/Research_on_Reading_files/RdTch93.pdf.

87 Hanford, "At a Loss for Words."

88 Student Achievement Partners, "Comparing Reading Research to Program Design,"
January 2020, https://achievethecore.org/content/upload/Comparing%20Read-
ing%20Research%20to%20Program%20Design_An%20Examination%20of%20
Teachers%20College%20Units%20of%20Study%20FINAL.pdf.

89 Hanford, "Experts Say Widely Used Reading Curriculum Is Failing Kids"; Student
Achievement Partners, "Comparing Reading Research to Program Design," p. 11.

90 Student Achievement Partners, "Comparing Reading Research to Program Design,"
p. 9.

91 Student Achievement Partners, "Comparing Reading Research to Program Design,"

p. 6; Cindy Jiban, "The Science of Reading Explained," NWEA, February 15, 2024, https://www.nwea.org/blog/2024/the-science-of-reading-explained/.

92 The Reading League, "What Is the Science of Reading," https://www.thereadingleague. org/what-is-the-science-of-reading/.

93 Emily Hanford, "Experts Say Widely Used Reading Curriculum Is Failing Kids," APM Reports, January 27, 2020, https://www.apmreports.org/episode/2020/01/27/ lucy-calkins-reading-materials-review.

94 E-mail and text exchange with teacher, multiple dates, March 2025 (teacher requested that name be withheld).

95 Teacher interview via e-mail with Jonathan Butcher, April 4, 2024 (teacher requested name be withheld).

96 Ibid.

97 Wise and Wise Bauer, p. 221.

98 Ibid.

99 Ibid., p. 224.

100 Ibid., p. 222.

101 Ibid., p. 168.

102 Wise and Wise Bauer, p. 223.

103 Karen Diegmueller, "Clinton Proposal Puts Attention on Early Reading Instruction," *Education Week*, September 11, 1996, https://www.edweek.org/teaching-learning/ clinton-proposal-puts-attention-on-early-reading-instruction/1996/09.

104 Emily Hanford, "Transcript of Sold a Story: Episode 2: The Idea," APM, October 20, 2022, https://www.apmreports.org/episode/2022/10/20/sold-a-story-e2-the-idea.

105 National Assessment of Educational Progress, "NAEP Reading: 4th Grade," https:// www.nationsreportcard.gov/reports/reading/2024/g4_8/national-trends/?grade=4. Scores changes are measured by levels of statistical significance. Scores are not statistically significantly different between 1992 and 2000.

106 Kim, p. 98.

107 P. David Pearson, "Reading the Whole-Language Movement," *The Elementary School Journal*, Vol. 90, No. 2, 1989, https://www.journals.uchicago.edu/doi/10.1086/461615.

108 Kim, p. 98.

109 Emily Hanford, "Sold a Story E5: The Company," November 10, 2022, https://www. apmreports.org/episode/2022/11/10/sold-a-story-e5-the-company.

110 Ibid.

111 Emily Hanford, "Sold a Story E3: The Battle," October 27, 2022, https://www. apmreports.org/episode/2022/10/27/sold-a-story-e3-the-battle.

112 Emily Schmidt, "Required Reading: How Textbook Adoption in 3 States Influences the Nation's K-12 Population," APM Research Lab, June 2, 2022, https://www. apmresearchlab.org/10x-textbook-adoption.

113 Coulson, p. 165.

114 Kim, p. 99.

115 Ibid.

116 Ibid., p. 100.

117 Ibid., p. 99.

118 Ibid., p. 100.

119 Diana Lambert, John Fensterwald, and Zaidee Stavely, "Bill to Mandate 'Science of Reading' in California Schools Faces Teacher Union Opposition," *EdSource*, April 5, 2024, https://edsource.org/2024/bill-to-mandate-science-of-reading-in-california-schools-faces-teachers-union-opposition/709193.

120 The Nation's Report Card, "2024 Reading State Snapshot Report: California," https://nces.ed.gov/nationsreportcard/subject/publications/stt2024/pdf/2024220CA4.pdf.

121 Emily Hanford, "Influential Literacy Expert Lucy Calkins Is Changing Her Views," APM Reports, October 16, 2020, https://www.apmreports.org/story/2020/10/16/influential-literacy-expert-lucy-calkins-is-changing-her-views.

122 Sarah Schwartz, "Teachers College to 'Dissolve' Lucy Calkins' Reading and Writing Project," *Education Week*, September 5, 2023, https://www.edweek.org/teaching-learning/teachers-college-to-dissolve-lucy-calkins-reading-and-writing-project/2023/09.

123 Ibid.

124 The Nation's Report Card, "Data Tools: State Profiles, 2013," https://www.nationsreportcard.gov/profiles/stateprofile?chort=1&sub=RED&sj=AL&sfj=NP&st=MN&year=2013R3; Associated Press, "Kids' Reading Scores Have Soared in Mississippi 'Miracle,'" PBS, May 17, 2023, https://www.pbs.org/newshour/education/kids-reading-scores-have-soared-in-mississippi-miracle.

125 Ibid.

126 Tim Daly, "Mississippi Can't Possibly Have Good Schools," *Education Next*, May 8, 2025, https://www.educationnext.org/mississippi-cant-possibly-have-good-schools/.

127 Barksdale Reading Institute, "About the Institute," https://www.msreads.org/about-the-institute/; Claiborne Barksdale, "How Jim Barksdale's $100 Million Gift to the State 25 Years Ago Led to 'the Mississippi Miracle,'" *Mississippi Today*, January 24, 2025, https://mississippitoday.org/2025/01/24/jim-barksdale-100-million-miracle/.

128 Ibid.

129 Mississippi Legislature, 2013 Regular Session, Senate Bill 2347, http://billstatus.ls.state.ms.us/documents/2013/html/SB/2300-2399/SB2347IN.htm; David Kaufman, "In Mississippi, a Broad Effort to Improve Literacy Is Yielding Results," *The New York Times*, October 6, 2022, https://www.nytimes.com/2022/10/06/education/learning/mississippi-schools-literacy.html.

130 Mississippi Legislature, 2013 Regular Session, House Bill 369, http://billstatus.ls.state.ms.us/2013/pdf/history/HB/HB0369.xml.

131 Mississippi Legislature 2015 Regular Session, Senate Bill 2695, http://billstatus.ls.state.ms.us/2015/pdf/history/SB/SB2695.xml.

132 Jonathan Butcher, "A Primer on Education Savings Accounts: Giving Every Child the Chance to Succeed," Heritage Foundation Backgrounder No. 3245, September 15, 2017, https://www.heritage.org/sites/default/files/2017-09/BG3245.pdf.

133 National Assessment of Educational Progress, "NAEP Report Card: Reading, State Average Scores," https://www.nationsreportcard.gov/reports/reading/2024/g4_8/state-district-trends/?grade=4#score-trends-by-state.

134 Erin Fahle et al., "Education Recovery Scorecard: The First Year of Pandemic Recovery: A District-Level Analysis," Center for Education Policy Research at Harvard University and The Educational Opportunity Project at Stanford University, January 2024, https://educationrecoveryscorecard.org/wp-content/uploads/2024/01/ERS-Report-Final-1.31.pdf.

135 National Assessment of Educational Progress, "NAEP Report Card: Reading, State Average Scores," https://www.nationsreportcard.gov/reading/states/scores/?grade=4/.

136 National Assessment of Educational Progress, "NAEP Report Card: Reading, State Student Group Scores," https://www.nationsreportcard.gov/reports/reading/2024/g4_8/performance-by-student-group/?grade=4#student-group-scores-state.

137 Jay P. Greene and Marcus A. Winters, "Revisiting Grade Retention: An Evaluation of Florida's Test-Based Promotion Policy," *Education Finance & Policy*, (2007), 2 (4): 319–340, https://direct.mit.edu/edfp/article/2/4/319/10061/Revisiting-Grade-Retention-An-Evaluation-of; Kirsten Slungaard Mumma, Ph.D., and Marcus A. Winters, Ph.D., "The Effect of Retention Under Mississippi's Test-Based Promotion Policy," Wheelock Education Policy Center, Working Paper 2023-1, Winter 2023, https://wheelockpolicycenter.org/wp-content/uploads/2023/02/MississippiRetention_WP.pdf.

138 U.S. Department of Education, *NAEP 2012: Trends in Academic Progress*, p. 2, https://nces.ed.gov/nationsreportcard/subject/publications/main2012/pdf/2013456.pdf.

139 Erik A. Hanushek, Paul E. Peterson, Laura M. Talpey, and Ludger Woessmann, "The Achievement Gap Fails to Close," *Education Next*, Summer 2019, https://www.educationnext.org/achievement-gap-fails-close-half-century-testing-shows-persistent-divide/.

140 Christopher Peak, "How Legislation on Reading Instruction is Changing Across the Country," APM Reports, November 17, 2022, https://www.apmreports.org/story/2022/11/17/reading-instruction-legislation-state-map.

141 The National Council on Teacher Quality counted 32 states by 2023 where such policies had been adopted. See National Council on Teacher Quality, "Five Policy Actions to Strengthen Implementation of the Science of Reading," March 2024, https://www.nctq.org/publications/State-of-the-States-2024-Five-Policy-Actions-to-Strengthen-Implementation-of-the-Science-of-Reading; *Education Week* said lawmakers in 40 states and Washington, D.C. had adopted such policies. See Sarah Schwartz, "Which States Have Passed 'Science of Reading Laws'? What's in Them?" *Education Week*, July 20, 2022, https://www.edweek.org/teaching-learning/which-states-have-passed-science-of-reading-laws-whats-in-them/2022/07.

142 Arizona Revised Statutes, 15-701 https://www.azleg.gov/viewdocument/?docName=https://www.azleg.gov/ars/15/00701.htm; Naaz Modan, "50 States of Ed Policy: Do 3rd Grade Reading Retention Policies Work?" *K-12 Dive*, July 30, 2019, https://www.k12dive.com/news/the-50-states-of-education-policy-do-3rd-grade-retention-policies-work/559741/; Mary Hennigan, "Rising 3rd Graders First Group to be Held Back if They Don't Meet Yet-to-be-Determined LEARNS Literacy Standards," *Arkansas Times*, May 16, 2025, https://arktimes.com/arkansas-blog/2025/05/16/rising-3rd-graders-first-group-to-be-held-back-if-they-dont-meet-yet-to-be-deter-

mined-learns-literacy-standards; Louisiana Revised Statutes, 17:21:11 §24.11, "Early Literacy Promotion to Fourth Grade," https://www.legis.la.gov/legis/Law.aspx?d=451839; Tennessee Department of Education, "Promotion & Retention Guidelines and Toolkit," January 2025, https://www.tn.gov/content/dam/tn/education/ccte/Promotion_Guidelines_and_Toolkit-Third_and_Fourth_Grade.pdf.

143　Step Up for Students, "New World Scholarship Accounts," available at https://www.stepupforstudents.org/scholarships/new-worlds-scholarship-accounts/.

144　Alli Aldis, "School Choice Participation, 2025 Edition," *Ed Choice*, January 6, 2025, https://www.edchoice.org/americas-school-choice-programs-ranked-by-participation-2025-edition/.

145　Jonathan Butcher and Jason Bedrick, "2023: The Year of Education Freedom," Heritage Foundation Backgrounder, September 11, 2023, https://www.heritage.org/education/report/2023-the-year-education-freedom; Jason Bedrick, "Louisiana Expands Education Choice to All," *The Daily Signal*, June 19, 2024, https://www.dailysignal.com/2024/06/19/louisiana-expands-education-choice-all/.

146　John Gramlich, "America's Incarceration Rate Falls to Lowest Level Since 1995," Pew Research, August 16, 2021, https://www.pewresearch.org/short-reads/2021/08/16/americas-incarceration-rate-lowest-since-1995/; Helen Fair and Roy Walmsley, "World Prison Population List," *World Prison Brief*, 13th ed., October 2021, https://www.prisonstudies.org/sites/default/files/resources/downloads/world_prison_population_list_13th_edition.pdf. Data are not available or incomplete for China, North Korea, Eritrea, and Somalia; Charles Stimson and Zack Smith, "The Myth of Mass Incarceration," Heritage Foundation Legal Memo No. 353, May 29, 2024, https://www.heritage.org/sites/default/files/2024-05/LM353.pdf.

147　Stimson and Smith, "The Myth of Mass Incarceration," pp. 12, 19.

148　Stimson and Smith, "The Myth of Mass Incarceration," p. 19.

149　World Literacy Foundation, "The Impact of Illiteracy and the Importance of Early Intervention," July 23, 2021, https://worldliteracyfoundation.org/early-intervention-reduces-illiteracy/; Early Literacy Foundation, "Early Literacy Connection to Incarceration," https://governorsfoundation.org/gelf-articles/early-literacy-connection-to-incarceration/.

150　Gerard Robinson, "Introduction," in *A Story to Tell*, Gerard Robinson, ed. (Charlottesville: Advanced Studies in Culture Foundation, 2021), p. 5, https://advancedstudiesinculture.org/wp-content/uploads/2021/03/a-story-to-tell_gerard_robinson4.pdf.

151　Associated Press, "Biden Announces New Steps to Tackle Racial Inequality in Government," PBS, February 16, 2023, https://www.pbs.org/newshour/politics/biden-announces-new-steps-to-tackle-racial-inequality-in-government; Center for American Progress, "Systematic Inequality," February 21, 2018, https://www.americanprogress.org/article/systematic-inequality/; Stimson and Smith review the literature on this subject in "The Myth of Mass Incarceration."

152　See NewJimCrow.com, "Praise," https://newjimcrow.com/praise-for-the-new-jim-crow.

153　Michelle Alexander, *The New Jim Crow* (New York: The New Press, 2012).

154 "Black Lives Matter Global Network demands Congress and the current Administration propose legislation truly intended to dramatically decrease mass incarceration centering the Black communities that continue to be disproportionately targeted by our criminal justice system." See Black Lives Matter, "Black Lives Matter Global Network Responds to the United States Senate Passage of the First Step Act, A Criminal Reform Package," December 20, 2018, https://blacklivesmatter.com/black-lives-matter-global-network-responds-to-the-united-states-senate-passage-of-the-first-step-act-a-criminal-reform-package/. See also Inimai Chettiar, "Why Mass Incarceration Really Is the New Jim Crow," ACLU, February 23, 2012, https://www.aclu.org/news/racial-justice/why-mass-incarceration-really-new-jim-crow.

155 Heather Mac Donald, "Tell the Truth about Law Enforcement and Crime," *City Journal*, November 13, 2023, https://www.city-journal.org/article/tell-the-truth-about-law-enforcement-and-crime.

156 Prison Policy Initiative, "Race and Ethnicity," https://www.prisonpolicy.org/research/race_and_ethnicity/.

157 Ibid.

158 Robinson, "Introduction," in *A Story to Tell*, p. 8.

159 Ibid.

160 Ibid., p. 8.

161 Ibid., p. 8.

162 See, for example, Inequality.org, "8 Ways States Can Fight Inequality and Build Worker Power," February 3, 2025, https://inequality.org/article/8-ways-states-can-fight-inequality/.

163 U.S. Department of Education, *Becoming a Nation of Readers*, p. vi.

CHAPTER THREE

1 Alexis de Tocqueville, Democracy in America, Translated by Henry Reeve (London: Saunders and Otley: 1835) p. 258.

2 Suparna Dutta phone interview with Jonathan Butcher, October 11, 2023.

3 Brittany Hunter, "Fighting for Equality: The Faces of Coalition for TJ," Pacific Legal Foundation, June 15, 2021, https://pacificlegal.org/the-faces-of-coalition-for-tj/.

4 Phone interview with Suparna Dutta and Jonathan Butcher, October 11, 2023.

5 Ibid.; Anna Bryson, "Senate Votes to Strip Youngkin Appointee to State Board of Education," *Richmond Times-Dispatch*, February 8, 2023, https://richmond.com/news/state-and-regional/govt-and-politics/ginni-thomas-urges-virginia-senators-to-confirm-youngkin-appointee-on-board-of-education/article_ec2a080c-a711-11ed-9c1b-33cf5a66cf66.html.

6 Dana Goldstein, "For Republican Governors, Civics Is the Latest Education Battleground," *The New York Times*, November 30, 2023, https://www.nytimes.com/2023/11/30/us/republican-governors-civics-education.html.

7 *The Republic of Plato*, Allan Bloom, trans. (New York: Basic Books, 2016 ed.), p. 105.

8 Bill of Rights Institute, "Principles and Virtues," available at https://billofrightsinstitute.org/resources/principles-and-virtues.

9 The Nation's Report Card, or National Assessment of Educational Progress, measures "students' knowledge and skills in democratic citizenship, government, and American constitutional democracy," a suitable summary of civics instruction. See National Center for Education Statistics, "National Assessment of Educational Progress: Civics, Overview of the Assessment," https://nces.ed.gov/nationsreportcard/civics/interpreting.aspx. See also The Jack Miller Center, "Why Civics?" https://www.jackmillercenter.org/why-civics.

10 Ibid.

11 Samuel Eagle Forman, *First Lessons in Civics: A Text-Book for Use in Schools* (New York: American Book Company, 1912), pp. 3–4.

12 Ibid.

13 Ibid., pp. 3–4.

14 Ibid., p. 3.

15 Peggy Noonan, "Teach Your Children to Love America," *The Wall Street Journal*, May 23, 2024, https://www.wsj.com/articles/teach-your-children-to-love-america-memorial-day-7c97666e.

16 Note the distinction, discussed in this chapter, between action civics and traditional civics instruction. See U.S. Department of Education, "Advancing Civic Learning and Engagement in Democracy: A Road Map and Call to Action," January 2012, https://www.ed.gov/media/document/road-map-call-actionpdf-81670.pdf, published under President Barrack Obama's administration, and President Donald Trump White House Archives, "1776 Report," January 2021, published under President Donald Trump's first administration, https://trumpwhitehouse.archives.gov/wp-content/uploads/2021/01/The-Presidents-Advisory-1776-Commission-Final-Report.pdf.

17 Ibid., p. 5.

18 Claudine Geoghegan, "Testimony to the U.S. House of Representatives Committee on the Judiciary Subcommittee on the Constitution and Limited Government," April 16, 2024, p. 2, https://www.iwf.org/wp-content/uploads/2024/04/Beanie-Geoghegan-written-testimony-House-Judiciary-4.16.2024.pdf.

19 Ibid., p. 5.

20 Melissa Jackson and Beanie Geoghegan, phone interview with Jonathan Butcher, October 27, 2023.

21 Ibid.

22 Freedom in Education, "Civics Education," https://freedomined.org/civics-education/.

23 Melissa Jackson and Beanie Geoghegan, interview with Jonathan Butcher, October 27, 2023.

24 Freedom in Education, "Civics Initiative," https://freedomined.org/civics-education/.

25 Freedom in Education, "About Us," https://freedomined.org/about/. For comparison, see Black Lives Matter at School, "Guiding Principles," https://www.blacklivesmatteratschool.com/guiding-principles.html.

26 Melissa Jackson and Beanie Geoghegan, interview with Jonathan Butcher, October 27, 2023.

27 Lindsey M. Burke, Ph.D., Jonathan Butcher, Emilie Gao, and Mike Gonzalez, "The

Culture of American K–12 Education: A National Survey of Parents and School Board Members," Heritage Foundation Special Report No. 241, January 11, 2021, https://www.heritage.org/sites/default/files/2021-01/SR241.pdf, p. 19.

28 Ibid.

29 Melissa Jackson and Beanie Geoghegan, interview with Jonathan Butcher, October 27, 2023.

30 National Center for Education Statistics, "NAEP Report Card: Civics," https://www.nationsreportcard.gov/civics/.

31 Ibid.

32 U.S. Department of Education, "Advancing Civic Learning and Engagement in Democracy," January 2012, p. 8.

33 Ibid.

34 Jonathan Butcher, *Splintered: Critical Race Theory and the Progressive War on Truth* (New York: Post Hill Press/Bombardier Books, 2022), pp. 99–102; Andre Perry, "Students Take Their Future into Their Own Hands on Climate Change Activism," The Hechinger Report, November 13, 2019, https://hechingerreport.org/students-take-their-future-into-their-own-hands-on-climate-change-activism/.

35 U.S. Department of Education, "Advancing Civic Learning and Engagement in Democracy," January 2012, p. 8.

36 President Donald Trump White House Archives, *The 1776 Report*.

37 Jonathan Butcher, "K–12 'Action Civics' Trained Students Encamped on College Campuses. Here's What Parents Need to Know," *The Daily Signal*, April 29, 2024, https://www.dailysignal.com/2024/04/29/K–12-action-civics-trained-students-encamped-on-college-campuses-heres-what-parents-need-to-know/.

38 Peter Baker, "Live Updates: College Students and Police Clash on Campuses Across Country," *The New York Times*, April 30, 2024, https://www.nytimes.com/live/2024/04/30/nyregion/columbia-protests-college; Jerusalem Post Staff, "Hamas' October 7 Massacre: Reliving the Day, Hour by Hour," *The Jerusalem Post*, October 7, 2024, https://www.jpost.com/israel-hamas-war/article-823396.

39 *Columbia Magazine*, "Henry S. Coleman, Popular Dean Held Captive During 1968 Protests, Dies at 79," Spring 2006, https://magazine.columbia.edu/article/henry-s-coleman-popular-dean-held-captive-during-1968-protests-dies-79.

40 Katie Cole and Willoughby Mariano, "118 Arrested As Police Forcibly Clear Emerson Encampment Protesting War in Gaza," WBUR, April 26, 2024, https://www.wbur.org/news/2024/04/25/boston-emerson-college-massachusetts-students-arrests.

41 Terry Chea and Olga R. Rodriguez, "Pro-Palestinian Protestors Arrested at Stanford University after Occupying President's Office," AP News, June 5, 2024, https://apnews.com/article/campus-protests-stanford-israel-gaza-f1ec47dcac1b55839e-96b5442ebcf00d.

42 In some states, the review cycle occurs every four years, while in other states, policymakers review standards every two years. See Jennifer Thomsen, "State Academic Standards," Education Commission of the States December 2014, https://files.eric.ed.gov/fulltext/ED560981.pdf.

43 Louisiana Department of Education, 2022 Louisiana Student Standards Social Studies, https://www.louisianabelieves.com/docs/default-source/academic-standards/02-08-2022---draft-louisiana-social-studies-standards.pdf?sfvrsn=52de6518_14; South Dakota Department of Education, "Social Studies Standards," April 17, 2023, https://doe.sd.gov/ContentStandards/documents/SS-Standards-2023.pdf.

44 Ibid., p. 9.

45 Ibid., pp. 4, 13.

46 Phone interview between Louisiana Superintendent Cade Brumley and Jonathan Butcher, February 2, 2025.

47 Ibid.

48 South Dakota Department of Education, "Social Studies Standards," April 17, 2023, https://doe.sd.gov/ContentStandards/documents/SS-Standards-2023.pdf.

49 Ibid., p. 2.

50 Ibid.

51 Ibid.

52 Ibid., p. 17.

53 See San Diego Unified School District, Ethnic Studies, https://www.sdusdethnic-studies.org; Los Angeles Unified School District, Ethnic Studies, https://www.lausd.org/EthnicStudies; Elissa Miolene, "Ethnic Studies Isn't Required Until 2025, So Why Is It Already a Mainstay at Bay Area High Schools?" *Mercury News*, August 26, 2023, https://www.mercurynews.com/2023/08/26/ethnic-studies-isnt-required-until-2025-so-why-is-it-already-a-mainstay-at-these-bay-area-high-schools/.

54 Eric He, "This High School Course Is Dividing Districts Across California," *Politico*, April 20, 2025, https://www.politico.com/news/2025/04/20/this-high-school-course-is-dividing-districts-across-california-00299498.

55 California State Board of Education, "Ethnic Studies Model Curriculum: Introduction," 2022, p. 9, https://www.cde.ca.gov/ci/cr/cf/documents/esmcchapter1.pdf; Kimberlé Williams Crenshaw, "Mapping the Margins: Intersectionality, Identity Politics, and Violence," in *Critical Race Theory: The Key Writings that Formed the Movement*, Kimberlé Crenshaw, Neil Gotanda, Gary Peller, and Kendall Thomas, eds. (New York: The New Press, 1995), pp. 357–383.

56 California State Board of Education, "Ethnic Studies Model Curriculum: Introduction," pp. 9–10.

57 California State Board of Education, "Ethnic Studies Model Curriculum," pp. 455, 474, 530.

58 Mary Graybar, *Debunking Howard Zinn: Exposing the Fake History that Turned a Generation against America* (Washington, D.C.: Regnery, 2019).

59 Howard Zinn, *A People's History of the United States* reissue (New York: Harper Perennial Modern Classics, 2015). The first edition was published in 1980.

60 Chris Williams, "Judge Approves Nearly All Updates to State Social Studies Standards," Education Minnesota, January 16, 2024, https://educationminnesota.org/news/press-release/judge-approves-updated-social-studies-standards/#:~:text=CHRIS%20WILLIAMS&text=Jan.,Specht%2C%20president%20of%20Education%20Minnesota.

61 Minnesota Department of Education, "2023 Legislative Impacts on Minnesota Social Studies Education," https://education.mn.gov/MDE/dse/stds/soc/#:~:text=In%20 2023%2C%20the%20Minnesota%20Legislature,02%2C%20subdivision%203.

62 Katherine Kersten, "Extremist Ideology Has Already Hijacked Minnesota's Social Studies Classes," *Star-Tribune*, April 6, 2024, https://www.startribune.com/kath- erine-kersten-extremist-ideology-has-already-hijacked-minnesotas-social-studies- classes/600356934/; Minnesota Department of Education, "Ethnic Studies," https:// education.mn.gov/MDE/dse/stds/EthnicStudies/index.htm.

63 Kersten, "Extremist Ideology Has Already Hijacked Minnesota's Social Studies Classes."

64 Katherine Kersten phone interview with Jonathan Butcher, April 30, 2024.

65 St. Paul Public Schools, "Ethnic Studies," https://www.spps.org/academics/teaching- learning/high-school-years/hs-ethnic-studies-curriculum-and-instruction.

66 Ibid.; see also Center for the American Experiment, "Bait and Switch," https://www. americanexperiment.org/bait-and-switch/.

67 Kersten, "Extremist Ideology Has Already Hijacked Minnesota's Social Studies Classes."

68 Mansoor, Ewe, and Moench, "Pro-Palestinian Encampments Take Over American College Campuses"; Marcus, "NYPD Riot Police Arrest Over 70 Pro-Palestine Protestors Occupying Columbia Library," *Yahoo News*.

69 James Lynch, "Columbia Backs Down After Setting Midnight Deadline for Anti- Israel Protestors to Disperse," *National Review Online*, April 24, 2024, https://www. nationalreview.com/news/columbia-backs-down-after-setting-midnight-deadline- for-anti-israel-protesters-to-disperse/.

70 Bari Weiss, "They Were Assaulted on Campus for Being Jews," *The Free Press*, April 21, 2024, https://www.thefp.com/p/they-were-assaulted-on-campus-for.

71 Katherine Kersten, "Doubling Down on CRT," Center of the American Experiment, *Thinking Minnesota*, Spring 2022, https://www.americanexperiment.org/magazine/ article/doubling-down-on-crt.

72 Katherine Kersten, "Tim Walz Brings 'Liberated' Ethnic Studies to Minnesota," *The Wall Street Journal*, August 21, 2024, https://www.wsj.com/opinion/tim-walz- brings-liberated-ethnic-studies-to-minnesota-radical-decolinization-election- 44a267ca?mod=article_inline.

73 Desheania Andrews, Chris Nesi, Reuven Fenton, and Alex Oliveira, "Columbia Uni- versity Refuses to Condemn Professor Who Called Hamas Attack 'Awesome,'" *New York Post*, October 16, 2024, https://nypost.com/2023/10/16/columbia-university- refuses-to-comment-on-growing-furor-over-professor-who-called-hamas-attack- awesome/.

74 Noah Lederman, "Jewish Students Are No Longer Safe at Columbia Univer- sity," *Haaretz*, April 25, 2024, https://www.haaretz.com/opinion/2024-04-25/ ty-article-opinion/.premium/jewish-students-are-no-longer-safe-at-columbia- university/0000018f-14e9-da70-a7bf-7debe6900000; NBC News, "Columbia Closed to Nonresidential Students, Remaining Protestors Face Suspension," April 30, 2024, https://www.nbcnews.com/news/us-news/live-blog/campus-protests- live-updates-students-occupy-columbia-university-rcna149926.

75 Forman, p. 4.

76 Katherine Kersten, "National Experts Highly Critical of Minnesota's Social Stud-
    ies Standards," Center of the American Experiment Policy Brief No. 20, February
    2024, p. 3, https://files.americanexperiment.org/wp-content/uploads/2024/02/
    National-Experts-Highly-Critical-of-Minnesotas-Social-Studies-Standards.
    pdf?v=1709057324.

77 Ibid.

78 Stanley Kurtz, "The Blue-State Education Nightmare," *National Review*, April 17,
    2024, https://www.nationalreview.com/corner/the-blue-state-education-nightmare/.

79 Kersten, "Extremist Ideology Has Already Hijacked Minnesota's Social Studies
    Classes."

80 Asra Q. Nomani, "Smearing a Hindu American Woman of Color as a 'White
    Supremacist,'" *RealClearPolitics*, February 18, 2023, https://www.realclearpolitics.
    com/articles/2023/02/18/smearing_a_hindu_american_woman_of_color_as_a_
    white_supremacist_148884.html.

81 Nick Minock, "Indian Mom Suparna Dutta Slams VA Dems Who Removed Her
    from Board of Ed, Called Her Racist," ABC 7 News, February 14, 2023, https://
    wjla.com/news/crisis-in-the-classrooms/virginia-board-of-education-suparna-dutta-
    interview-removal-governor-glenn-youngking-va-democrats-meeting-vote-senator-
    ghazala-hashmi-standards-of-learning-schools-terry-mcauliffe.

82 Ibid.; Suparna Dutta phone interview with Jonathan Butcher, October 11, 2023.

83 Minock, "Indian Mom Suparna Dutta Slams VA Dems Who Removed Her from
    Board of Ed, Called Her Racist."

84 Suparna Dutta phone interview with Jonathan Butcher, October 11, 2023.

85 Jonathan W. Emord, "Virginia Board of Education Controversy Rages on," PJ Media,
    March 16, 2023, https://pjmedia.com/jonathanemord/2023/03/16/virginia-board-
    of-education-controversy-rages-on-n1679066; for evidence debunking these views of
    our founding documents, see Sean Wilenz, including *No Property in Man: Slavery and
    Antislavery at the Nation's Founding* (Cambridge: Harvard University Press, 2018).

86 Suparna Dutta phone interview with Jonathan Butcher, October 11, 2023.

87 Pacific Legal Foundation, "Fighting Race-Based Discrimination at Nation's Top-
    Ranked High School," https://pacificlegal.org/case/coalition_for_tj/.

88 Ibid.

89 Ibid.

90 Suparna Dutta phone interview with Jonathan Butcher, October 11, 2023.

91 Pacific Legal Foundation, "Fighting Race-Based Discrimination at Nation's Top-
    Ranked High School."

92 Suparna Dutta phone interview with Jonathan Butcher, October 11, 2023.

93 Nomani, "Smearing a Hindu American Woman of Color as a 'White Supremacist,'"

94 Ibid.

95 Ibid.

96 Suparna Dutta phone interview with Jonathan Butcher, October 11, 2023.

97 Ibid.

98 Ibid.

99 601 U.S. ___ (2024) (Alito, J., dissenting in denial of certiorari), https://www.supremecourt.gov/opinions/23pdf/23-170_7l48.pdf.

100 Ibid.

101 Ibid., p. 1.

102 Ibid., p. 3.

103 Ibid., p.5.

104 President Donald Trump White House Archives, *The 1776 Report*.

105 White House Executive Orders, "Ending Radical Indoctrination in K–12 Schooling," January 29, 2025, https://www.whitehouse.gov/presidential-actions/2025/01/ending-radical-indoctrination-in-K–12-schooling/.

106 Gov. Ron DeSantis, "Governor Ron DeSantis Launches National Model Civic Learning Initiative," press release, July 13, 2021, https://www.flgov.com/eog/news/press/2021/governor-ron-desantis-launches-national-model-civic-literacy-initiative.

107 Tiffany Hoben phone interview with Jonathan Butcher, March 7, 2025.

108 Ibid.

109 Florida Department of Education, "Florida Civics Seal of Excellence Course: Module 2," https://www.civicsliteracy.org/civics/course?courseversion=regular-course.

110 Ibid.

111 Goldstein, "For Republican Governors, Civics Is the Latest Education Battleground."

112 Forman, p. 6.

113 Ibid., p. 5.

114 Ibid.

115 Ibid., pp. 5–6.

116 Forman, p. 13.

117 Ibid., p. 5.

118 Ibid., p. 6.

119 U.S. Department of Justice, "Special Report: Profile of Prison Inmates, 2016," Office of Justice Programs, December 2021, p. 20, https://bjs.ojp.gov/content/pub/pdf/ppi16.pdf.

120 Mark E. Courtney, Sherri Terao, and Noel Bost, "Midwest Evaluation of the Adult Functioning of Foster Youth: Conditions of Youth Preparing to Leave State Care," Chapin Hall Center for Children at the University of Chicago Discussion Paper, 2004, p. 9, https://www.chapinhall.org/wp-content/uploads/Midwest-Study-Youth-Preparing-to-Leave-Care-Brief.pdf.

121 Joseph P. Ryan and Mark F. Testa, "Children Maltreatment and Juvenile Delinquency," *Children and Youth Services Review*, Vol. 27, Issue 3, March 2005, pp. 227–249, https://www.sciencedirect.com/science/article/abs/pii/S0190740904002026.

122 Mark E. Courtney et al., "Midwest Evaluation of the Adult Functioning of Former Foster Youth: Outcomes at Age 26," Chapin Hall Center at the University of Chicago, 2011, p. 91, https://www.chapinhall.org/wp-content/uploads/Midwest-Eval-Outcomes-at-Age-26.pdf.

123 Ibid., p. 92.

124 U.S. Department of Justice, "Special Report: Profile of Prison Inmates, 2016."

125 Nicholas Zill, "The Resurgence of the Two-Parent Family," Institute for Family Studies, January 10, 2024, https://ifstudies.org/blog/the-resurgence-of-the-two-parent-family.

126 Brad Wilcox and Wendy Wang, "The Power of the Success Sequence," AEI Report, May 26, 2022, https://www.aei.org/research-products/report/the-power-of-the-success-sequence/.

127 Burke et al., "The Culture of American K–12 Education: A National Survey of Parents and School Board Members," p. 6.

128 Wilcox and Wang, "The Power of the Success Sequence," American Enterprise Institute, p 2.

129 Ibid., p. 3.

130 AEI–Brookings Working Group on Childhood in the United States, "Rebalancing: Children First," p. 12, https://www.brookings.edu/wp-content/uploads/2022/02/ES_20220228_Rebalancing_Children_First.pdf.

131 Ibid., p. 22.

132 Ibid.

133 Anna J. Egalite, "How Family Background Influences Student Achievement," *Education Next*, Vol. 16, No. 2, https://www.educationnext.org/how-family-background-influences-student-achievement/.

134 Ibid.

135 Brian Goesling, Hande Inanc, and Angela Rachidi, "Success Sequence: A Synthesis of the Literature," Administration for Children and Families, OPRE Report No. 2020-41, December 2020, p. 15, https://www.acf.hhs.gov/sites/default/files/documents/opre/Success_sequence_review_2020_508_0.pdf.

136 AEI–Brookings Working Group on Childhood in the United States, "Rebalancing: Children First," p. 27; and Melissa S. Kearney, *The Two-Parent Privilege: How Americans Stopped Getting Married and Started Falling Behind* (Chicago: University of Chicago Press, 2023), p. 45.

137 Patrick Fagan et al., "The Positive Effects of Marriage: A Book of Charts," The Heritage Foundation, April 2002, p. 25, https://www.heritage.org/sites/default/files/2017-09/positive_effects_of_marriage.pdf; and Brad Wilcox, *Get Married: Why Americans Must Defy the Elites, Forge Strong Families, and Save Civilization* (New York: Broadside Books, 2024), p. 52.

138 Robert Rector, Testimony before the U.S. House of Representatives' Subcommittee on Health Care and Financial Services Committee on Oversight and Government Reform, February 11, 2025, https://oversight.house.gov/wp-content/uploads/2025/02/Rector-Written-Testimony.pdf.

139 Wilcox, *Get Married: Why Americans Must Defy the Elites, Forge Strong Families, and Save Civilization*; and Cynthia C. Harper and Sara S. McLanahan, "Father Absence and Youth Incarceration," *Journal of Research on Adolescence*, Vol. 14, No. 3 (September 2004), p. 382.

140 Brad Wilcox, Wendy Wang, and Ian Rowe, "Less Poverty, Less Prison, More Col-

lege: What Two Parents Mean for Black and White Children," Institute for Family Studies, June 17, 2021, https://ifstudies.org/blog/less-poverty-less-prison-more-college-what-two-parents-mean-for-black-and-white-children.

141 Angela Rachidi, "The Success Sequence for Unmarried Mothers," American Enterprise Institute, January 9, 2024, https://www.aei.org/op-eds/the-success-sequence-for-unmarried-mothers/#:~:text=As%20covered%20on%20these%20pages,young%20people%20to%20avoid%20poverty.

142 Rachidi, "The Success Sequence for Unmarried Mothers."

143 Angela Rachidi, "Dynamics of Families After a Nonmarital Birth," American Enterprise Institute, January 8, 2024, https://www.aei.org/research-products/report/dynamics-of-families-after-a-nonmarital-birth/.

CHAPTER FOUR

1 Calvin Coolidge, "The Press Under a Free Government," January 17, 1925, Calvin Coolidge Foundation, https://coolidgefoundation.org/resources/the-press-under-a-free-government/.

2 Phone interview with anonymous and Jonathan Butcher, April 2, 2024.

3 Kathleen Stock, *Material Girls* (London: Fleet, 2021), p. 5.

4 Federal Register, "Nondiscrimination on the Basis of Sex in Education Programs or Activities Receiving Federal Financial Assistance," Docket ID ED-2021-OCR-0166, July 12, 2022, https://www.federalregister.gov/documents/2022/07/12/2022-13734/nondiscrimination-on-the-basis-of-sex-in-education-programs-or-activities-receiving-federal. In Gayle Rubin's essay, "Thinking Sex: Notes for a Radical Theory of the Politics of Sexuality," one of the defining essays of queer theory or critical gender studies, Rubin argues that regulations on pornography and non-homosexual relationships violate "sexual civil liberties" and explains the Marxist roots of queer theory. See Gayle Rubin, "Thinking Sex: Notes for a Radical Theory of the Politics of Sexuality," in *Culture, Society and Sexuality*, Richard Parker and Peter Aggleton, eds. (London: Routledge, 2007), p. 146, 158, 169, available at https://bpb-us-e2.wpmucdn.com/sites.middlebury.edu/dist/2/3378/files/2015/01/Rubin-Thinking-Sex.pdf.

5 Ibid.; The White House, "Defending Women from Gender Ideology Extremism and Restoring Biological Truth to the Federal Government," Presidential Actions, January 20, 2025, https://www.whitehouse.gov/presidential-actions/2025/01/defending-women-from-gender-ideology-extremism-and-restoring-biological-truth-to-the-federal-government/; Matt Lavietes, "Over 20 GOP-Led States Sue Biden Administration Over Title IX Rules for LGTBQ Students," NBC News, May 8, 2024, https://www.nbcnews.com/nbc-out/out-politics-and-policy/20-gop-led-states-sue-biden-administration-title-ix-rules-lgbtq-studen-rcna151247.

6 Shauneen Miranda, "Over Half of States Sue to Block Biden Title IX Rule Protecting LGTBQ+ Students," *West Virginia Watch*, May 22, 2024, https://www.msn.com/en-us/news/us/over-half-of-states-sue-to-block-biden-title-ix-rule-protecting-lgbtq-students/ar-BB1mNwdQ; Jay Richards, "What Is Gender Ideology?" *The American Conservative*, July 3, 2023, https://www.theamericanconservative.com/what-is-gender-ideology/.

7 Associated Press, "Transcript of President Donald Trump's Speech to a Joint Session

of Congress," March 5, 2025, https://apnews.com/article/trump-speech-congress-transcript-751b5891a3265ff1e5c1409c391fef7c.

8   Associated Press, "Transgender Issues Are a Strength for Trump, New Poll Finds," NBC News, May 12, 2025, https://www.nbcnews.com/nbc-out/out-politics-and-policy/transgender-issues-are-strength-trump-new-poll-finds-rcna206265.

9   See, for example, Florida Senate, 2022 Session, HB 1557, https://www.flsenate.gov/Session/Bill/2022/1557/BillText/er/PDF; Iowa Legislature, 2023 Session, SF 496, https://www.legis.iowa.gov/legislation/BillBook?ga=90&ba=SF496; Arkansas Legislature, 94th General Assembly, Regular Session, SB 294, p. 23, https://arkleg.state.ar.us/Home/FTPDocument?path=%2FACTS%2F2023R%2FPublic%2FACT237.pdf.

10   See, for example, Texas Legislature, 2023 Session, SB 14, https://capitol.texas.gov/BillLookup/History.aspx?LegSess=88R&Bill=SB14; Florida Senate, 2023 Session, SB 254, https://www.flsenate.gov/Session/Bill/2023/254; West Virginia Legislature, 2023 Regular Session, House Bill 2007, https://www.wvlegislature.gov/Bill_Status/bills_text.cfm?billdoc=hb2007%20intr.htm&yr=2023&sesstype=RS&i=2007.

11   Robert Schmad, "Hospitals Conducting Transgender Procedures on Children Supported by Billions in Taxpayer Dollars," *Washington Examiner*, February 27, 2025, https://www.msn.com/en-us/news/us/hospitals-conducting-transgender-procedures-on-children-supported-by-billions-in-taxpayer-dollars/ar-AA1zMaYv.

12   Ibid.; Do No Harm, "About Us," https://donoharmmedicine.org/about/.

13   Schmad, "Hospitals Conducting Transgender Procedures on Children Supported by Billions in Taxpayer Dollars."

14   Parents Defending Education, "List of School Transgender—Gender Nonconforming Student Policies," last updated April 21, 2025, https://defendinged.org/investigations/list-of-school-district-transgender-gender-nonconforming-student-policies/.

15   Richards, "What Is Gender Ideology?"

16   Etymonline, "Gender," available at https://www.etymonline.com/word/gender.

17   Richards, "What Is Gender Ideology?"

18   David Artavia, "Logan Brown, A Pregnant Transgender Man, Is on the Cover of 'Glamour' Magazine. 'I Do Exist,' He Says—and so Do Others," *Yahoo News*, June 2, 2023, https://www.yahoo.com/lifestyle/logan-brown-pregnant-transgender-man-182112724.html.

19   "The number of children who started on puberty-blockers or hormones totaled 17,683 over the five-year period, rising from 2,394 in 2017 to 5,063 in 2021, according to the analysis." Chad Terhune, Robin Respaut, and Michelle Conlin, "As More Transgender Children See Medical Care, Families Confront Many Unknowns," Reuters, October 6, 2022, https://www.reuters.com/investigates/special-report/usa-transyouth-care/.

20   Abigail Shrier, *Irreversible Damage* (Washington, DC: Regnery, 2020), p. 25; *The Economist*, "Our Books of the Year," December 3, 2020, https://www.economist.com/books-and-arts/2020/12/03/our-books-of-the-year.

21   Stock, *Material Girls*, p. 4.

22   Akosua Mireku, "Legal Challenges Put Off Label Use of Gender Affirming Care Drugs in Jeopardy," Pharmaceutical Technology, March 16, 2023, https://www.pharmaceutical-technology.com/features/legal-challenges-put-off-label-use-of-gender-

affirming-care-drugs-in-jeopardy/; Jamie Reed, "I Thought I Was Saving Trans Kids. Now I'm Blowing the Whistle," *The Free Press*, February 9, 2023, https://www.thefp.com/p/i-thought-i-was-saving-trans-kids.

23 Kelsey B. Eitel, M.D., et al., "Leuprolide Acetate for Puberty Suppression in Transgender and Gender Diverse Youth: A Comparison of Subcutaneous Eligard Versus Intramuscular Lupron," *Journal of Adolescent Health*, November 18, 2022, https://www.jahonline.org/article/S1054-139X(22)00686-3/fulltext; Abigail Shrier, "Affirmative Abandonment," *City Journal*, June 23, 2020, https://www.city-journal.org/article/affirmative-abandonment.

24 LupronDepot, available at https://www.lupron.com/; *MedicalNewsToday*, "What to Expect from Lupron Treatment," https://www.medicalnewstoday.com/articles/324480#:~:text=Lupron%20is%20a%20type%20of,radiation%20therapy%20or%20following%20surgery.

25 University of California San Francisco, "Overview of Feminizing Hormone Therapy," June 17, 2016, https://transcare.ucsf.edu/guidelines/feminizing-hormone-therapy; Mayo Clinic, "Spironolactone," https://www.mayoclinic.org/drugs-supplements/spironolactone-oral-route/description/drg-20071534#:~:text=Spironolactone%20is%20used%20in%20combination,for%20hospitalization%20for%20heart%20failure.

26 Terhune, Respaut, and Conlin, "As More Transgender Children See Medical Care, Families Confront Many Unknowns."

27 Ibid.

28 Spencer Lindquist, "EXCLUSIVE: Health Centers at Seattle Public Schools Offer 'Gender-Affirming' Hormone Therapy to Children," *The Daily Wire*, May 21, 2024, https://www.dailywire.com/news/exclusive-health-centers-at-seattle-public-schools-offer-gender-affirming-hormone-therapy-to-children.

29 Lindquist, "EXCLUSIVE: Health Centers at Seattle Public Schools Offer 'Gender-Affirming' Hormone Therapy to Children"; NeighborCare Health, "About Us," https://neighborcare.org/about-us/.

30 Olympia School District, "Transgender and Gender Non-Conforming Students," p. 2, https://go.boarddocs.com/wa/osd111/Board.nsf/files/BQM2AF013832/$file/3211PRO_Draft_AC.pdf; Seattle Public Schools, "School Board Action Report," May 10, 2020, p. 3, https://www.seattleschools.org/wp-content/uploads/2021/07/I09_20200624_Approval-of-new-BP-No.-3211-Gender-Inclusive-Schools.pdf.

31 Phone interview with anonymous and Jonathan Butcher, April 2, 2024.

32 Cass, H., "Independent review of gender identity services for children and young people: Final report," 2024, https://cass.independent-review.uk/home/publications/final-report/.

33 Max Colchester and Stephanie Armour, "U.K. Study Criticizes Puberty Blockers for Gender Dysphoria in Minors," *The Wall Street Journal*, April 10, 2024, https://www.wsj.com/world/uk/uk-study-criticizes-puberty-blockers-for-gender-dysphoria-in-minors-703c2ad7?mod=Searchresults_pos1&page=1; James Beal, "Hilary Cass: I Can't Travel on Public Transport After Gender Report," *The Times*, April 19, 2024, https://www.thetimes.co.uk/article/hilary-cass-i-cant-travel-on-public-transport-any-more-35pt0mvnh.

34 Cass Review, "Independent review of gender identity services for children and young people: Final report," p. 13.

35 Cass Review, p. 21.

36 Emilie Kao, "Safeguarding Parental Rights and Protecting Children from Federally Mandated Gender Ideology," The Heritage Foundation Backgrounder No. 3744, January 10, 2023, https://www.heritage.org/sites/default/files/2023-01/BG3744_0.pdf; Jay W. Richards, Ph.D. and Emilie Kao, "California Attacks Parents' Rights Under the Guise of Medical Care," The Heritage Foundation, September 30, 2022, https://www.heritage.org/gender/commentary/california-attacks-parents-rights-under-the-guise-medical-care.

37 Cass Review, p. 21.

38 Cass Review, p. 21–22.

39 Ibid., p. 22.

40 Terhune, Respaut, and Conlin, "As More Transgender Children See Medical Care, Families Confront Many Unknowns."

41 Beal, "Hilary Cass: I Can't Travel on Public Transport After Gender Report."

42 Miroshnychenko A., Roldan Y, Ibrahim S., et al., "Puberty blockers for gender dysphoria in youth: A systematic review and meta-analysis," Archives of Disease in Childhood, Published Online First: January 24, 2025, doi: 10.1136/archdischild-2024-327909.

43 Miroshnychenko A., Ibrahim S., Roldan Y., et al., "Gender affirming hormone therapy for individuals with gender dysphoria aged <26 years: a systematic review and meta-analysis," Archives of Disease in Childhood, January 2025, doi: 10.1136/archdischild-2024-327921.

44 Joshua E. Lewis et al., "Examining Gender-Specific Mental Health Risks after Gender-Affirming Surgery: A National Database Study," The Journal of Sexual Medicine, February 25, 2025, https://academic.oup.com/jsm/advance-article-abstract/doi/10.1093/jsxmed/qdaf026/8042063?redirectedFrom=fulltext.

45 Society for Evidence Based Gender Medicine, "Treatment of Gender-Diverse Youth," available at https://segm.org/.

46 Phone interview with anonymous and Jonathan Butcher, April 2, 2024.

47 Lawmakers in California and New Jersey, for example, have adopted policies that prevent educators from informing parents when their minor-aged child expresses sexual confusion at school. See California Department of Education, "Protections for LGTBQ+ Students: AB 1955," https://www.cde.ca.gov/ci/pl/ab-1955-sum-of-prov.asp; New Jersey Department of Education, "Transgender Student Guidance for School Districts," https://www.nj.gov/education/safety/sandp/climate/docs/Guidance.pdf.

48 Defending Education tracks the school districts that withhold student health information concerning sexual confusion from parents. See Defending Education, "List of School District Transgender—Gender Nonconforming Student Policies," last updated April 21, 2025, https://defendinged.org/investigations/list-of-school-district-transgender-gender-nonconforming-student-policies/.

49 Shrier, Irreversible Damage; Mary Margaret Olohan, Detrans: True Stories of Escaping the Gender Ideology Cult (Washington, D.C.: Regnery, 2024); Stock, Material Girls; Ryan T. Anderson, When Harry Became Sally (New York: Encounter, 2018).

50 Phone interview with anonymous and Jonathan Butcher, April 2, 2024.

51 David Artavia, "J.K. Rowling Says She Faces Threats by 'Hundreds' of Trans Activists Amid Controversy," *Yahoo News*, July 20, 2021, https://www.yahoo.com/entertainment/jk-rowling-says-threats-trans-activists-203717514.html.

52 Jeffrey M. Jones, "More Say Birth Gender Should Dictate Sports Participation," June 12, 2023, https://news.gallup.com/poll/507023/say-birth-gender-dictate-sports-participation.aspx.

53 PRRI Staff, "The Politics of Gender, Pronouns, and Public Education," PRRI, June 8, 2023, https://www.prri.org/research/the-politics-of-gender-pronouns-and-public-education/; for partnerships, see PRRI, "About," https://www.prri.org/about/.

54 Ibid.

55 Stock, p. 14.

56 "The cultural fusion of gender with sexuality has given rise to the idea that a theory of sexuality may be derived directly out of a theory of gender." See Rubin, "Thinking Sex: Notes for a Radical Theory of the Politics of Sexuality," p. 169.

57 Butler, Judith. "Performative Acts and Gender Constitution: An Essay in Phenomenology and Feminist Theory." *Theatre Journal* 40, no. 4 (1988): 519–31, https://doi.org/10.2307/3207893.

58 Richards, "What Is Gender Ideology?"

59 Leonard Sax, "How Common Is Intersex? A Response to Anne Fausto-Sterling," *Journal of Sex Research* 30 (2002), pp. 174–178, https://www.tandfonline.com/doi/abs/10.1080/00224490209552139.

60 Jay Richards, "Why States Must Define Sex Precisely," The Heritage Foundation, March 31, 2023, https://www.heritage.org/gender/commentary/why-states-must-define-sex-precisely; see also Ryan Anderson, "The Philosophical Contradictions of the Transgender Worldview," *Public Discourse*, February 1, 2018, https://www.thepublicdiscourse.com/2018/02/20971/ .

61 New York Times/Siena Poll, September 2022, https://www.nytimes.com/interactive/2022/09/16/upshot/september-2022-times-siena-poll-crosstabs.html.

62 Florida Gov. Ron DeSantis, "Governor Ron DeSantis Signs Historic Bill to Protect Parental Rights in Education," press release, March 28, 2022, https://www.flgov.com/2022/03/28/governor-ron-desantis-signs-historic-bill-to-protect-parental-rights-in-education/.

63 Joseph Ax, "Florida Education Board Extends Ban on Gender Identity Lessons to all Grades," Reuters, April 19, 2023, https://www.reuters.com/world/us/florida-education-board-vote-extending-ban-gender-identity-lessons-2023-04-19/.

64 Andrew DeMillo, "Other States Are Copying Florida's 'Don't Say Gay' Efforts," Associated Press, March 23, 2023, https://apnews.com/article/huckabee-sanders-desantis-dont-say-gay-lgbtq-702fd5dc9633a7c93432f582de51a5fb.

65 PEN America, "Book Bans," https://pen.org/book-bans/.

66 Jay P. Greene, Max Eden, and Madison Marino, "The Book Ban Mirage," Education Freedom Institute, July 2023, https://www.aei.org/wp-content/uploads/2023/07/EFI-Book_Ban_Mirage-2.pdf?x91208.

67 Ibid.

68 Ibid.

69 Phone interview with Erin Friday and Jonathan Butcher, April 4, 2024.

70 Ibid.

71 Jonathan wrote more about the AMA's new glossary in "The Critical Contagion: Gender and Critical Race Theories," Journal of Interdisciplinary Studies, Vol. 36, 2024, https://jis3.org/contents2024/. See also, American Medical Association, "Advancing Health Equity: A Guide to Language, Narrative, and Concepts," https://www.ama-assn.org/system/files/ama-aamc-equity-guide.pdf.

72 Ibid., p. 7.

73 Ibid.

74 Ibid., p. 15.

75 Ibid., p. 7.

76 Ibid., p. 6.

77 Phone interview with Erin Friday and Jonathan Butcher, April 4, 2024.

78 Ibid.

79 New York Public Radio, "I'd Rather Have a Living Son than a Dead Daughter," August 2, 2016, https://www.wnycstudios.org/podcasts/onlyhuman/episodes/id-rather-have-living-son-dead-daughter.

80 Jay Greene, Ph.D., "Puberty Blockers, Cross-Sex Hormones, and Youth Suicide," Heritage Foundation Backgrounder No. 3712, June 13, 2022, https://www.heritage.org/sites/default/files/2022-06/BG3712_0.pdf; Jonathan Butcher, "New Jersey Schools Want to Talk to Kids about Sex—and Keep It a Secret," Fox News, April 14, 2022, https://www.foxnews.com/opinion/new-jersey-schools-phil-murphy-sex-education-jonathan-butcher; Mackenzie Mays, "Newsom Signs Bill Banning Schools from Notifying Parents about Student Gender Identity," The Los Angeles Times," July 15, 2024, https://www.latimes.com/california/story/2024-07-15/newsom-bans-schools-from-requiring-that-parents-are-notified-about-student-gender-identity.

81 "A superior research design shows that easing access to puberty blockers and cross-sex hormones by minors without parental consent increases suicide rates." See Greene, "Puberty Blockers, Cross-Sex Hormones, and Youth Suicide."

82 Phone interview with anonymous and Jonathan Butcher, April 2, 2024.

83 Phone interview with Erin Friday and Jonathan Butcher, April 4, 2024.

84 Ibid.

85 Virginia Allen, "Mom Explains What It Took to Rescue Daughter from Transgenderism," The Daily Signal, January 30, 2023, https://www.dailysignal.com/2023/01/30/activist-mom-explains-what-it-took-to-rescue-daughter-from-transgenderism/.

86 Phone interview with Erin Friday and Jonathan Butcher, April 4, 2024.

87 Dominic Yeatman, "Feminist Campaigner Says She Stopped Supporting Trans Rights After Being Beaten and Raped by Transgender Woman," Daily Mail, May 22, 2024, https://www.dailymail.co.uk/news/article-13445629/raped-transgender-woman-lgbt-oklahoma-tulsa.html.

88 Ibid.

89 Bailey Gallion, "Transgender Sexual Assault Claims at Brevard Public Schools Could Bring New State Rules," *USA Today*, August 19, 2022, https://www.floridatoday.com/story/news/education/2022/08/19/transgender-sexual-assault-report-bathroom-brevard-randy-fine-fdoe-could-bring-new-state-rules/10356216002/.

90 J. K. Rowling, "J.K. Rowling Writes about Her Reasons for Speaking Out on Sex and Gender Issues," jkrowling.com, June 10, 2020, https://www.jkrowling.com/opinions/j-k-rowling-writes-about-her-reasons-for-speaking-out-on-sex-and-gender-issues/.

91 Katy Steinmetz, "Why LGBT Advocates Say Bathroom 'Predators' Argument Is a Red Herring," *Time*, May 2, 2016, https://time.com/4314896/transgender-bathroom-bill-male-predators-argument/.

92 German Lopez, "Anti-Transgender Bathroom Hysteria, Explained," *Vox*, February 22, 2017, https://www.vox.com/2016/5/5/11592908/transgender-bathroom-laws-rights.

93 AP, "Virginia Family Sues School System for $30 million Over Student's Sexual Assault in Bathroom," October 6, 2023, https://apnews.com/article/loudoun-virginia-lawsuit-transgender-bathroom-sexual-assault-a26168568cc20c2aa6cec9bef50e7c3f.

94 Hannah Natanson, "Loudoun Fires Superintendent after Grand Jury Blasts Schools' Handling of Sex Assaults," *The Washington Post*, December 7, 2022, https://www.washingtonpost.com/education/2022/12/07/loudoun-superintendent-scott-ziegler-fired/.

95 Briana Oser, "Young Girl Is Raped in School Bathroom by Transgender Peer," *Washington Examiner*, June 20, 2023, https://www.washingtonexaminer.com/opinion/1974562/young-girl-is-raped-in-school-bathroom-by-transgender-peer/.

96 *Daily Mail*, "'I'm Trans by the Way': Wisconsin High School Is Under Fire after Trans Woman, 18, 'Exposed Their Male Genitalia to Four Freshmen Girls, 14, in Locker Room Showers' After a Swim Class," October 9, 2023, https://www.dailymail.co.uk/news/article-12000615/Wisconsin-high-school-fire-trans-woman-18-exposed-genitalia-freshmen-girls-shower.html.

97 Dana Kennedy, "17-year-Old Scolded for Crying Over Transgender Woman's Penis at YMCA," *New York Post*, January 14, 2023, https://nypost.com/2023/01/14/sighting-of-trans-womans-penis-in-ymca-locker-room-sparks-tears/.

98 Dominic Yeatman, "Horrific Violence Erupts at South Carolina Women's Shelter After Staff Unwittingly Let Transgender Woman Move In," *Daily Mail*, July 29, 2024, https://www.dailymail.co.uk/news/article-13685741/shelter-vulnerable-women-children-transgender-attack-miracle-hill-ministries.html.

99 Zipporah Osei, "Swampscott Field Hockey Injury Has Readers Questioning Mixed-Gender Youth Sports," *Boston.com*, November 14, 2023, https://www.boston.com/community/readers-say/swampscott-field-hockey-injury-has-readers-questioning-mixed-gender-youth-sports/.

100 Letter to U.S. Department of Education Secretary Miguel Cardona, Docket ID ED-2021-OCR-0166, August 2, 2022, https://static.heritage.org/2022/Butcher_Burke_TitleIX.pdf; Luke Gentile, "WATCH: Transgender Rugby Player Slams Female Athletes, Coach Says Three Injured," *Washington Examiner*, April 14, 2022, https://www.washingtonexaminer.com/news/1065633/watch-transgender-rugby-player-slams-female-athletes-coach-says-three-injured/.

101 Steven Rondina, "MMA Fighter Paints Her Opponent Red After Slashing Elbow, Violent Slam," *Bleacher Report*, March 24, 2018, https://bleacherreport.com/articles/2766462-mma-fighterpaints-her-opponent-red-after-slashing-elbow-violent-slam; Monique Curet, "Social Media Posts Mislead about Transgender MMA Fighter's Injuries to Opponents," *PolitiFact*, March 16, 2021, https://www.politifact.com/factchecks/2021/mar/16/facebook-posts/social-media-posts-mislead-about-transgender-mma-f/.

102 See Riley Gaines, "Save Women's Sports," Independent Women's Forum, https://www.iwf.org/save-womens-sports-riley-gaines/.

103 Houston Keene, "Riley Gaines Hits Back at 'Squad' Dem Calling Her Testimony 'Transphobic': You're a 'Misogynist,'" Fox News, December 5, 2023, https://www.foxnews.com/politics/riley-gaines-hits-back-squad-dem-calling-her-testimony-transphobic-youre-misogynist.

104 Jones, "More Say Birth Gender Should Dictate Sports Participation."

105 Sophie Mann, "Outrage as Five Transgender Students Dominate the Volleyball Court at a Women's College Varsity Game—as Biological Females are Kicked Down the Bench," *Daily Mail*, February 6, 2024, https://www.dailymail.co.uk/news/article-13051969/Outrage-FIVE-transgender-students-dominate-volleyball-court-womens-college-varsity-game-biological-females-kicked-bench.html.

106 Shauneen Miranda, "Over Half of States Sue to Block Biden Title IX Rule Protecting LGBTQ+ Students," *West Virginia Watch*, May 21, 2024, https://www.msn.com/en-us/news/us/over-half-of-states-sue-to-block-biden-title-ix-rule-protecting-lgbtq-students/ar-BB1mNwdQ.

107 Memorandum from Dr. Cade Brumley to School System Leaders & Schools [*sic*] Boards, April 22, 2024, https://doe.louisiana.gov/docs/default-source/newsroom/dr--cade-brumley_title-ix-memo-4_22_2024.pdf?sfvrsn=beae6e18_0.

108 Cade Brumley phone interview with Jonathan Butcher, February 4, 2025.

109 Ibid.

110 Ibid.

111 Phone interview with anonymous and Jonathan Butcher, April 2, 2024.

112 Phone interview with Erin Friday and Jonathan Butcher, April 4, 2024.

113 California Family Council, "Protect Kids CA Launches Petition to Repeal Transgender Policies and Protect Parent Rights," December 18, 2023, https://www.californiafamily.org/2023/12/protect-kids-ca-launches-petition-to-repeal-transgender-policies-and-protect-parent-rights/.

114 Ibid.

115 Phone interview with Erin Friday and Jonathan Butcher, April 4, 2024.

116 Fifty-sixth Arizona Legislature, HB 1511, March 11, 2024 hearing, https://www.azleg.gov/videoplayer/?eventID=2024031032&startStreamAt=10365.

117 Ibid.

118 American Federation of Teachers, "Defeat Anti-LGBTQIA+ 'Don't Say Gay' and Anti-Transgender Bills and Attacks with Mass Pride and Mass Action," AFT Reso-

lution, https://www.aft.org/resolution/defeat-anti-lgbtqia-dont-say-gay-and-anti-transgender-bills-and-attacks-mass-pride-and.

119 American Federation of Teachers, "AFT's Weingarten on Biden Administration's Proposed Title IX Rule," press release, April 6, 2023, https://www.aft.org/press-release/afts-weingarten-biden-administrations-proposed-title-ix-rule.

120 National Education Association, "NEA LGBTQ+ Resources," https://www.nea.org/resource-library/nea-lgbtq-resources.

121 Mary Ellen Flannery, "Great Summer Reads for Educators!" NEA News, June 5, 2023, https://www.nea.org/nea-today/all-news-articles/great-summer-reads-educators.

122 American Federation of Teachers, "Celebrate Pride with the AFT," https://www.aft.org/pride.

CHAPTER FIVE

1 Ronald Reagan, "Radio Address to the Nation on Education," Ronald Reagan Presidential Library and Museum, March 12, 1983, https://www.reaganlibrary.gov/archives/speech/radio-address-nation-education-1.

2 The 2025 "Annual Meeting and Representative Assembly" was held in Portland, Oregon. See "NEA's Annual Meeting and Representative Assembly," available at https://www.nea.org/professional-excellence/conferences-events/annual-meeting-and-representative-assembly.

3 National Education Association, "2024–2025 NEA Resolutions," pp. 92–93, 104, 106, available at https://www.nea.org/sites/default/files/2024-10/nea-resolutions_2024-2025.pdf.

4 Ibid., p. 106.

5 Lindsey M. Burke, Ph.D., Jonathan Butcher, Emilie Kao, and Mike Gonzalez, "The Culture of American K-12 Education: A National Survey of Parents and School Board Members," Heritage Foundation Special Report No. 241, January 11, 2021, p. 17, https://www.heritage.org/sites/default/files/2021-01/SR241.pdf.

6 Ibid.

7 Emily Peck, "'The Backlash Is Real': Behind DEI's Rise and Fall," Axios, April 2, 2024, https://www.axios.com/2024/04/02/dei-backlash-diversity; Erica Pandey, "Colleges Dismantle DEI," Axios, December 7, 2024, https://www.axios.com/2024/12/07/colleges-end-dei-programs-florida-michigan-utah; Jonathan Butcher, "Restoring Equality in Employment: Sinking the DEI Ship," Heritage Foundation Backgrounder No. 3875, November 27, 2024, https://www.heritage.org/progressivism/report/restoring-equality-employment-sinking-the-dei-ship; for a map tracking the legislation prohibiting DEI in state government, with a focus on higher education, see The Heritage Foundation, "DEI: A State Legislation Tracker," Data Visualizations, https://datavisualizations.heritage.org/education/dei-a-state-legislation-tracker/.

8 The White House, "Ending Radical and Wasteful Government DEI Programs and Preferencing," Presidential Actions, January 20, 2025, https://www.whitehouse.gov/presidential-actions/2025/01/ending-radical-and-wasteful-government-dei-programs-and-preferencing/.

9 National Education Association, "2023-2024 NEA Resolutions," p. 107, https://www.nea.org/sites/default/files/2023-08/nea-resolutions_2023-2024.pdf.

10 Matthew M. Chingos, "Does Expanding School Choice Increase Segregation?" Brookings Institution, May 15, 2013, https://www.brookings.edu/articles/does-expanding-school-choice-increase-segregation/; Greg Forster, "What the Data Show on School Choice and Segregation," Ed Choice, March 23, 2017, https://www.edchoice.org/data-show-school-choice-segregation/.

11 Phillip W. Magness, "School Choice's Antiracist History," The Wall Street Journal, October 18, 2021, https://www.wsj.com/opinion/school-choice-antiracist-history-integration-funding-segregation-11634568700; see also Phillip Magness and Chris W. Surprenant, "School Vouchers, Segregation, and Consumer Sovereignty," Journal of School Choice, Volume 13, No. 3, 2019, https://www.tandfonline.com/doi/full/10.1080/15582159.2019.1591157?needAccess=true.

12 Forster, https://www.educationnext.org/what-data-show-on-school-choice-and-segregation/.

13 Education Next, "Results from the 2022 Education Next Survey: Support for Choice," https://www.educationnext.org/2022-ednext-poll-interactive/.

14 Ibid.

15 Ibid.

16 National Education Association, "2023-2024 NEA Resolutions," p. 104.

17 Heritage Foundation Data Visualizations, "Education Power for Parents: A State Legislation Tracker: Given Name Act," https://datavisualizations.heritage.org/education/education-power-for-parents-a-state-legislation-tracker/.

18 Katie Millard and Natalie Fahmy, "Ohio 'Given Name Act' Proposes Strict Rules for Names, Pronouns in Schools," NBC 4, March 31, 2025, https://www.nbc4i.com/news/politics/ohio-given-name-act-proposes-strict-rules-for-names-pronouns-in-schools/.

19 Federal Bureau of Investigation, "Summary and Timeline Related to Parkland Shooting Investigation," March 20, 2018, https://www.fbi.gov/news/speeches-and-testimony/summary-and-timeline-related-to-parkland-shooting-investigation; Metropolitan Nashville Police Department, "MNPD Concludes Covenant School Mass Murder Investigation," April 2, 2025, https://www.nashville.gov/departments/police/news/mnpd-concludes-covenant-school-mass-murder-investigation.

20 For a review of the research and data on school discipline, see Federal Commission on School Safety, "Final Report," U.S. Department of Education, U.S. Department of Health and Human Services, U.S. Department of Homeland Security, and U.S. Department of Justice, December 2018, https://www.schoolsafety.gov/resource/final-report-federal-commission-school-safety.

21 National Education Association, 2023-2024 Resolutions, p. 44.

22 Brooke Schultz, "Restorative Justice in Schools," Education Week, May 31, 2024, https://www.edweek.org/leadership/restorative-justice-in-schools-explained/2024/05.

23 U.S. Department of Justice and U.S. Department of Education, Dear Colleague Letter on the Nondiscriminatory Administration of School Discipline, January 8, 2014, https://www2.ed.gov/about/offices/list/ocr/letters/colleague-201401-title-vi.pdf.

24 *People Who Care v. Rockford Bd. of Educ.*, 851 F. Supp. 905 (N.D. Ill. 1994); Jonathan
    Butcher, "The U.S. Department of Education Should Rescind 2014 Federal School-
    Discipline Guidance," The Heritage Foundation Issue Brief No. 4833, March 28,
    2018, https://www.heritage.org/education/report/the-us-department-education-
    should-rescind-2014-federal-school-discipline-guidance.

25 News release, "Educators Gather at the White House to Rethink School Discipline,"
    U.S. Department of Education, July 22, 2015, retrieved from https://web.archive.
    org/web/20150727001541/https://www.ed.gov/news/press-releases/educators-
    gather-white-house-rethink-school-discipline. For example, the Obama administration
    praised Broward County School District (Florida) for its PROMISE program, a
    student discipline program that tried to limit student interaction with law enforce-
    ment and used restorative justice practices instead.

26 U.S. Department of Education and U.S. Department of Justice, Dear Colleague Let-
    ter, OCR-000113, December 21, 2018, https://www.ed.gov/sites/ed/files/about/
    offices/list/ocr/letters/colleague-201812.pdf; U.S. Department of Education, "Guid-
    ing Principles for Creating Safe, Inclusive, Supportive, and Fair School Climates,"
    March 2023, https://www.ed.gov/sites/ed/files/policy/gen/guid/school-discipline/
    guiding-principles.pdf.

27 Center on Gender Justice and Opportunity, "School-Based Restorative Justice: State-
    by-State Analysis," https://genderjusticeandopportunity.georgetown.edu/report/
    school-based-restorative-justice-state-by-state-analysis/; National Center for Educa-
    tion Statistics, "More Than 80 Percent of U.S. Public Schools Report Pandemic Has
    Negatively Impacted Student Behavior and Socio-Emotional Development," July 6,
    2022, https://nces.ed.gov/whatsnew/press_releases/07_06_2022.asp.

28 National Center for Education Statistics, "More Than 80 Percent of U.S. Public
    Schools Report Pandemic Has Negatively Impacted Student Behavior and Socio-
    Emotional Development."

29 Ibid.

30 Arianna Prothero, "Student Behavior Isn't Getting Any Better, Survey Shows," Educa-
    tion Week, April 20, 2023, https://www.edweek.org/leadership/student-behavior-
    isnt-getting-any-better-survey-shows/2023/04.

31 Ibid.

32 Government of Canada, "The Effects of Restorative Justice Programming: A Review
    of the Empirical [sic]," available at https://www.justice.gc.ca/eng/rp-pr/csj-sjc/jsp-
    sjp/rr00_16/p2.html.

33 Joe Hudson, "Contemporary Origins of Restorative Justice Programming: The Min-
    nesota Restitution Center," *Federal Probation*, Vol. 76, No. 2, https://www.uscourts.
    gov/sites/default/files/76_2_9_0.pdf.

34 Ibid., p. 2.

35 Ibid.

36 neaToday, "How Restorative Practices Work for Students and Educators," June 13,
    2019, https://www.nea.org/nea-today/all-news-articles/how-restorative-practices-
    work-students-and-educators.

37 Ibid.

38 We Are Teachers, "What Is Restorative Justice," August 29, 2023, https://www.
    weareteachers.com/restorative-justice/#:~:text=Restorative%20justice%20encour-
    ages%20kids%20to,the%20traumas%20they%20have%20faced.

39 Abigail M. Gray et al., "Discipline in Context: Suspension, Climate, and PBIS in
    the School District of Philadelphia," CPRE Research Reports, 2017, https://files.
    eric.ed.gov/fulltext/ED586779.pdf; Matthew P. Steinberg and Johanna Lacoe, "The
    Academic and Behavioral Consequences of Discipline Policy Reform: Evidence
    from Philadelphia," The Thomas B. Fordham Institute, December 5, 2017, available
    at https://stopradicaled.com/wp-content/uploads/2020/10/The-Academic-and-
    Behavioral-Consequences-of-Discipline-Policy-Reform-Evidence-from-Philadelphia.
    pdf.

40 Gray et al., "Discipline in Context: Suspension, Climate, and PBIS in the School
    District of Philadelphia," p. 21.

41 Catherine H. Augustine et al., *Restorative Practices Help Reduce Student Suspensions*
    (Santa Monica, CA: RAND Corporation, 2018), https://www.rand.org/pubs/
    research_briefs/RB10051.html.

42 Ibid., p. 3.

43 Lauren Sartain et al., "Suspending Chicago's Students," The University of Chicago
    Consortium on Chicago School Research, September 2015, p. 5, https://consortium.
    uchicago.edu/sites/default/files/2023-06/Suspending%20Chicago%E2%80%99s%20
    Students-Sep2015-Consortium.pdf.

44 *Phi Delta Kappan*, "Frustration in the Schools," September 2019, p. K18, https://
    pdkpoll.org/wp-content/uploads/2020/05/pdkpoll51-2019.pdf.

45 Ibid., p. K20.

46 *Education Next*, "2019 Education Next Poll Interactive," https://www.educationnext.
    org/2019-ednext-poll-interactive/.

47 Butcher, "The U.S. Department of Education Should Rescind 2014 Federal School-
    Discipline Guidance"; see also Andrew Pollack and Max Eden, *Why Meadow Died:
    The People and the Policies that Created the Parkland Shooter and Endanger America's
    Students* (Nashville: Post Hill Press, 2019).

48 Mark Keierleber, "Embattled Florida School Superintendent Runcie to Step Down
    After Perjury Arrest Tied to Parkland Shooting Inquiry," the74, April 29, 2021,
    https://www.the74million.org/article/embattled-florida-school-superintendent-
    runcie-to-step-down-after-perjury-arrest-tied-to-parkland-shooting-inquiry/; Scott
    Travis, "Perjury Case of ex-Broward Schools Chief Robert Runcie Set for Trial in
    June," *Sun-Sentinel*, March 14, 2025, https://www.sun-sentinel.com/2025/03/14/
    perjury-case-of-ex-broward-schools-chief-robert-runcie-set-for-trial-in-june/.

49 News release, "Educators Gather at the White House to Rethink School Discipline."

50 Pollack and Eden, *Why Meadow Died*.

51 National Education Association, 2023-2024 NEA Resolutions, p. 92.

52 Ibid.

53 Open Secrets, "Teacher Unions Summary," https://www.opensecrets.org/industries/
    indus?ind=L1300.

54 Gallup, "Party Affiliation," 2024, at https://news.gallup.com/poll/15370/party-affiliation.aspx

55 National Center for Education Statistics, "Characteristics of Public School Teachers," May 2023, https://nces.ed.gov/programs/coe/indicator/clr/public-school-teachers.

56 EdWeek Research Center, "Educator Political Perceptions: A National Survey," December 2017, https://epe.brightspotcdn.com/be/2b/1bc98850470e9fecf8f80 85a3284/educator-political-perceptions-education-week-12-12-2017.pdf.

57 Americans for Fair Treatment, "NEA: Where Do Your Union Dues Go?" https://americansforfairtreatment.org/resources-and-data/nea-where-do-your-union-dues-go/.

58 American Federation of Teachers, "Randi Weingarten," https://www.aft.org/about/leadership/randi-weingarten.

59 Jon Brown, "Randi Weingarten Takes Flak on Social Media for Ukraine Trip as US Schools Struggle," Fox News, October 10, 2022, at https://www.foxnews.com/us/randi-weingarten-takes-flak-social-media-ukraine-trip-us-schools-struggle

60 Jon Levine, "Powerful Teachers Union Influenced CDC on School Reopenings, Emails Show," *New York Post*, May 1, 2021, https://nypost.com/2021/05/01/teachers-union-collaborated-with-cdc-on-school-reopening-emails/.

61 John E. Chubb, "The System," in *A Primer on America's Public Schools*, Terry M. Moe, ed. (Stanford: Hoover Institution Press, 2001), pp. 25–27.

62 Ibid.

63 Marc Porter Magee, Teacher Unions and the Influence of Special Interests in Local Elections, *FutureEd*, March 18, 2021, at https://www.future-ed.org/teacher-unions-and-the-outsized-influence-of-special-interests-in-local-elections/

64 Ibid.

65 Chubb, "The System," p. 24.

66 Hartney, Michael T., and Vladimir Kogan, The Politics of Teachers' Union Endorsements. (EdWorkingPaper: 23-841), 2024, Retrieved from Annenberg Institute at Brown University: https://doi.org/10.26300/9ygx-5730

67 Michael T. Hartney, "Students or Salaries? How Unions Choose School Board Candidates," Manhattan Institute, November 2023, p. 1, https://files.eric.ed.gov/fulltext/ED660942.pdf.

68 Ibid.

69 Hartney, Michael T., and Leslie K. Finger, Politics, Markets, and Pandemics: Public Education's Response to COVID-19. (EdWorkingPaper: 20-304, 2020, Retrieved from Annenberg Institute at Brown University: https://doi.org/10.26300/8ff8-3945.

70 Virginia Allen, "The Real Harm of Teachers Union's Decision to Keep Schools Closed," *The Daily Signal*, January 29, 2021, at https://www.dailysignal.com/2021/01/29/the-real-harm-of-teachers-unions-decision-to-keep-schools-closed/.

71 Jonathan Butcher, "Unions Are Keeping Students and Teachers Out of the Classroom. Here's What Lawmakers Can Do About It," *The Daily Signal*, February 16, 2021, at https://www.heritage.org/education/commentary/unions-are-keeping-students-and-teachers-out-the-classroom-heres-what

72 Jonathan Butcher, "Union Activities Beg the Question: How, Specifically, Is This Going to Make the Education of Children Better?" *NextSteps*, August 27, 2020, at https://www.redefinedonline.org/2020/08/union-activities-beg-the-question-how-specifically-is-this-going-to-make-the-education-of-children-better/

73 Mike Antonucci, "The Long Reach of Teachers Unions," *Education Next*, Fall 2010, at http://educationnext.org/the-long-reach-of-teachers-unions/

74 Ibid.; Open Secrets, National Education Association, 2024 Cycle, https://www.opensecrets.org/orgs/national-education-assn/recipients?id=d000000064.

75 The White House, "Improving Education Outcomes by Empowering Parents, States, and Communities," Executive Orders, March 20, 2025, https://www.whitehouse.gov/presidential-actions/2025/03/improving-education-outcomes-by-empowering-parents-states-and-communities/.

76 National Education Association, "NEA and ACLU Sue U.S. Department of Education Over Unlawful Attack on Educational Equity," press release, March 5, 2025, https://www.neari.org/about-neari/media-center/press-releases/nea-and-aclu-sue-us-department-education-over-unlawful; Brooke Schultz, "NEA, AFT, Sue to Block Trump's Education Department Dismantling," *Education Week*, March 24, 2025, https://www.edweek.org/policy-politics/nea-aft-sue-to-block-trumps-education-department-dismantling/2025/03.

77 Andrew Coulson, *Market Education: The Unknown History* (New Brunswick: Transaction, 1999), pp. 107–176.

78 Charles Leslie Glenn, *The Myth of the Common School* (Boston: University of Massachusetts Press, 1988); Mass Moments, "Massachusetts Passes First Education Law," https://www.massmoments.org/moment-details/massachusetts-passes-first-education-law.html; see also David Carleton, "Old Deluder Satan Act of 1647," Free Speech Center at Middle Tennessee State University, updated July 2, 2024, https://firstamendment.mtsu.edu/article/old-deluder-satan-act-of-1647/.

79 David Carleton, "Old Deluder Satan Act of 1647."

80 Glenn, *The Myth of the Common School*, p. 64.

81 Glenn, *The Myth of the Common School*, pp. 133–135.

82 Mann, H., Twelfth annual report to the secretary of the Massachusetts State Board of Education. (Boston: Dutton and Wentworth, State Printers, 1848), Retrieved from https://faculty.etsu.edu/history/documents/hmann.htm.

83 Ibid.

84 Coulson, pp. 110–115; Glenn, pp. 5–10, 249–251.

85 U.S. Department of Education, "An Overview of the U.S. Department of Education," available at https://www.ed.gov/about/ed-overview/an-overview-of-the-us-department-of-education--pg-1.

86 Gordon W. Gunderson, "History of the National School Lunch Program," available at https://www.fns.usda.gov/nslp/program-history.

87 "Federal Education Policy and the States, 1945–2009: A Brief Synopsis," New York State Archives, January 2006, p. 11, available at https://www.academia.edu/36680252/Federal_Education_Policy_and_the_States_1945_2009_A_Brief_Synopsis_States_Impact_on_Federal_Education_Policy_Project.

88 Ibid.

89 Ibid., p. 11.

90 Ibid., p. 12.

91 Ibid., p. 12.

92 Ibid., p. 16; see also Lindsey M. Burke and Jonathan Butcher, eds., *The Not So Great Society* (Washington, D.C.: 2019).

93 Lyndon B. Johnson, "The Great Society," speech at the University of Michigan, May 22, 1964, https://www.presidency.ucsb.edu/documents/remarks-the-university-michigan. The first two places that LBJ had in mind were the cities and the countryside; Burke and Butcher, eds., *The Not-So-Great Society*.

94 Ibid.

95 See Burke and Butcher, eds., *The Not-So-Great Society*.

96 Ben Scafidi, Ph.D., "The Productivity Decline in American Public Schools Since the 1965 ESEA: Trends in Spending, Staffing and Achievement," in *The Not-So-Great Society*, Lindsey M. Burke, Ph.D., and Jonathan Butcher, eds., pp. 27–36.

97 Michael Puma et al., "Third Grade Follow Up to the Head Start Impact Study," Final Report, OPRE No. 2012-45, U.S. Department of Health and Human Services, October 2012, https://files.eric.ed.gov/fulltext/ED539264.pdf.

98 Paul E. Peterson, Ph.D., "Student Achievement Gap Fails to Close for Nearly 50 Years—It's Time to Focus on Teacher Quality," in *The Not-So-Great Society*, Lindsey M. Burke, Ph.D., and Jonathan Butcher, eds., pp. 87–94.

99 Benjamin Scafidi, "Back to the Staffing Surge," *EdChoice*, May 2017, at https://www.edchoice.org/wp-content/uploads/2017/05/Back-to-the-Staffing-Surge-by-Ben-Scafidi.pdf

100 U.S. Department of Education, National Center for Education Statistics, Common Core of Data (CCD), "State Nonfiscal Survey of Public Elementary/Secondary Education," 2012–2013 through 2022–2023. (This table was prepared January 2024), https://nces.ed.gov/programs/digest/d23/tables/dt23_213.40.asp

101 Jeannette Smyth, "The Education of Shirley Mount Hufstedler," *The Washington Post*, January 27, 1980, https://www.washingtonpost.com/archive/lifestyle/1980/01/27/the-education-of-shirley-mount-hufstedler/53577ec5-9548-4ac4-86d5-ffa9f0bd60b6/; David Stephens, "President Carter, the Congress, and NEA: Creating the Department of Education," *Political Science Quarterly*, Vol. 98, No. 4 (Winter 1983–1984), pp. 641-663, available at https://www.jstor.org/stable/2149722.

102 Ibid.

103 Stephens, "President Carter, the Congress, and NEA: Creating the Department of Education," p. 644.

104 Frank Thompson, Jr., *The Presidential Campaign 1976: Jimmy Carter*, Vol. 1, Part 1 (Washington, DC: U.S. Government Printing Office, 1978), p. 252–253, https://books.google.com/books?id=gHNAAAAAIAAJ&pg=PA1155&lpg=PA1155&dq=Walter+Mondale+speech+to+National+Education+Association+1976&source=bl&ots=1kvy3nzxsE&sig=ACfU3U3_F4SkFLLMcvLaOkQFJhYSmzNFUA&

hl=en&sa=X&ved=2ahUKEwiW-p2AgcXoAhVUlHIEHah8B9AQ6AEwBHoE-
CAsQAQ#v=snippet&q=National%20Education&f=false

105 Stephens, "President Carter, the Congress, and NEA: Creating the Department of Education," p. 643.

106 Stephens, "President Carter, the Congress, and NEA: Creating the Department of Education," pp. 655, 657.

107 96th Congress, S.210, An Act to Establish a Department of Education, and for Other Purposes, https://www.congress.gov/bill/96th-congress/senate-bill/210 and The American Presidency Project, Executive Order 12212—The Department of Education, https://www.presidency.ucsb.edu/documents/executive-order-12212-the-department-education.

108 One Hundred Fifth Congress, Second Session, "Education at a Crossroads: What Works and What's Wasted in Education Today," Subcommittee Report by the Subcommittee on Oversight and Investigations of the Committee on Education and the Workforce, U.S. House of Representatives, July 17, 1998, https://files.eric.ed.gov/fulltext/ED431238.pdf.

109 Ibid., p. 13.

110 Ibid., p. 12.

111 Ibid., p. 13.

112 Edmund Burke, *Reflections on the Revolution in France*, Vol. 1, found in *The British Prose Writers*, vol. XXI (London: John Sharpe, Piccadilly), p. 64; Alexis de Tocqueville, *Democracy in America* (Chicago: University of Chicago Press, 2002) (vol. 1 first printed 1835 and vol. 2 in 1840).

CONCLUSION

1 E. J. Dionne Jr. and Thomas E. Mann, "Polling & Public Opinion: The Good, the Bad, and the Ugly," Brookings Institution, June 1, 2003, https://www.brookings.edu/articles/polling-public-opinion-the-good-the-bad-and-the-ugly.

2 U.S. Department of Education, "U.S. Department of Education Cuts Over $600 Million in Divisive Teacher Training Grants," press release, February 17, 2025, https://www.ed.gov/about/news/press-release/us-department-of-education-cuts-over-600-million-divisive-teacher-training-grants.

3 See, for example, Elena Moore, "Trump Administration Cancels $400 Million in Federal Dollars for Columbia University," NPR, March 7, 2025, https://www.npr.org/2025/03/07/nx-s1-5321326/trump-administration-columbia-university-400-million-cancelled; U.S. Department of Education, "DOG, HHS, ED, and GSA Announce Initial Cancelation of Grants and Contracts to Columbia University Worth $400 Million," press release, March 7, 2025, https://www.ed.gov/about/news/press-release/doj-hhs-ed-and-gsa-announce-initial-cancelation-of-grants-and-contracts-columbia-university-worth-400-million.

4 "U.S. Department of Education Initiates Reduction in Force," U.S. Department of Education, March 11, 2025, at https://www.ed.gov/about/news/press-release/us-department-of-education-initiates-reduction-force.

5 "Improving Education Outcomes by Empowering Parents, States, and Communities,"

Executive Order, March 20, 2025, at https://www.whitehouse.gov/presidential-actions/2025/03/improving-education-outcomes-by-empowering-parents-states-and-communities/.

6 Rapid Response 47 [@RapidResponse47], "President Trump announces that the SBA will begin handling student loans -- and that HHS will handle the special needs and nutrition programs.'Coming out of the Department of Education immediately.'" Twitter, March 21, 2025, https://x.com/RapidResponse47/status/1903109579895963703.

7 *Firing Line*, "Presidential Hopeful Ronald Reagan," January 14, 1980, https://www.youtube.com/watch?v=lTyZAul60ok; Bernd Debusmann, Jr., "Trump's Move to Dismantle Education Department Was a Conservative Dream for Decades," BBC, March 20, 2025, https://www.bbc.com/news/articles/ckg80x2rw58o.

8 Ronald Reagan, weekly radio address, *The New York Times*, March 13, 1983, at https://www.nytimes.com/1983/03/13/us/reagan-in-talk-on-education-calls-for-ending-department.html

9 ComoTV, "Milton Friedman on Government Agencies," YouTube, n.d., https://www.youtube.com/watch?v=aZ8LkRLuEDk.

10 Mark Pitsch, "Dole Campaign Weighs Options on Education," *Education Week*, May 1, 1996, at https://www.edweek.org/policy-politics/dole-campaign-weighs-options-on-education/1996/05.

11 Statement by Joe Lockhart, National Press Secretary, Clinton/Gore96 release, September 9, 1996, at https://www.livingroomcandidate.org/websites/cg96/dole909.html; see also Sarah G. Boyce, "The Obsolescence of *Antonio v. Rodriguez* in the Wake of the Federal Government's Quest to Leave No Child Behind," *Duke Law Journal*, Vol. 61 (2012): 1025, 1039, https://scholarship.law.duke.edu/cgi/viewcontent.cgi?article=1527&context=dlj.

12 William Bennett and Lamar Alexander, "We Both Ran the Education Department and There Are 3 Things We Should Keep," Fox News, March 20, 2025, at https://www.foxnews.com/opinion/william-bennett-lamar-alexander-we-both-ran-education-dept-3-things-keep.

13 104th Congress, H.R.1883 – To strengthen parental, local, and State control of education in the United States by eliminating the Department of Education and redefining the Federal role in education, June 16, 1995, at https://www.congress.gov/bill/104th-congress/house-bill/1883/text.

14 Ibid.

15 "Officials Debate Plans to Scrap or Demote E.D.," *Education Week*, June 14, 1995, at https://www.edweek.org/education/officials-debate-plans-to-scrap-or-demote-e-d/1995/06; Sam Stein, "McCain Backed Abolishing The Department of Education," *Huffington Post*, October 10, 2008, at https://www.huffpost.com/entry/mccain-backed-abolishing_n_125096; Shauneen Miranda, "Only Congress Can Close the Department of Education, and Republicans Are Going to Try," *Georgia Recorder*, March 21, 2025, at https://georgiarecorder.com/2025/03/21/repub/only-congress-can-close-the-department-of-education-and-republicans-are-going-to-try/; Lindsey McPherson and Alex Miller, "Congress' push to eliminate Education Department gains steam under Trump," *Washington Times*, at https://www.washingtontimes.com/

news/2025/mar/26/congress-push-eliminate-education-department-gains-steam-trump/; Lexi Lonas Cochran, "2024 Republicans want to eliminate the Education Department. What would that look like?" *The Hill*, August 27, 2024, at https://thehill.com/homenews/education/4171756-2024-republicans-want-to-eliminate-the-education-department-what-would-that-look-like/.

16 Author was in attendance.

17 Ibid.

18 Peter Pinedo, "Education Leaders Say Trump Dismantling Key Government Agency 'Saved Education,'" Fox News, March 19, 2025, at https://www.foxnews.com/politics/education-leaders-say-trump-dismantling-key-government-agency-saved-education.

19 Jake Stofan, "'Get That Funding Where It Needs To Go': Florida Education Commissioner Weighs in on DOE Dismantling," *Action News Jax*, March 21, 2025, at https://www.actionnewsjax.com/news/local/get-that-funding-where-it-needs-go-florida-education-commissioner-weighs-doe-dismantling/VWASAT5GGRCY3JUOXKZM-PLC2KY/.

20 Joe Gallinaro, "Superintendent Cade Brumley Supports the Dismantling of the U.S. Department Of Education," *Louisiana Radio Network*, March 12, 2025, at https://louisianaradionetwork.com/2025/03/12/superintendent-cade-brumley-supports-the-dismantling-of-the-u-s-department-of-education/.

21 For a review of the research, overall, on increasing taxpayer spending and student success, see Jay P. Greene, *New Yorkers for Students' Educational Rights, et al, v. The State of New York: Expert Report of Jay P. Greene, Ph.D.*, September 13, 2023, available at https://www.heritage.org/sites/default/files/2023-09/Greene%20NY%20Expert%20Report_0.pdf.

22 William J. Bennett, "Our Greedy Colleges," *The New York Times*, February 18, 1987, https://www.nytimes.com/1987/02/18/opinion/our-greedy-colleges.html.

23 Ibid.

24 Ibid.

25 Preston Cooper, "Why College is Too Expensive – And How Competition Can Fix It, Foundation for Research on Equal Opportunity," March 5, 2021, at https://freopp.org/why-college-is-too-expensive-and-how-competition-can-fix-itcb2eb901521b.

26 David O. Lucca, Taylor Nadauld, and Karen Shen, "Credit Supply and the Rise in College Tuition: Evidence from the Expansion in Federal Student Aid Programs," Federal Reserve Bank of New York Staff Reports No. 733, February 2017, https://www.newyorkfed.org/medialibrary/media/research/staff_reports/sr733.pdfb.

27 Douglas Belkin and Scott Thrum, "Deans List: Hiring Spree Fattens College Bureaucracy – And Tuition," *The Wall Street Journal*, December 28, 2012, at https://www.wsj.com/articles/SB10001424127887323316804578161490716042814. Belkin and Thrum describe non-teaching staff as "employees hired by colleges and universities to manage or administer people, programs and regulations."

28 See Benjamin Ginsberg, *The Fall of the Faculty: The Rise of the All-Administrative University and Why it Matters* (Oxford: Oxford University Press, 2011), pp. 24–25 as cited in "Critical Care: Policy Recommendations to Restore American Higher

Education after the 2020 Coronavirus Shutdown," National Association of Scholars, April 18, 2020, at https://www.nas.org/reports/critical-care/full-report.

29 Cooper, "Why College is Too Expensive – And How Competition Can Fix It, "Foundation for Research on Equal Opportunity."

30 Ibid.

31 National Center for Education Statistics, "Fast Facts: Undergraduate Graduation Rates," https://nces.ed.gov/FastFacts/display.asp?id=40.

32 Lindsey M. Burke, Mary Clare Amselem, and Jamie Hall, "Big Debt, Little Study: What Taxpayers Should Know about College Students' Time Use," The Heritage *Foundation,* July 19, 2016, at https://www.heritage.org/node/10537/print-display.

33 Jaison R. Abel, Richard Deitz, and Yaquin Su, "Are Recent College Graduates Finding Good Jobs?" *Current Issues in Economics and Finance,* Federal Reserve Bank of New York, Vol. 20, No. 1 (2014), p. 4, at https://www.newyorkfed.org/medialibrary/media/research/%20current_issues/ci20-1.pdf

34 Abel, Deitz, and Su, p. 6.

35 Dana Wilkie, "Employers Say College Grads Lack Hard Skills, Too," SHRM, October 21, 2019, at https://www.shrm.org/resourcesandtools/hr-topics/employee-relations/pages/employers-say-college-grads-lack-hard-skills-too.aspx.

36 Jeremy Bauer-Wolf, "Overconfident Students, Dubious Employers," *Inside Higher Ed,* February 23, 2018, at https://www.insidehighered.com/news/2018/02/23/study-students-believe-they-are-prepared-workplace-employers-disagree

37 *Education at a Crossroads: What Works and What's Wasted in Education Today.* Subcommittee Report, Subcommittee on Oversight and Investigations of the Committee on Education and the Workforce, U.S. House of Representatives, One Hundred Fifth Congress, Second Session, July 17, 1998, pp. 11–15, https://files.eric.ed.gov/fulltext/ED431238.pdf.

38 The phrase "laboratories of democracy" comes from the late Supreme Court Justice Louis Brandeis, who said, "It is one of the happy incidents of the federal system that a single courageous State may, if its citizens choose, serve as a laboratory; and try novel social and economic experiments without risk to the rest of the country." See *New State Ice Co. v. Liebmann,* 285 U.S. 262 (1932), available at https://supreme.justia.com/cases/federal/us/285/262/.

39 Wisconsin Statutes, Chapter 119, First Class City School System, 119.23, available at https://docs.legis.wisconsin.gov/statutes/statutes/119/i/23.

40 Ibid.

41 Ohio Department of Education and the Workforce, "Scholarship Historical Information," https://education.ohio.gov/Topics/Other-Resources/Scholarships/Additional-Scholarship-Resources/Historical-Information; Anthony Rebora, "The Cleveland Voucher Program: A Backgrounder," *Education Week,* October 3, 2001, https://www.edweek.org/education/the-cleveland-voucher-program-a-backgrounder/2001/10#:~:text=vouchers%20of%20up%20to%20$2250%20for%20a,first%20to%20allow%20tuition%20vouchers%20to%20be.

42 American Federation for Children, "2015-2016 School Choice Yearbook," p. 16, https://www.federationforchildren.org/wp-content/uploads/2016/09/2015-16-School-Choice-Yearbook-4_27.pdf.

43 Ibid.; *Zelman v. Simmons-Harris*, 536 U.S. 639 (2002).

44 Jonathan Butcher, "A Primer on Education Savings Accounts," Heritage Foundation Backgrounder No. 3245, September 15, 2017, https://www.heritage.org/sites/default/files/2017-09/BG3245.pdf.

45 Ibid. Nevada lawmakers also adopted the accounts, but the program was never implemented.

46 See West Virginia Code, §18-8-1, https://code.wvlegislature.gov/18-8-1/; §18-9A-25, https://code.wvlegislature.gov/18-9A/; and §18-31, https://code.wvlegislature.gov/18-31/.

47 Jason Bedrick, "Gov. Ayotte Delivers for New Hampshire Parents," *The Daily Signal*, June 11, 2025, https://www.dailysignal.com/2025/06/11/gov-ayotte-delivers-for-new-hampshire-parents/. For a list of ESA programs, with details on eligibility and year of adoption, see EdChoice, "What Is an Education Savings Account," https://www.edchoice.org/school-choice/education-savings-account/.

48 EdChoice, "123s of School Choice," 2024 ed., p. 10, available at https://www.edchoice.org/wp-content/uploads/2024/06/2024-123s-of-School-Choice.pdf.

49 Ibid., p. 6.

50 Ibid., p. 10.

51 Matthew H. Lee, Jonathan Mills, and Patrick Wolf, "Heterogeneous Impacts Across Schools in the First Four Years of the Louisiana Scholarship Program," April 23, 2019, EDRE Working Paper No. 2019-11. Research finds that a large share of private schools that had diminishing enrollment figures—a sign of poor student outcomes—participated in the program, which depressed student outcomes.

52 EdChoice, "123s of School Choice," p. 10.

53 Ibid.

54 Ibid.

55 Ibid.

56 Patrick J. Wolf, "Civics Exam: Schools of Choice Boost Civic Values," *Education Next*, Vol. 7, No. 3 (Summer 2007), pp. 66–73, available at https://www.educationnext.org/civics-exam/.

57 Corey DeAngelis and Patrick J. Wolf, "Private School Choice and Crime: Evidence from Milwaukee," *Social Science Quarterly*, July 7, 2019, https://onlinelibrary.wiley.com/doi/abs/10.1111/ssqu.12698.

58 Ann Webber, Ning Rui, Roberta Garrison-Mogren, Robert B. Olsen, Babette Gutmann, and Meredith Bachman, "Evaluation of the D.C. Opportunity Scholarship Program: Impacts Three Years After Students Applied," *Institute of Education Sciences*, May 2019, at https://files.eric.ed.gov/fulltext/ED594875.pdf.

59 Eric Bettinger and Robert Slonim, "Using Experimental Economics to Measure the Effects of a Natural Educational Experiment on Altruism," *Journal of Public Economics*, Vol. 90, No 809 (2006), pp. 1625–1648; David J. Fleming, William Mitchell, and

Michael McNally, "Can Markets Make Citizens? School Vouchers, Political Tolerance, and Civic Engagement," *Journal of School Choice*, Vol. 8, No. 2 (2014), pp. 213–236; Corey A. DeAngelis and Patrick J. Wolf, "Will Democracy Endure Private School Choice? The Effect of the Milwaukee Parental School Choice Program on Adult Voting Behavior," *The Journal of Private Enterprise*, Vol. 34, No. 3 (Summer 2019), pp. 1–21.

60 The Heritage Foundation, "Protecting K-12 Students from Discrimination," Model Legislation, https://www.heritage.org/model-legislation/protecting-k-12-students-discrimination.

61 Heritage Data Visualizations, "Education Power for Parents: A State Legislation Tracker: Rejecting CRT's Discrimination," updated May 2, 2025, https://datavisualizations.heritage.org/education/education-power-for-parents-a-state-legislation-tracker/.

62 The Heritage Foundation, "Rejecting Racism in Postsecondary Institutions and Postsecondary Accreditation," Model Legislation, https://www.heritage.org/model-legislation/rejecting-racism-higher-education.

63 Jeff Bleiler, "U-M Announces Important Changes to DEI Programs," March 28, 2025, https://michigantoday.umich.edu/2025/03/28/u-m-announces-important-changes-to-dei-programs/; Jay P. Greene, Ph.D., "Diversity University: DEI Bloat in the Academy," Heritage Foundation Backgrounder No. 3641, July 27, 2021, https://www.heritage.org/sites/default/files/2021-07/BG3641_0.pdf.

64 The Heritage Foundation, "The Given Name Act," Model Legislation, https://www.heritage.org/model-legislation/the-given-name-act.

65 U.S. Department of Justice, "Duty to Report Suspected Child Abuse Under 42 U.S.C. § 13031," available at https://www.justice.gov/file/147491-0/dl.

66 See FACTS Management, https://factsmgt.com/; Anthology, https://www.blackboard.com/?lang=en-us; Daily Connect Childcare Management Software, https://www.dailyconnect.com/; Parent Square, https://www.parentsquare.com/signin.

67 The 2018 Federal Commission on School Safety has a catalogue of such disciplinary practices, along with case studies, available at https://www.ed.gov/sites/ed/files/documents/school-safety/school-safety-reportpdf.pdf.

68 Ibid.

69 The Heritage Foundation, "Model Bill for State Teacher Certification," https://www.heritage.org/model-legislation/model-bill-state-teacher-certification; Mehta, J., & Teles, S., "Professionalization 2.0: The case for plural professionalization in education," in *Teacher quality 2.0: Toward a new era in education reform*, F. M. Hess & M. Q. McShane, eds. (Cambridge, Massachusetts: Harvard Education Press, 2014), pp. 109–131, https://dash.harvard.edu/server/api/core/bitstreams/7312037e-3033-6bd4-e053-0100007fdf3b/content.

70 Thomas J. Kane, Jonah E. Rockoff, and Douglas O. Staiger, "What Does Certification Tell Us about Teacher Effectiveness? Evidence from New York City," NBER Working Paper Series, Working Paper 12155, April 2006, p. 41, at https://www.nber.org/system/files/working_papers/w12155/w12155.pdf.

71 Kane, Rockoff, and Staiger (2008).

72 The Heritage Foundation, "Teaching the Success Sequence to Help Every Child Succeed in School and in Life," Model Legislation, November 16, 2023, https://www.heritage.org/model-legislation/teaching-the-success-sequence-help-every-child-succeed-school-and-life-model-statedistrict.

73 Tennessee General Assembly, HB 178, https://wapp.capitol.tn.gov/apps/BillInfo/default.aspx?BillNumber=HB0178&GA=114; Alabama Senate, SB 289, which became Act Number 2025-411, https://arc-sos.state.al.us/cgi/actdetail.mbr/detail?page=act&year=2025&act=411.

74 Heritage Foundation Data Visualizations, "Education Power for Parents: A State Legislation Tracker: Parents' Bill of Rights."